In 2000, I was invited to Singapore by Insoo Kim Berg to offer training and supervision for a graduate diploma in solution-focused brief therapy. In 2004, three from that initial group set up the Academy of Solution Focused Training. It is a testimony to the sustained level of their enthusiasm and dedication, and that of later associates, that the Academy continues offering graduate courses; that training is being exported to other countries; that successful international conferences have been organised; and that now this book has been published, containing 50 chapters by 48 authors representing 11 countries in Asia. The breadth of applications of the solution-focused approach attests to the excitement and creativity generated in the region by those who have continued this work. This book is a worthy tribute.

Brian Cade, BA, CSW, MFT
Brief and Family Therapist
Private practice
Cirencester, UK

This book is a celebration of solution focused practice. It is full of gems: simple stories, both practical and inspirational, which take the reader on a journey through street gangs, hospitals, boardrooms and many other places where solution focused work can be found. Examples range from how to engage disaffected youth, create a better work-life balance, improve performances or manage an impossibly busy workload by developing the 10 minute session. This is a showcase book, a convincing account of how a solution focused approach can be applied to almost any area of life in any part of the world. Do not hide this book. Keep it in view, not on a bookshelf!

Chris Iveson, BSc
Therapist, Coach, Trainer
BRIEF
London, UK

This book is a must have for any clinician who wants to use the solution focused approach in today's society in any country with any population. This compilation of work provides the reader with explanations and applications of the solution focused approach in a multitude of settings. Written clearly with case studies, lists of questions and concepts of the solution focused approach, the reader will find virtually any situation in mental health typically brought to therapy in this book. The use of case studies in business, schools, hospitals, agencies and more shows how the model is versatile and usable when its core tenets are used to construct valuable questions. Those new to the solution focused approach will efficiently learn how the approach works. Seasoned solution focused practitioners will find themselves smiling at the end of each case description.

Linda Metcalf, PhD
Director, Graduate Counseling Programs
Texas Wesleyan University
Fort Worth, TX, USA

This is an impressive book. It's impressive through the span of the work presented, the number of people who are doing it, the diversity of the use of solution focused brief therapy techniques in so many diverse settings and with such diversity of practitioners' experience.

As I read this book I was reminded of something Steve de Shazer once said to me:

> Solution focus is a slow virus. Sometimes someone tells me that they heard about this stuff 10 years ago, didn't like it, thought it was oversimplistic and now it has eaten itself into their practice in such a way that they can't stop doing it.

I think Asia is infected.

Harry Korman, MD
Specialist in Child and Adolescent Psychiatry
Family Therapist and Supervisor in Family Therapy
Trainer and Supervisor in SFBT
SIKT, Malmö, Sweden

This book is more than yet another book on SF practice: It is a comprehensive collection of examples of the many and varied applications of the SF approach across many countries within the Asia-Pacific region.

There is something for everyone within this book, whether it be SF therapy, supervision, school counselling, coaching, training, consulting or managing change.

I have found many of the chapters most interesting, and one which I like particularly is a Singaporean one, written by a senior school counsellor. It deals with the 'I don't know' response that so many of us get when working with young people. It outlines how persistence pays off when the firm belief is held by the counsellor that perhaps the young person does know really, or eventually, they will know.

Debbie, Dave, Jane and Alan have achieved a mammoth task, in both editing the book and writing their own offerings, to make this such a wonderful collection of SF practice stories. Furthermore, among SF texts generally, my belief is that it will soon be regarded as a seminal work.

John Henden, BA
Psychotherapist, Trainer
Managing Director
John Henden Consultancy
Taunton, UK

SOLUTION FOCUSED PRACTICE IN ASIA

This book is a collection of solution focused practice across Asia, offering case examples from the fields of therapy, supervision, education, coaching and organisation consulting. It demonstrates the usefulness of the solution focused approach in the Asian context by providing practice-based evidence, and highlights the diversity of application. By sharing real case examples in action across Asia, it is the aim of this book to stimulate the curious and inspire the converted. It gives readers a taste of what it is like to use this approach within an Asian context, in different areas of practice and within a broad spectrum of clinical issues. The examples offer exciting and creative ways in which solution focused practice can be used within the Asian context – with the hope that more practitioners will be curious enough to give solution focused practice serious consideration as a viable, evidence-based practice.

Debbie Hogan is Managing Director at the Academy of Solution Focused Training Pte Ltd.

Dave Hogan is Director at the Academy of Solution Focused Training Pte Ltd.

Jane Tuomola is a lecturer in clinical psychology at James Cook University, Singapore.

Alan K.L. Yeo is a consultant at Balanced Consulting.

SOLUTION FOCUSED PRACTICE IN ASIA

SOLUTION FOCUSED PRACTICE IN ASIA

*Edited by Debbie Hogan, Dave Hogan,
Jane Tuomola and Alan K.L. Yeo*

For Brandi + Penny
with love and admiration
and deep gratitude for the
amazing work you have done
in Singapore,

Dave + Debbie

21 June 2017

Routledge
Taylor & Francis Group

LONDON AND NEW YORK

First published 2017
by Routledge
2 Park Square, Milton Park, Abingdon, Oxon OX14 4RN

and by Routledge
711 Third Avenue, New York, NY 10017

Routledge is an imprint of the Taylor & Francis Group, an informa business

British Library Cataloguing in Publication Data
A catalogue record for this book is available from the British Library

Library of Congress Cataloging in Publication Data
Names: Hogan, Debbie, editor. | Hogan, Dave, editor. | Tuomola, Jane, editor. |
    Yeo, Alan, editor.
Title: Solution focused practice in Asia / edited by Debbie Hogan, Dave Hogan,
    Jane Tuomola and Alan Yeo.
Description: Abingdon, Oxon : New York, NY : Routledge is an imprint of the
    Taylor & Francis Group, an Informa Business, [2017] | Includes bibliographical
    references and index.
Identifiers: LCCN 2016025680 | ISBN 9781138188112 (hbk : alk. paper) |
    ISBN 9781315642697 (ebk : alk. paper) | ISBN 9781138188129 (pbk. : alk. paper)
Subjects: LCSH: Solution-focused brief therapy—Asia—Case studies.
Classification: LCC RC489.S65 S68 2017 | DDC 616.89/147095—dc23
LC record available at https://lccn.loc.gov/2016025680

ISBN: 978-1-138-18811-2 (hbk)
ISBN: 978-1-138-18812-9 (pbk)
ISBN: 978-1-315-64269-7 (ebk)

Typeset in Bembo
by Apex CoVantage, LLC

Debbie Hogan

To my husband, Dave, who is my best supporter and encourager in life and in work and loves me unconditionally. To my daughter, Breda, who has touched my life so profoundly and so deeply and the gift she continues to be in my life. To Insoo Kim Berg, who inspired me and encouraged me to keep going. And I never turned back.

Dave Hogan

To Debbie, my best friend and partner in life, who through her dogged, disciplined and dedicated determination 'dragged' me into the amazing Solution Focused world and introduced me to new friends and opened new doors of joyful collaboration together.

Jane Tuomola

To my husband, Petri, who is always there for me; my daughter Sophia, whom I miss more than words can say and who inspires me to make the most out of life; my daughter Alexandra who brings untold joy and laughter into our lives; and my growing bump, whose imminent arrival has helped push this project through to completion – we can't wait to meet you!

Alan K.L. Yeo

To my dad and late mum; the love you have given me will last me several lifetimes. To Debbie, for teaching me that the best gifts are the ones we can pass on.

CONTENTS

SECTION 2
Solution focused practice in supervision in Asia   83

FOREWORD

This book gives us the opportunity to walk through a wonderful garden where we can admire what becomes possible when the soil, the irrigation and the fertilising is perfectly adjusted to the need of every single plant. In other words, it is a testament to the huge work that has been done by all the people who have been trained in the solution-focused (SF) approach in Asia. It is a testament to their flexibility and their competence to make the essentials of the solution-focused approach work, embedded in different environments with various values and belief systems. What impresses me most is the high level of awareness to not leave footsteps behind and the big effort to use language that can be understood and that is filled with the sense of the cultural context the clients live in. This work has been successfully done in many different fields: therapy, supervision, in schools, coaching and organisational development.

All this would not be possible without the little SF plant that Insoo and Steve planted at the beginning of this century in this part of the world and the way Debbie and Dave Hogan nurtured this seedling with devotion, passion, endurance and high professional skill to make it grow to the Asian SF tree of today.

Since 2004 the Academy of Solution Focused Training has offered multiple trainings in Singapore as well as abroad. It also offers a lot of SF supervision, a necessary core experience for everyone that starts to work in a solution-focused way. Here, I wish to highlight another step Debbie and Dave took—to my understanding, a very altruistic step. They encouraged people to offer local SF training possibilities, for instance in the Philippines as well as in Indonesia.

All these enormous efforts the two made, and with them many former trainees, created the preconditions so that the knowledge of the model, or let me call it the SF virus, could spread in Asia as fast as it did.

Yet, there is even more to discover in this book: If you listen to the different authors' thoughts on how they made cultural adaptations it is like listening to a new description of the model you are very familiar with, and this turns out to be a big enrichment. Besides that, you will find many inspiring new ideas on how SF work can be done, in ways that will work throughout the world. It is like a box that holds many little and big treasures for anyone that gives support from the SF stance.

A big thanks to you, Debbie and Dave, my dear friends, and all the co-editors and authors for the wonderful job you have done and still do.

Therese Steiner, MD
Child and Adolescent Psychiatrist
Private Practice and NGO Terre des Hommes Basel
Embrach, Switzerland

BIOGRAPHIES OF THE EDITORS

Debbie Hogan, originally from the US, has lived in Singapore for 28 years. She has a BS in Psychology, an MS in Counselling and an Advanced Certificate in Ericksonian Psychotherapy and Hypnotherapy. She is Board Certified with the American Psychotherapy Association, with over 30 years of experience as a psychotherapist, and is a Master Clinical Member and Supervisor with the Singapore Association for Counselling. Debbie trained with Insoo Kim Berg and Steve de Shazer and earned a Graduate Diploma in Solution Focused Brief Therapy. As a family therapist in private practice, she works with a wide range of clinical issues. Debbie is a Professional Certified Coach and Mentor Coach with the International Coach Federation and coaches executives and individuals from the private sector. Debbie is the Managing Director of the Academy of Solution Focused Training and conducts training in the solution focused model in therapy, education and coaching, leading to professional certification. She is a Supervisor and Examiner with the Canadian Council of Professional Certification and the International Alliance of Solution Focused Teaching Institutes. Debbie has been interviewed on the radio and has contributed to numerous magazine articles and book chapters, including *The Art of Solution Focused Therapy* and *Encounters with Steve de Shazer and Insoo Kim Berg*.

Dave Hogan has an MTh in Theology and a BA in French, with a specialisation in Coaching and Counselling. He is originally from the US and has been involved in spiritual development and leadership training and development in Asia for more that 30 years. As a consultant he has worked with many organisations in team building, organisational development and change management. Dave is a Professional Certified Coach with the International Coach Federation and a qualified user of the Myers Briggs Type Indicator. As an executive and life coach, he works with CEOs and executives from the private and public sectors. He is a trainer and conducts workshops for organisations on Team Building, Leadership Coaching and Career Development. Dave is the Director of the Academy of Solution Focused Training and conducts solution focused training in coaching and education, leading to professional certification. Dave is a Certified Solution Focused Therapist and Coach and Supervisor with the Canadian Council of Professional Certification and Master Solution Focused Practitioner and founding member of the International Alliance of Solution Focused Teaching Institutes.

Dr Jane Tuomola is a Clinical Psychologist, originally from the UK, who has lived and worked in Singapore for the last eight years. She completed her Doctorate in Clinical Psychology at the University of Sheffield. Following that, she worked for several years in the NHS, specialising in adult mental health with an interest in psychosis. She has supervised for over 10 years, including trainee and qualified clinical psychologists, nurses, social workers and case managers, in both individual and group supervision. In Singapore she has worked in private practice, and as a Lecturer in Clinical Psychology at James Cook University, teaching on the Masters and Doctorate in Clinical Psychology Courses. She supervised interns on clinical placements as well as supervising research theses. She completed a graduate diploma in solution focused therapy in 2010. As well as using this model with clients, she has supervised others in the approach and taught a basic introduction to solution focused therapy course to psychology students. She is also a consultant to the Early Psychosis Intervention Programme at the Institute of Mental Health. She is a Master Solution Focused Practitioner (International Alliance of Solution-Focused Teaching Institutes) and Certified Solution Focused Therapist (Canadian Council of Professional Certification). She is a Practitioner Psychologist with the Health Professions Council UK, an Associate Fellow of the British Psychological Society and on the Singapore Psychological Society Register of Psychologists.

Alan K. L. Yeo has a BSc (Hons) in Psychology, an MA in Experimental Psychology and an MEd. He also has an Advanced Certificate in Eriksonian Hypnotherapy. He is an Associate of the Academy of Solution Focused Training, Singapore. He is a Registered Counsellor and Registered Clinical Supervisor with the Singapore Association for Counselling, and a Life Member of the Singapore Psychological Society. Alan has been in private practice in Singapore since 2003. He was among the pioneer batch of cohorts trained under Insoo Kim Berg, Steve de Shazer and their associates in 2000. He has held appointments of Counsellor for Staff at a local university and polytechnic. He lectures at various tertiary counselling programs, supervises interns and practitioners, and conducts counselling workshops. He is among 20 Singapore-based therapists featured in the book *Lessons From Therapy* by Toh Hwee Boon (2011). Alan was the Editorial Consultant for a teen magazine, and contributes to various local periodicals. Alan is a Master SF Practitioner (International Alliance of Solution-Focused Teaching Institutes), Certified SF Therapist and SF Coach (Canadian Council of Professional Certification). Alan recently ended a 10-year appointment on the Film Consultative Panel, Media Development Authority, Ministry of Communications and Information, Singapore.

THE CONTRIBUTORS

Yasuteru AOKI, BA
President
Solution Focus Inc.
Tokyo, Japan

Raymond W.C. AU, PhD
Occupational Therapist
Union Christian Hospital
Hospital Authority
Hong Kong

Terese BARETH, MA
Founder, CEO, Coach, Consultant, Trainer
Bareth Management Consultants (Shanghai) Co. Ltd.
Shanghai, China

Bradley BARRETT, BS, MA
School Counselor
Asian Hope International
Phnom Penh, Cambodia

David BLAKELY, MA
Mental Health Counselor
Colorado, USA

Natalie BRODERICK, PhD
Director Student Services
Hong Kong International School
Hong Kong

Maria Aurora Assumpta D. CATIPON, MA
Registered Psychologist
In Touch Community Services
AAAI Assessment Psychologists
Metro Manila, Philippines

Joe CHAN, BA
Social Worker
Centre Head, Youth
REACH Community Services Society
Singapore

Simon Tak-mau CHAN, PhD, RSW
Assistant Professor
Hong Kong Baptist University
Hong Kong

Edwin CHOY, MS
Coach, Trainer
Resourcefull
Singapore

Ada Yee Lin CHUNG, BSW, RSW, MSocSc
Head of Mrs Wong Kwok Leong Student Wellness Centre
Singapore Management University
Singapore

Andrew DA ROZA, BA (Law) (Hons), LLM (Law), EMBA, MA (Counselling)
Addictions Therapist, Promises
Director, We Care
Singapore

Kirsten DIEROLF, MA
Director
SolutionsAcademy
Germany

Vania M.N. DJOHAN, MBA
Member of the Advisory Board
PT Lentera Kasih Internasional
Jakarta, Indonesia

Kotaro FUJIOKA, MD
Vice-director of Yahata Kohsei Hospital
Vice-director of Hatakeyama Clinic
Chairman of Solution Academy
Kitakyushu Fukuoka, Japan

Isabelle HANSEN, MA
Director
Europe Asia Business Services
Hamburg, Germany

Dave HOGAN BA, MTh
Coach, Consultant and Trainer
Academy of Solution Focused Training
Singapore

Debbie HOGAN BS, MS
Psychotherapist, Coach and Trainer
Academy of Solution Focused Training
Singapore

Wei-Su HSU, PhD
Professor
National Taiwan Normal University
Taipei, Taiwan

Lilian ING, BA, BA (Hons), MA (Clinical Psychology)
Consultant Psychologist and Supervisor
ithaka consulting
Singapore

Amanda JEWITT, BSc (Hons) Psych, MSocSc (Counselling)
Counsellor, Therapist, Coach
Hathaways Counselling
Westcliff-on-Sea, UK

Patricia JOUDREY, MEd
Middle School Counselor
American International School
Chennai, India

Anisha KAUL, BSc (Hons) Psychology, MSc Org Psych
Founder and Director
Mindspring TCC Pte Ltd
Singapore

Yunjoo KIM (MSW)
Social Worker
Solution Center
South Korea

Ben C.H. KUO, PhD
Professor of Clinical Psychology
University of Windsor
Windsor, Ontario, Canada

Yi Ping LEE, BPsych
Senior Case Manager
Early Psychosis Intervention Programme
Institute of Mental Health
Singapore

Valerie P.C. LIM, B Sp Path (Hons), M App Sc (Research), PhD
Senior Principal Speech Therapist
Singapore General Hospital
Singapore

Karen McDonald LOUIS, MS
Program Developer and Consultant
Louis Counselling and Training Services Pte Ltd
Singapore

Joan LOW, MASocSc
Senior School Counsellor
Yishun Junior College
Singapore

Petra MAIERHÖFER, BSc (OT)
Occupational Therapist
In Touch Community Services
Metro Manila, Philippines

Mark MCKERGOW, MBA, PhD
Director
Sfwork, London, UK
And Director HESIAN
University of Hertfordshire, UK

Emily MEADOWS, BA, Med, MHSc
Professional School Counselor
Hong Kong International School
Hong Kong

Ann MOIR-BUSSY, BEd, MA, PhD
Senior Lecturer and Program Coordinator of Counselling
School of Social Sciences, University of Sunshine Coast
Queensland, Australia

Agnes Hautea NANO, BA
Life Coach
In Touch Community Services
Metro Manila, Philippines

Cheryl NG, BA (Hons), PGDE, MSc
Senior Speech-Language Therapist
Singapore General Hospital
Singapore

Yana RICART, BSc, MSc
School Counselor
Chatsworth International School
Singapore

Harliem SALIM, MBA
Consultant, Coach, Trainer
Kuningan Family and Community Center
Jakarta, Indonesia

Eunice Limin SEAH, BA (Hons)
Psychologist
Institute of Mental Health
Singapore

Jayne SIM, BA
Women's Coach, Mentor
Hope Worldwide
Singapore and Malaysia

Colleen STEIGERWALD, MEd, M Couns
School Counselor
Singapore American School
Singapore

Peter SZABO, PhD (Law)
Solutionsurfer
Solutionsurfers Intl.
Switzerland

Jane TUOMOLA, BA, MA, DClinPsy
Clinical Psychologist, Supervisor
Early Psychosis Intervention Programme Institute of Mental Health
Singapore

Marjanne VAN DER HELM, MSc
Consultant, Coach
QMJ Consultancy
Singapore

Arvind WABLE, MA, MBA
Brand Consultant, Coach
PYXS Partners
New Delhi, India

Maurice S.H. WAN, MSocS
Occupational Therapist
Union Christian Hospital
Hospital Authority
Hong Kong

Indry WARDHANI, MA
Psychologist, Coach
Vlinder Indonesia
Jakarta, Indonesia

Denise WRIGHT, BSSc
Leadership Facilitator, Coach
Xtend Coaching International
Singapore

Alan K.L. YEO, BSc (Hons), MA, MEd
Counsellor, Clinical Supervisor and Trainer
Balanced Consulting
Singapore

FOREWORD

For many reasons, it is an honour and a pleasure to provide this foreword to *Solution Focused Practice in Asia*, edited by our dear friends and much admired colleagues, Debbie and Dave Hogan, and their associates, Jane Tuomola and Alan Yeo. This is an extremely ambitious and satisfying work which demonstrates how professionals in Asia have fully embraced the SF approach, adapting it beautifully to the cultures and customs of Asia. One of the hallmarks of the SF approach is its adaptability to different situations and populations, and this theme is apparent throughout the chapters.

The topic of SF practices in Asia has special meaning to us because of many conversations on this topic with our long-time colleagues and dear friends, the late Insoo Kim Berg and Steve de Shazer. They watched the growing development and utilisation of the SF approach in Asia with keen interest. Oftentimes, we would meet for dinner just after they returned from teaching trips throughout Asia. It was a long journey to Asia from their home in Milwaukee, Wisconsin, and these trips typically involved multiple stops accompanied by gruelling teaching schedules. Yet, Steve and Insoo always came home energised and enthusiastic and told wonderful stories about the excellent work being done by their many colleagues and friends throughout Asia. They also spoke warmly about the wonderful hospitality and kindness. Steve, an avid and very gifted cook, often returned with a new recipe or some special seasoning ingredient that tasted wonderfully exotic to us back here in the American Midwest.

In the mid 1990s, when I (YD) accompanied Insoo on a multi-stop teaching trip through Japan and Korea, and during subsequent trips to Singapore and Hong Kong, it quickly became clear why she and Steve had such deep respect and warm feelings for their Asian SF colleagues.

Like many visitors from the West, I was initially overwhelmed by the rich history and unique cultural complexity of the many countries that define Asia, and quickly recognised that one could spend a lifetime studying the many different customs, languages, religions and traditions of the amazing continent without arriving at anything approaching a complete and accurate understanding.

Early on during my first teaching trip with Insoo to Japan, I was worried that I would make some cultural blunder when presenting the SF approach. During the first day of our workshop, I kept silent while Insoo did most of the teaching, but then my heart sank when she asked me to do a live session with a father and son. During the tea break that preceded the live session, I begged her to give me some advice, or better yet, to do the session herself (!) explaining that my understanding of the Japanese culture was far too superficial.

Insoo gently agreed that my understanding of the Japanese culture was superficial, and limited, but reminded me that it is the clients, not the therapist, who determine the goal of an SF session and the solution development process and it was important to always remain mindful of this fact. She went on to remind me that because SF goals are necessarily based upon the hopes and desires described by the client, the goals naturally reflect the unique cultural, familial and religious traditions that characterise each client's life experiences. In inviting clients to search for exceptions and resources that already exist or at least have the potential to exist in the context of their everyday life, it is the clients themselves who ensure that the resulting solutions are going to be both culturally and personally relevant and achievable. Over the years, we (TT and YD) have found Insoo's explanation of SF 'cultural fit' to be very meaningful and helpful, so we were particularly pleased to note that the various chapters in this book beautifully embody this way of working mindfully so as to deeply respect and honour each client's unique life experience.

This book is a monumental work whose scope goes well beyond merely chronicling solution focused brief therapy in Asia. The 50 chapters provide one of the most comprehensive contemporary examinations of the state of the art of SF practices available. This book can and should be read by *anyone* interested in understanding the full scope of SF practices, including therapy, supervision, in education, coaching, and organisations, be it in Asia, or anywhere in the world.

Yvonne Dolan, MA
Founding Director
Institute for Solution- Focused Therapy
Chicago, IL, USA

Terry S. Trepper, PhD
Professor Emeritus of Psychology
Purdue University Northwest
Hammond, IN, USA

ACKNOWLEDGEMENTS FROM THE EDITORS

The editors would like to personally thank all the authors who contributed to this book. It was a massive project, and without their contributions it would not be possible. It is a celebration of their work. The editors would also like to express appreciation to the mentors, reviewers and the international SF family for their support, on whose shoulders we stand, for those who have nurtured our work and interest in doing this project.

During the last stage of this book project, the editors faced many challenges and personal crises – complicated pregnancy, health crisis and surgery, family crisis and the unexpected death of a close friend. It is a testimony to the dedication and commitment to the book project that it was completed. It served as a reminder that through the challenges of life, individuals are called to draw from their most inner resources and support system. This is a profound truth that is so relevant to what this book is about. This book acknowledges the hard work and resilience of the clients, for whom this book is written, and how their stories are a reflection of the ability of the human spirit to keep going and bounce back.

The editors would like to give special acknowledgement to our mentors and key supporters. Thanks to Therese Steiner, Yvonne Dolan and Terry Trepper, who have become close friends and collaborators. Thanks to Brian Cade, Chris Iveson, Linda Metcalf, Harry Korman and John Henden for writing endorsements, believing in us and investing in the work in Asia. Thanks to Mark McKergow and Peter Szabo, who have contributed greatly to the development of coaching and consulting work in Asia. A special word of gratitude to Insoo Kim Berg and Steve de Shazer for bringing solution-focused practice to Asia and leaving their indelible footprints across this vast area.

Finally, a special thanks to our families, who were patient and understanding when we were 'otherwise engaged' in book writing and editing.

With much gratitude,
Dave Hogan
Debbie Hogan
Jane Tuomola
Alan K.L. Yeo

CONFIDENTIALITY

Protecting client confidentiality has been of the utmost concern to the authors and editors in the preparation of this book. The majority of the client examples (whether these are therapy clients, supervisees, schools, coaching clients or organisations) are based on actual client work done by the authors. In these cases, the clients have read the relevant chapter that their story appears in and given written consent for their story to be included. Various demographic characteristics (e.g., names, ages, occupations) have been changed to protect the clients' anonymity. All organisations that are mentioned by name (e.g., specific hospitals, schools, companies) have also read the chapters and given written consent for the name of the organisation to be mentioned in the chapter. To further de-identify their clients, some authors use composite cases drawn from several clinical experiences but based on real clinical cases. As such, any resemblance to real clients is purely coincidental.

1

INTRODUCTION TO SOLUTION FOCUSED PRACTICE IN ASIA

Creative applications across diverse fields

Debbie Hogan

This book is an ambitious project, and very timely. With the growing interest in the solution focused (SF) approach in Asia, this book is a celebration to honour the growing number of solution focused practitioners across Asia and their inspiring work.

This chapter begins with the significance of this book on the SF approach in Asia and highlights the chapters in five key sections – therapy, supervision, education, coaching and organisational work. It offers the reader a brief overview of the history and development of the SF approach and the key solution building tools that characterise this approach. It ends with a brief overview of the applications of SF work in Asia and areas for further development and firmly establishes the Asian presence in the international network of SF practitioners.

Its time has come – the significance of this book

My first workshop in solution focused brief therapy (SFBT) with Insoo Kim Berg and Steve de Shazer was in 1999, and in 2000 I took a full program with Insoo and other trainers, many of whom are part of this book project. It radically changed my clinical practice and impacted my personal life. A few years down the road, I started collecting impressive stories from my supervisees and trainees, thinking someone should write a book on SFBT in Asia. Some were stories from my own cases, which I thought were amazing examples of how clients can change so dramatically with this approach. I remember saying to John Henden that someone needs to write this book. He responded in a very gentle and convincing way that I should do it. Dave, my husband and business partner, met Insoo at our 2006 Asia Pacific Solution Focused Approach Conference and was already a 'convert' of the SF approach. We talked often about our appreciation for the SF approach and its impact on our work, and we started to talk about writing a book. Alan Yeo and I had become close friends when we attended the training with Insoo. Dr. Jane Tuomola, a clinical psychologist, attended our SFBT training in 2010 and became highly skilled and a strong advocate for SFBT. A few years later, I knew the time was right when Jane and Alan agreed to partner with me and Dave as editors of this book.

In the twelve years that I've been teaching the SF approach in Asia, one of the most frequently asked questions during training has been, 'Yes, but does it work in Asia?' Since SF practice was developed in the United States, sometimes there is a hesitation to accept it as relevant within the Asian context. My typical response was, 'Let's find out. Experiment with it, and I'm curious what you discover.' Now, we can definitely say that, 'Yes, it does work in Asia and here is how.' We have a growing body of work and experienced practitioners who have found creative ways in which this approach can be applied.

Five areas of practice

This book has five key sections, which highlight SF practice in Asia – therapy, supervision, education, coaching and organisational consulting. We invited SF practitioners we knew across Asia to share their experiences and how they adapted it to their cultural context.

This is a seminal book, a collection of 50 chapters by 48 different authors, and their work represents 11 countries across Asia – Singapore, Malaysia, Indonesia, China, Japan, the Philippines, Cambodia, India, Hong Kong, Korea and Taiwan. This is only a small step in representing SF practice in Asia and limited to only what the editors are aware of. Undoubtedly, the scope and breadth of SF practice in Asia is much more than what can be covered in this book. We hope this is just the beginning of more to come.

Therapy. The largest section includes 12 chapters on SF therapy in private practice, general hospitals, psychiatric hospitals, community settings and outpatient clinics. The chapters describe SF work with adults, children, couples and families with a variety of presenting problems such as psychiatric diagnoses and psychological issues, parenting issues, communication issues, relationship issues, school based issues, and health issues including speech problems. The professionals writing the chapters include psychiatrists, psychologists, counsellors, social workers, speech therapists, occupational therapists, trainers, coaches, consultants and business owners.

Supervision. There is growing interest and recognition that supervision needs to be part of good clinical practice. Seven practitioners describe their supervision experience in different situations: group supervision, peer supervision, supervision of teams and staff and individual supervision.

Education. Using solution focused practice in education has been one of the most successful applications of the model, besides in therapy. Eight different chapters highlight the benefits of this approach in schools from different vantage points: from working with primary school children to adolescents, dealing with school bullying, and at risk youth, to working with multiple stakeholders including the school, parents and students.

Coaching. The interest in coaching is exploding in Asia. Eight coaches describe their experience in different coaching contexts: with executives, CEOs and business owners; using metaphors in coaching; using coaching in occupational therapy; team coaching; cultural adaptability and the importance of correct translation for coaching in China.

Organisations. Using solution focused approaches in organisational development involves a multi-layered approach to address the entire organisation at many levels of engagement. Eight authors share their experiences in working in children's homes, big conglomerate organisations, dealing with change management, integrating systems thinking, and facilitating leadership development.

Overview of solution focused practice

Brief history

Solution focused brief therapy was developed by Insoo Kim Berg, Steve de Shazer and their colleagues at the Brief Family Therapy Center in Milwaukee, Wisconsin, in the late 1970s. It has its roots in the early work at the Mental Research Institute in Palo Alto, California, and was fluenced by the work of the innovative psychiatrist, Milton Erickson. Insoo and Steve were drawn to finding a way of working that was effective and efficient, and that helped people to make progress on what was important to them. They began in an inner city outpatient mental health centre, working with mostly psychiatric clients. For over 20 years they observed their sessions, noting what helped people to change and what sustained those changes.

What is SFBT?

Solution focused brief therapy, also known as solution focused practice, is a goal-oriented, future-focused approach to brief therapy. While there is great respect for the client and their problematic state, there is a strong emphasis on co-construction of their desired outcome based on what the client wants to be made better or changed. SFBT is known for its attention to language and how questions are constructed. The focus is on listening to clients' words and language that support what they want in their lives. Listening for what is important and what clients value is central as these are key motivators for client change. Identifying and utilising clients' strengths and capabilities remind the clients that they possess competencies that can be leveraged. SFBT requires discipline. Instead of formulating theories about the nature of the problem, the practitioner remains curious and interested in what the client wants to be made better.

Major tenets of SFBT

These three tenets serve as a guideline and characterise the basic philosophy of SFBT.

- *If it isn't broken, don't fix it.* If something is working well, there is no need to change it. If the client has already solved the problem, don't intervene.
- *If it works, do more of it.* Find what is working for the client and encourage them to continue. Sometimes clients don't realise their own brilliance.
- *If it doesn't work, do something different.* No matter how good a solution sounds, if it does not work, do something else. Working creatively to explore what 'different' looks like is key. It has to be a difference that makes a difference.

Key solution focused process tools

Goals

What needs to happen in this session so that it will have been worthwhile for you?

Good goal construction is a key foundation. Knowing what the client wants, or at least having an idea of what they want, is important for good collaboration. Most clients know what they don't want.

It takes time to help the client articulate what they do want. Often, clients have not been asked what they want from the session that will lead to progress outside of the therapy room.

Miracle question

Suppose tonight after you go to bed, while you are sleeping, a miracle happens and all these things we've been talking about are solved. You don't know the miracle occurred. How would you discover that it had? What would be the first small clue that something was different?

This is an invitation for the client to imagine life without the problem. This process enables the client to access creative imagination to construct life as they would experience it with all the blocks removed. It helps the client create useful information about what they would do when the problem has been solved. As more details are revealed, the preferred future is created.

Scaling questions

On a scale of 1–10, where '10' represents you at your best, and '1' being the opposite, where are you today?

Scaling allows the client to view where they are in relation to where they want to be. You can scale progress, confidence, ability to manage, completion of a task, coping, etc. Ten is always the presence of what is desired, and 1 is the opposite.

Exception questions

When was the most recent time that you could have overslept but you managed to get up on time?

These are powerful questions that explore times when the problem could have occurred but didn't. It draws from the client's past experiences, when the problem was absent and encourages them to consider what they did that contributed to the positive difference. It becomes a gentle reminder that if they did it once, they can do it again.

Relationship questions

Suppose you did keep silent when your son comes home late, instead of scolding him. What difference would that make for him?

SFBT is based on the interactional view that when one person responds differently, it changes the pattern in the relationship and new patterns can be developed. These questions evoke creative thinking that opens up possibilities.

End of session review

The therapist wraps up the session by affirming the client's strengths and capabilities and things the client has done that contribute to what the client wants and co-creates a small step that will help the client stay on track with the progress they want to make.

Follow-up sessions

What's been better since our last session?

The therapist remains curious about small signs of improvement and seeks information on what the client did and how they did it. Being persistent in exploring small changes in the right direction helps the client stay focused on information that supports the changes they want.

The key assumptions of SFBT and the therapist's stance on 'not knowing' embody the philosophy and spirit of this approach.

Full details of solution focused brief therapy can be found in *Interviewing for Solutions* by Peter De Jong and Insoo Kim Berg (2013). In most areas of practice, the same core ideas and tools are applied. For coaching and organisational consulting, refer to Paul Z Jackson and Mark McKergow's *The Solutions Focus: Making Coaching and Change SIMPLE* (2007).

Applications in Asia

Solution focused practice was initially developed in the therapy context. Its impact and wide appeal quickly became apparent as it spread into education, schools, supervision, coaching and the corporate world. It spread beyond the borders of the USA into Europe, Africa, Central and South America and Asia.

The solution focused approach has been embraced in many different areas and settings in Asia. SF therapists have worked within a wide spectrum of clinical issues, such as depression, anxiety, stress, phobias, eating disorders, self-harming, suicide, obsessive-compulsive disorders, Tourette's syndrome, trichotillomania, schizophrenia and bi-polar disorders. In fact, the clinical experience in Asia is the same as what you would expect in other countries. SF practice can be found in primary and secondary schools, polytechnics and universities, social services, the civil service, prison services, the police force, hospitals, family courts, juvenile homes, government agencies, career guidance and private and group practices. Coaches and consultants are using this approach in banks, human resources firms, insurance companies, the oil and gas industry, hotel management and manufacturing. The list goes on. SF practice has indeed germinated the landscape in Asia.

In talking to different practitioners in Asia and abroad, it is not clear how and when SF practice was established in the various countries in Asia. My best attempts at piecing this together found that, generally, SF practice was introduced to Asia in a first wave in the late 1980s and a second wave around the year 2000. I do know that during Insoo and Steve's trips abroad, they included doing training in Asia. For many Asian countries, it is not known if SF is practised there. I do think it is spreading, because of new inquires around Asia, most recently from the Maldives and Bangladesh.

Research

SF practice is an evidence-based practice, which has been studied since the early 1980s, with over 2,300 publications annually, with an impressive body of research that continues to grow (see http://www.solutionsdoc.co.uk/sft.htm for an up-to-date list of worldwide publications). It is one of the few approaches in psychotherapy that began as 'evidence-based,' instead of being 'theory-driven' like many models. While many of the studies about Asians are done outside Asia, a growing body of research is being done in Asia about Asians, and there is a need for many more relevant studies.

Enjoy the buffet

In Singapore, where I've lived for the past 28 years, a common greeting among the Chinese majority is 'Have you eaten?' which culturally means, 'How are you?' Embedded in this common greeting is a central focus around food, social interaction and well-being. In the spirit of this social greeting, we invite the reader to our Asian buffet. It's only a little teaser, an exotic mix to tantalise your taste buds and give you an experience of the SF flavours the authors have prepared.

We hope the reader will enjoy the stories, be inspired and perhaps become curious as to how they might adapt solution focused practice into their area of work.

References

De Jong, P., & Berg, I.K. (2013). *Interviewing for solutions* (4th ed.). Belmont CA: Brooks/Cole, Cengage Learning.

Macdonald, A. (2015, November 18). *Solution-focused brief therapy evaluation list*. Retrieved from: www .solutionsdoc.co.uk/sft.html.

Jackson, P. Z., & McKergow, M. (2007). *The solutions focus: Making coaching and change SIMPLE* (2nd ed.). London, UK: Nicholas Brealey International.

Solution focused practice in therapeutic settings in Asia

2

INTRODUCTION TO SOLUTION FOCUSED PRACTICE IN THERAPEUTIC SETTINGS IN ASIA

Jane Tuomola

Introduction

When I moved to Singapore from the UK eight years ago, one of my first questions to my colleagues was how cognitive behavioural therapy (my approach at the time) could be adapted to clients in Asia. I was surprised that while I was offered some advice, or sent one or two papers, there was very little that was tangible for me to use.

After training in SFBT five years ago I had the same question. Shifting from working as a clinical psychologist used to assessment, formulation and intervention within more problem based frameworks, to take on board the philosophy of SFBT was a complete paradigm shift. I therefore needed evidence to convince me that it works – both in general and within Asia.

In the introduction to this book, Debbie Hogan has outlined the history of SFBT and key techniques of the model. In this chapter, I will focus more on the evidence base of SFBT, Asian psychology and values and the importance of adapting therapy across cultures. I will then describe the 12 chapters in this section that offer creative ideas for using SFBT in Asia.

The evidence base for SFBT

The evidence base for the effectiveness of SFBT is expanding rapidly, with more rigorous outcome studies being published. For example, a recent systematic review of all available controlled outcome studies on SFBT found SFBT to be an effective treatment for a variety of behavioural and psychological problems, and as effective as other established alternative approaches (Gingerich & Peterson, 2013).

Only 6 of the 43 studies in the Gingerich and Peterson (2013) review were, however, carried out in Asia, and the results were not analysed by race or culture. There has been a recent meta-analysis of the effectiveness of SFBT in Mainland China (Kim et al., 2015). Nine studies met the inclusion criteria and showed that, overall, SFBT in China showed a very large treatment effect favouring SFBT. The authors note, however, that future research needs to show both treatment fidelity to the SFBT model while adapting the approach to the cultural and ethnic values of the Chinese population. Clearly more research needs to be done across a wider range of countries, cultures and ethnic groups within Asia to build on these results.

Evidence based practice is more than just following results from the latest meta-analysis or systematic review. It is 'a process of clinical decision-making that integrates research evidence, clinical expertise and patient preferences and characteristics' (Spring, 2007, p. 611). That is, we must use our clinical expertise to apply the latest research in a way that takes into account the context of our work and decide how best to apply the research evidence with each and every client in a way that respects and honours their values.

The research evidence indicates that while there is some evidence that SFBT works in Asia, in addition to knowing *that* it works, clinicians need to know *whether and how* to adapt the model to their specific clients and cultural setting.

This is especially important as a growing body of research indicates that 'cross-cultural competence facilitates therapy and improves assessment' (see, e.g., Hays, 2006, p. 5). The American Psychological Association also states that 'services are most effective when responsive to the patient's specific problems, strengths, personality, sociocultural context and preferences' (APA Presidential Task Force, 2006, p. 284). Not taking culture into account can lead to barriers between therapists and their clients, even leading to premature termination of therapy. Insoo Kim Berg wrote about the importance of culture and taking both 'an ecosystemic view of how the ethnic and cultural experience of the client affect treatment while not losing site of the micro view of how these cultural traits are experienced at the individual level' (Berg & Miller, 1992, p. 356). Writing from an SFBT perspective more recently, Kim (2014) suggests that understanding the cultural context of clients can help clinicians structure questions related to specific cultural values and experiences and help clients use their unique cultural strengths and experiences to build on solutions.

Asian psychology and values

The field of Asian psychology is vast and growing rapidly, with the recognition that individuals of Asian descent differ from those from other parts of the world, for example, as to how they think, feel and behave (Saw & Okazaki, 2012). However there is not just one 'Asian psychology' as each ethnic group has common as well as unique cultural characteristics, which are influenced by religious beliefs (for example, Buddhism, Confucianism, Hinduism and Taoism), as well as historical and social processes.

There has been great debate as to what constitutes core Asian values, and the field of Asian indigenous psychology has moved on from previous overly simplistic East–West comparisons to provide analyses of key values held by Asians from an Asian perspective (Saw & Okazaki, 2012).

While it is important not to use broad generalisations and overlook more specific cultural nuances, there are some values regarded as commonly held within Asia, which include a collectivist orientation, social harmony, filial piety and moral obligation to the family, and saving face (Kim, 2014, p. 55), and these are often linked to shared value systems such as kapwa, Confucianism and Taoism (Saw & Okazaki, 2012).

Adapting therapy in Asia

One of the difficulties for practitioners working in Asia has been the lack of availability and accessibility of appropriate resources adapted to their context. Other therapeutic models have recently focused on the importance of adapting their approaches to clients in Asia. For example, Oei and Tang (2008) bring together a collection of papers on the research and adaptations of the cognitive behavioural approach within an Asian context. Potash, Chan and Kalmanowitz (2012) pull together perspectives and effective approaches in art therapy developed by practitioners in Asia. They aim to demonstrate ways of adapting and assimilating theory, research and practice developed in the West with ideas from Chinese medicine and Eastern philosophy, spirituality and art traditions. Gerlach, Hooke and Varvin (2013) have focused on psychoanalysis in Asia and the importance of the development of this within separate Asian countries, as each has different socio-political historical contexts and cultural textures.

It is therefore timely that SFBT follows suit with other therapeutic modalities, and offers a book of resources to practitioners relevant to the Asian context.

There is already some literature on the use of SFBT both with Asians outside Asia as well as within Asia. Kim's (2014) book focuses on working with various minority client groups within the US, including chapters on Asian American clients and Asian immigrant clients. However, some of the ideas are less relevant for Asian therapists working in Asia with Asian clients of the majority culture.

Various papers have described the practice of SFBT in Asia, and some of the most recent are listed here. Lee and Mjelde-Mossey (2004) describe how to use SFBT to facilitate family harmony when there are clashes of cultural values between generations. Hsu and Wang (2011) describe how to integrate Asian clients' filial piety beliefs into SFBT in Taiwan. Mishima (2012) outlines the use of SFBT by nurses offering health interviews in Japan. Moir-Bussy (2014) reports the use of SFBT by counselling students in Hong Kong and how to adapt SFBT to the cultural context. Liu et al. (2015) review the literature on the use of SFBT in China, and describe how SFBT spread to China. They found over 100 papers using SFBT across a variety of settings such as education, mental health care and social services and conclude that it is effective with the Chinese population.

We are now adding to the literature on SFBT in Asia by bringing together several chapters from practitioners working in Asia. The chapters offer wonderful case examples and reflections on cultural issues with very practical advice on how to adapt SFBT in these settings.

Contributions by authors

The chapters cover many different settings where SFBT is used, including private practice; general hospitals; psychiatric hospitals; community settings and outpatient clinics. The chapters describe working with individual adults, children and families with a variety of presenting problems such as psychiatric diagnoses and psychological issues (e.g., anxiety, OCD, depression, psychoses, addictions), parenting issues, communication issues, relationship issues, school based issues, and health issues including speech problems. The professionals writing the chapters include psychiatrists, psychologists, counsellors, social workers, speech therapists and occupational therapists.

There are 15 authors who contribute 12 chapters in this section. The first three authors provide examples of working with clients from Chinese cultural backgrounds in Singapore and Hong Kong. Lilian Ing has several years' experience working in Singapore and describes how language and wording of traditional SFBT questions were adapted to fit the cultural context of her clients. Simon Tak-mau Chan and Ada Yee Lin Chung describe Chinese cultural values such as collectivism, hierarchy and harmony that have been influenced by Confucianism. Taking each in turn, they describe how SFBT either fits or needs to be adapted to respect these cultural values for clients in Hong Kong. Andrew da Roza describes how many Chinese cultural values can lead to the precipitants and perpetuators of addictions – shame and isolation. He shares how SFBT can be used effectively to overcome these issues, offering those with addictions new hope and empowerment.

Three authors write about using SFBT in psychiatric settings including hospital and outpatient clinics, and how the model was adapted to the cultural setting. Eunice Limin Seah writes about her psychological work with clients at a large psychiatric hospital. She gives four case examples covering a range of psychiatric diagnoses, which highlight the range of problems and cultural backgrounds with which SFBT was effective. Jane Tuomola and Yi Ping Lee describe how case managers use SFBT with clients with psychosis. This chapter focuses on the difference SFBT made to the case managers' work, offering a sense of hope and empowerment to both the case managers and their clients. Kotaro Fujioka outlines the 10-minute solution building approach designed to fit the need for very brief sessions in psychiatric outpatient clinics in Japan, which can be applicable to almost any setting where time is limited.

Cheryl Ng outlines how SFBT is a useful adjunct to traditional speech and language therapy to help clients move beyond their impairments and focus on the goals that are important to them.

Two authors describe their work in the Philippines. Petra Maierhöfer describes some of the cultural and economic conditions in the Philippines that make SFBT a good fit in this context saving clients 'face', time and money. Maria Catipon describes how she integrated SFBT with play therapy, to help children feel ready to engage and express themselves, an important adaptation in addressing the cultural discomfort with therapy in this setting.

Two authors focus on working with families and relationship issues. David Blakely describes a creative visual technique, the solution balloon, to use with families. He describes how well this fits in the Singaporean culture where practical steps forward are valued and meaningful change can be highlighted without dwelling on flaws. Wei-Su Hsu and Ben Kuo describe working with mother-daughter relationships in Taiwan. They describe how to use SFBT techniques to balance the needs of the daughter, the mother and the relationship in a way that respects the cultural context of this type of relationship.

Lastly, Amanda Jewitt describes working in private practice and highlights the importance of gathering details to work towards clients' solutions. She highlights how the SF process of gathering details is respectful of the cultural context of the client.

Conclusions

What stands out to me as the editor of this section is that while all the authors wrote their chapters without knowledge or reference to each other, there is a commonality of ideas expressed in their chapters. Those familiar with the SFBT approach will clearly recognise the techniques as used anywhere in the world. The approach itself automatically respects and allows for cultural differences – as the goals always come from the clients' frame of reference. However there are specific adaptations of the SFBT model needed when working with Asian clients, for example, wording of the miracle question or being cautious with giving compliments. These mirror the findings reported by Liu et al. (2015). To me, using SFBT in Asia is summed up by a wonderful Asian expression: 'Same, same but different.'

We hope that these stories will provide a wealth of practice based evidence to help those currently in undergraduate training courses where SFBT is covered or those doing specific postgraduate training in SFBT, to learn how to adapt the SF approach, as well as inspiriting experienced practitioners with new ideas.

References

APA Presidential Task Force on Evidence Based Practice. (2006). Evidence based practice in psychology. *American Psychologist, 61*, 271–285.

Berg, I.K., & Miller, S.D. (1992). Working with Asian American clients: One person at a time. *Families in Society, 73*(6), 356–63.

Gerlach, A., Hooke, M.T. S., & Varvin, S. (Eds.) (2013). *Psychoanalysis in Asia*. London, UK: Karnac Books.

Gingerich, W.J., & Peterson, L.T. (2013). Effectiveness of solution-focused brief therapy: A systematic qualitative review of controlled outcome studies. *Research on Social Work Practice, 23*(3): 266–283.

Hays, P.A. (2006). Introduction: Developing culturally responsive cognitive-behavioral therapies. In P.A. Hays & G.Y. Iwamasa (Eds.), *Culturally responsive cognitive behavioural therapy: Assessment, practice and supervision* (pp. 3–19). Washington, DC: American Psychological Association.

Hsu, W.S., & Wang, C.D.C. (2011). Integrating Asian clients' filial piety beliefs into solution-focused brief therapy. *International Journal of Advanced Counselling, 33*, 322–334.

Kim, J. S (2014). *Solution-focused brief therapy: A multicultural approach*. Thousand Oaks, CA: Sage Publications Inc.

Kim, J.S., Franklin, C., Zhang, Y., Liu, W., Qu, Y., & Chen, H. (2015) Solution-focused brief therapy in China: A meta-analysis. *Journal of Ethnic and Cultural Diversity in Social Work, 24*(3), 187–201.

Lee, M.Y., & Mjelde-Mossey, L. (2004). Cultural dissonance among generations: a solution-focused approach with east Asian elders and their families. *Journal of Marital and Family Therapy, 30*(4), 497–513.

Liu, X., Zhang, Y.P., Franklin, C., Qu, Y., Chen, H., & Kim, J.S. (2015). The practice of solution-focused brief therapy in Mainland China. *Health and Social Work, 40*(2), 84–90.

Mishima, N. (2012). Applying a solution-focused approach to health interviews in Japan. In C. Franklin, T.S. Trepper, W. Gingerich & E. McCollum (Eds.). *Solution focused brief therapy: A handbook of evidenced-based practice* (pp. 327–341). New York, NY: Oxford University Press.

Moir-Bussy, A. (2014). Using SFBT in Hong Kong: Initiatives from Hong Kong master of counselling psychology students and implications for cultural contexts in Australia. *Journal of Solution-Focused Brief Therapy, 1(1),* 30–45.

Oei, T.P., & Tang, S.K.C. (Eds.) (2008). *Current research and practices on cognitive behaviour therapy in Asia*. Singapore: PH Productions Ltd.

Potash, J.S., Chan, S.M., & Kalmanowitz, D.L. (Eds.) (2012). *Art therapy in Asia: To the bone or wrapped in silk*. London, UK: Jessica Kingsley Publishers

Saw, A., & Okazaki, S. (2012). What is the psychology of Asians? In E.C. Chang (Ed.). *Handbook of adult psychopathology in Asians* (pp. 15–29). New York, NY: Oxford University Press.

Spring, B. (2007). Evidence-based practice in clinical psychology: What it is, why it matters, what you need to know. *Journal of Clinical Psychology, 63*, 611–631.

3

THE SOLUTION-FOCUSED APPROACH IN THERAPEUTIC SETTINGS

From cannot to can—like a dream come true

Lilian Ing

Introduction

This chapter describes my therapeutic work with Chinese Singaporean clients, which took me on a journey of learning what worked for them. In learning Mandarin, I was able to access the culture and the language that might work for them in therapy, to convey the heart of the solution-focused brief therapy (SFBT) approach. The chapter provides vignettes of how I used the SFBT approach, the language used and the impact on clients.

The Chinese term for crisis is 'danger-opportunity' (危機). Co-existing with any opportunity is danger and risk, of failure, but also success! This implies that, in the midst of change, it is possible to take advantage of the situation and gain from this. At the heart of the SFBT approach lies how we journey with the client from problem to solution. The problem, the turmoil, the pain that brings a client into our ambit, brings with it the opportunity to do something different.

We are co-constructers of our reality and our relationships, and the SFBT conversation enables clients to change both their perspective and their behaviour through participating in these conversations. This interactional model has worked for me and my supervisees, in our work with a predominantly Asian population in Singapore. Eight strategies are explained below.

1 Accepting problem talk while listening for strengths

The 19-year-old woman sitting before me is in crisis. She hesitantly starts on her problem-exposing journey. She feels shame but needs to share her burden. She wants to excel academically, to bring honour to her family.

I affirm her courage in her time of need. I listen. I offer her this space.

How are you managing every day? To do everything you need to do?

I focus on what she has been doing to manage herself, and the strengths and resources that have kept her going.

Of all the things you do to keep going, what is most helpful?

Who are your greatest supports?

What do they do that helps?

What do you do that stops the problem from getting worse?

This is the start of her discovery that she is not the incompetent, unfaithful daughter she perceives. We build a platform of acceptance and trust. The problem and the pain have been contained, and she has some inkling of resources for the journey.

Before she leaves I check in with her about her experience of our time together.

Of all the things we have talked about today, what has been most helpful?

She tells me that I am the first person she has spoken to, and it was helpful, to talk, without being 'scolded' and instructed what to do, as she fears from her parents. Instead, she has had a very different experience. Our dialogue is counter-cultural and provides a welcome space in her pain.

2 Living in the now

Using solution-focused (SF) pre-suppositional language, we ask the client to suspend judgement and 'suppose' what *would* be happening if the problem *were* no more.

This use of the subjunctive verb 'were' and 'would' is correct English. My experience with people of Chinese ethnicity in Singapore is that the word 'would' is often used in place of the present tense 'will'. So use of this word 'would' is understood by many of my clients as 'will'.

In Mandarin, there are no conjugations of verbs, and all verbs mean simultaneously, 'to be' and 'being', as well as 'has been' and 'will be'. There are other words and context that indicate present, future and past. Time is. As in the brain, memories of the past, thoughts of the future and the experience of the present all are experienced as in the now.

The questions I have learned to ask are therefore always in the present tense and suggest that change is happening as we speak!

Suppose the problem *is* no more, what is happening instead?

The casually dressed mother of two frowns.

'That's a very interesting question!'

She begins to describe in detail her preferred future, in the present tense, as if it were already happening, of her best hopes, when the problem is no more.

3 You make your luck

Luck is what happens when preparation meets opportunity.

(Elmer G Letterman)

After a number of times of being met by a blank stare and a request to repeat the miracle question, or *'Do you mean when something you only ever dreamed, happens?'* *'My lucky day?'* I experimented with what phrase worked for my clients to describe life in the absence of the problem.

Both O'Hanlon and Weiner-Davis (1989) and Henden (2008) have given examples of alternatives to the miracle question. In my experience, using a culturally relevant approach for an individual is most helpful. The phrases that were most helpful for my clients are as follows:

Suppose that one night while you are asleep . . . your deepest wishes are granted/ your luck changes/ the problem is solved, like a dream come true . . .

I worked with a client before the Chinese Lunar New Year. I used this context to paint the picture of going home for her reunion dinner, celebrating with family, and then returning to work on the Monday, to find that her 'luck' had changed and her problem was no more. She entered into the moment completely to create a delicate net in which her dreams could be captured.

4   It's not inside, it's on top

McKergow and Korman (2009) describe solution-focused therapists as needing to '*stay on the surface*'.

An advertisement for coffee creamer speaks volumes. A man searches for coffee creamer. He rummages through a fridge, muttering: 'Where does she hide the creamer?' Finally, his patience wears thin and he shouts at his wife: 'There's no creamer in the fridge!' She shouts back: 'It's not inside, it's on top'. He shouts back: 'It's not inside', raises his eyes and sees it on top of the fridge and in a muted tone adds, 'it's on top!'

The traumatised teenager sits hunched self-protectively in her chair. She does not want to go over the attack because each time she has felt as if it were happening again. We do not try to analyse her trauma. We focus on the life she wants instead:

Tell me what is happening.

What do you discover?

She whispers, her voice ragged with pain, 'I have my old self back'. She pauses, and describes what she sees herself being able to do instead and the steps she will take to get there.

This has been helpful for clients who have been raised in a culture where self-awareness, identifying emotions or analysing thoughts has not been encouraged; rather, a pragmatic approach as to what to do has been promoted.

5   What gets measured gets done

My experience in Singapore suggests that measurement of how one is performing against a standard is part of the landscape. Thus scaling, as measurement, is easy to introduce.

The woman is well groomed and in her mid-fifties. She experienced the loss of her only child and has felt very isolated and angry with friends who she feels have not heard or understood her. She talks and it seems clear that she is frustrated at her limited progress, since she too wants to move on.

On a scale that measures from 1–10, where 10 stands for the day after your lucky day . . .

Where do you stand now in your situation?

Have you been lower? Where did you stand then?

How do you come back to where you are now on the scale?

What number will satisfy you?

When you achieve your satisfaction level, what do you discover?

So when you measure (n+1), what do you discover?

> She initially describes wanting to get as close to a 10 as she can! Then she revises this to an 8 as she will be doing all those things that she has not been interested in since her loss. She notices that she feels some of her 'old' passion. She is ready to do some more work together.

6 Discovering hidden treasures

Many of my clients in Singapore have explained that the focus tends to be not on what they already do well, but rather on what they need to do better. The market for enrichment and improvement is lucrative. Therefore, using the SF question 'What's better?' can unintentionally reinforce this focus on achievement. I devised a process of discovery, which leads to a very different conversation.

The young man sinks into the sofa and comments:

> *'I love the atmosphere here. I can relax and be real. . . . I don't have to keep striving. . . .'*

What do you discover instead?

What do you see that's different?

> *'I discover what I can do, what I really want. Here I have rediscovered my passion.'*

He goes on to describe his day and what his parents and friends see him doing. He is discovering what he wants, what he is already doing, that he has choices. He is starting to *rediscover* parts of himself that he has forgotten.

Using the concept of 'discovery' also suggests finding something new that you had not seen before, had overlooked or had taken for granted. Perhaps this is like an explorer, setting off in search of something, focusing the search, and paying attention only to the clues that point to the treasure.

When you leave here, what tiny things do you discover that show you that you are going in the direction you want?

> He is off on his adventure again. His view is on the *things he discovers as he takes small steps*, and he focuses on the signposts that point the way to the hidden treasure.

7 Revisiting moments of satisfaction

The framework I used to explore exceptions, or times when the problems were less, when it seems as if their lucky day has dawned, draws pragmatically on describing what is already in place. It assumes that, despite difficulties, we do have and *have had* moments of respite, or times when we engage in helpful behaviours that work. So there may be a need not to learn new behaviours, but rather, to do more of what already works, to engage the client's strengths, resources and competencies in service of their solution.

Tell me when this happened before.

Tell me about those moments when you already have your luck/ when you achieved your satisfaction level.

The woman sitting in front of me leans forward. She has already described moving on with her life as well as the routine she wants, something she has avoided since her husband left her. She continues:

'I never thought I could change. Now, I'm not so sure. Those dreams I had . . . Now when I think of picking up where I left off, I feel excited, like there's life after him . . . and it's good! I am in charge of myself again. I am a very disciplined person.'

Helping to frame these times as 'moments of satisfaction' injects a dose of hope into even the darkest night. When we draw on our memories of previous dawns, we know that this too shall pass.

8   *Highlighting strengths*

My Asian colleagues explained to me that fulsome praise does not sit well with those who have grown up in Chinese families. There is a resistance to accepting the compliment. Instead, there is a need to be modest. Direct and even indirect praise may not be welcome, and the client may not accept the comments as indicative of their strengths.

Instead, taking a low-key approach and simply *reflecting* the client's strengths, enables the client to also reflect and consider their strength.

A middle-aged man who has been passed over for promotion, due to his perceived lack of authority and impact with senior management, tells of his loss of motivation, which is impacting his performance.

As we talk, I become aware that although he is modest, there are many areas in which he shines in his life.

I notice that you . . .

I see that this 'crisis' presents the opportunity for you to. . . .

How does this happen?

He pauses. Then, he begins to talk about the times he does show up with authority and impact. His response suggests he has accepted these 'compliments' as a perspective of himself that he perhaps has forgotten.

'I think I have forgotten to do that in the company as well. Thank you for reminding me.'

He is taking the first steps to getting back on track.

Reflections

This is how I have learned to apply SFBT in a way that works for my clients in Singapore. Enabling clients to focus on a future in which the client's problems and *'cannot'* have been eclipsed by the solution they want has required focusing on helping the client to identify their preferred solution, to leverage the client's resources, strengths and competence (*'can'*-do) in service of their preferred outcome, and to support them in taking small steps on the path to achieving their preferred outcome.

Acknowledgements

With heartfelt thanks to all my clients who shared their lives with me and enabled me to learn what works with them; to Clara and Ada, who shared their work and gave me access to how to 'think Singapore', and to TK, who explained the radical root of Chinese characters, so that I might access Chinese culture.

References

Henden, J. (2008). *Preventing suicide: The solution-focused approach*. Chichester, UK: John Wiley & Sons Ltd.
McKergow, M., & Korman H. (2009). Inbetween – neither inside nor outside. The radical simplicity of solution-focused brief therapy. *Journal of Systemic Therapies, 28*, 34–49.
O'Hanlon, W.H., & Weiner-Davis, M. (1989). *In search of solutions: A new direction in psychotherapy*. New York, NY: Norton.

4

CHINESE CULTURAL VALUES AND SOLUTION FOCUSED THERAPY

Simon Tak-mau Chan and Ada Yee Lin Chung

Introduction

Indigenous and cultural considerations have been extensively discussed in the field of psychotherapy for the past two decades, (Kuo, 2004; Duan et al., 2011; Moir-Bussy, 2014). Thus, when we apply solution focused therapy (SFT) to Chinese clients in Hong Kong, we have to first understand Chinese cultural values. In this chapter, we will share some of the important cultural values that affect the counselling of Chinese clients and the appropriateness of SFT in the Chinese cultural context. We will also share clinical examples of using SFT in Hong Kong that will illustrate the use and adaptation of the approach as needed so as to sensitively and effectively take the cultural values into account.

Chinese cultural context

Whereas self-actualisation and independence are emphasised in western society, the Chinese focus on different values that are profoundly influenced by Confucianism, e.g., collectivism, hierarchy and harmony (Kuo & Gingrich, 2005; Duan et al., 2011). These differences in values warrant the need to modify western based therapies to fit the Chinese cultural context. Some of these values are discussed below.

Independent vs. interdependent self construals

The concept of collectivism, which is influenced by Confucianism, is so prevalent in Chinese society that the self/person (rén, 人) is seen as part of a larger group (zhòng, 众): '(t)he concept of self is often derided and played down in favour of group considerations' (Bond & Hwang, 1990, p. 236). Chinese people place much importance on family bonds and unity, and emphasise reserve and formality in social relationships. Individuality, independence and self-reliance are given less importance. Since people are interdependent and interconnected, individual problems are seen as family problems, and personal success and failure are not individual issues, but attributed to a group, clan or family (Kuo, 2004; Duan et al. 2011).

Interdependence and SFT

Since the Chinese prioritise family, they are therefore concerned about the reactions of their family members, and any impact of their problems on them. Consequently, it is appropriate to ask questions that concern relationships in SFT. For example, 'If I ask your mother, what would she say about your strengths?' This question aligns with the Chinese context, which emphasises interpersonal relationships and also facilitates the client to reflect on their concerns from the perspective of another person.

Therapist: What are your best hopes from our session today?
Tony: I don't know. My dad told me to come.
Therapist: If I were to ask your father the same question, what would he tell me?
Tony: I think he would say that I need to improve my grades. We always disagree about my school work.

In this case, the therapist asked Tony to respond based on the perspective of his father, which would improve his sense of linkage to his family member in the SFT session.

Face

According to Yuan (2013, p. 93), face (liǎn, 脸) 'is the respect of the group for an individual with a good moral reputation'. To lose face is a serious matter because a person is then judged badly by their community. This loss of face not only affects the individual, but also their clan or family. Thus, an individual is expected to give higher priority to the needs, feelings and face of their family especially when there is conflict between the self and family. Therefore, individuals tend to take into consideration the response of other people about their own actions and are very careful to act appropriately so that they will not lose face.

Face and help seeking

Personal problems, especially mental and emotional issues, are seen as signs of weakness. They are also viewed as a failure of the family because an individual is losing face, which also causes the family to lose face. Thus, Chinese people will rarely talk about personal problems or seek help since it is shameful to tell the outsider about one's own family's problem (Yuan, 2013). In fact, face is so important that even when clients overcome their personal barriers to seeking help and are in the therapy room, they may assume sole responsibility for the problem so as to preserve the reputation of their family. SFT therefore works well in this situation as the aim of this therapy is not to understand the cause of the problem, but to explore ways to move forward. The therapist would need to simultaneously explore moving forward from the viewpoint of both the client and their family, so that their needs are both met. It is also helpful to invite the client to use family resources in working towards a solution.

Case example

Tony is 8 years old. His father, Mr Wong, and teachers are concerned that he could have ADHD. Mr Wong is worried about Tony's situation and hopes that the therapist can provide more information that would help him with the behaviour of his son. If a perspective of pathology is used, the focus would be on the diagnosis and behaviour issues of Tony and treatment would be provided accordingly.

SFT, however, focuses on helping the client to recognise what it is they want and what they are already able to do. For example, scaling questions can be used.

Therapist: Let's say that 10 is the perfect day, 1 is the opposite. What would you score today?
Mr Wong: 3.
Tony: I would say 4.
Therapist: Imagine that there is an increase of 1 point, what will be different?

With the use of scaling questions, the therapist is evaluating the perception of the circumstances of Mr Wong and Tony. When they are asked to imagine a 1-point improvement, this allows them to envision the possible changes and how both father and son can contribute to the changes.

The therapist has also changed the direction of the discourse to eliminate any complaints about Tony's performance at school. This helped preserve the 'face' of the client and also his family.

Filial piety

Filial piety (xiào, 孝) is an important element for understanding how the Chinese perceive themselves, others and the world (Hsu & Wang, 2011). The crux of filial piety is that relationships are ordered through a social hierarchy. Parents or elderly/senior family members (grandparents, aunts, uncles, etc.) have a higher position and more authority, and therefore, are respected, are obeyed and command great respect from the younger generation due to their vast life experience and social standing. Filial piety is also extended to other parental or authority figures such as teachers.

Filial piety and expectations of counselling

Filial piety also influences the role of clients and therapists, and expectations from counselling sessions (Saner-Yiu & Saner-Yiu, 1985; Snider, 2005). Chinese clients situate their therapist as an authority figure who can provide solutions. Indeed the Chinese translation of counselling (fǔ dǎo, 辅导) means direction and guidance. Solution focused therapists, however, see clients as the experts in their own lives and believe that they have the competency to solve their own problems. Therefore, it is important that solution focused therapists help clients to understand that they are simply assisting in the therapeutic process, rather than providing 'the answers' or solutions.

Filial piety and SFT

Due to the influence of filial piety, it can be especially difficult for children and youths to voice their opinions to those who have seniority and their parents, especially if their opinions are conflicting.

A strength-based approach like SFT can help these clients to relax and speak up during the counselling process. Younger clients will feel more comfortable in expressing their views and have the capacity to better understand the viewpoints of their parents, especially when relationship questions are used (Hsu & Wang, 2011) as the focus is on coping, and positive examples are used to demonstrate viable options.

Therapist: Tony, what has your father has done to help improve your school work?
Tony: Sometimes he checks my homework at night.
Therapist: How is that helpful?

Tony is able to share the contributions from his father towards improvement in his school work in the counselling session. Prompted by his therapist, he can also express his appreciation towards the efforts of his father, which could have been previously suppressed and not acknowledged.

Modesty

The Chinese have the tendency to be diligent in meeting their responsibilities and often do not like to take much credit for success (Anderson, 1999). Therefore, Chinese people tend to demonstrate modesty (qiān xùn, 谦逊) when asked about their strengths. While acknowledging success or strengths means that one's ability is recognised, it is also an honour to the family. One's strength is also defined by others, especially through the collective strength of family members, as evidenced by family support. However, one should not be overly demonstrative of one's strengths, and it is good to be modest because this also reflects well on the parents and family (Yip, 2008). Thus, recognition of ability is good as this brings honour to the family, but at the same time, it is not good to flaunt one's strengths.

Modesty and compliments in SFT

The use of compliments is essential in SFT, that is, acknowledgement and reinforcement of clients' strengths and what they are doing well. There are three kinds of compliments: direct, indirect and self. The Chinese are more receptive to indirect compliments that highlight their accomplishments, as this fits with the concept of modesty, rather than direct compliments, which may make them feel uneasy. Indirect compliments also work well when the client feels uncomfortable with self-complimenting. According to Moir-Bussy (2014), clients benefit most from compliments that focus on their efforts and personal qualities, and also those that are culturally appropriate.

Therapist: Both of you are willing to improve Tony's school work. Tony, you acknowledge that your father helps you with math. You are able to put yourself in your father's situation and improve your school work to meet his expectations. Mr Wong, you have attempted to help your son and provide resources for his studies. And your son has acknowledged your efforts.

The compliment comes from restating in their own words what the client and his father have done. The acknowledgment of the actions taken to improve the father-son relationship and Tony's academic performance also considers the family as a whole in the process rather than attributing the success at an individual level.

Pragmatism

During the counselling process, Chinese clients tend to seek practical advice because they value pragmatism (shí yòng zhǔ yì, 实用主义). They prefer to know 'how' to do something rather than 'why' or the reason that something happened. Chinese clients normally want an immediate outcome within a certain period of time, and therefore prefer their therapist to be directive and efficient (Chong & Hung, 2002).

Pragmatism and SFT

Chinese clients therefore value therapy that is goal-oriented and able to solve their problems. This fits well with SFT, which emphasises solution building in a short time frame and focuses on moving forward rather than understanding the cause of the problems. Scaling questions can therefore guide these clients to work towards solutions in a stepwise manner, which is appropriate for Chinese clients because they prefer a practical approach with foreseeable outcomes.

Conclusion

Every culture has its own unique characteristics, and these cultural contexts are crucial to bear in mind when carrying out therapy. Although SFT originated in the United States, we have demonstrated that many of the principles fit very well in the Chinese context, although some of the techniques require slight amendments. When therapists are sensitive to cultural differences and adapt the approach to take these into consideration as outlined above, SFT can indeed be very effective in this setting.

References

Anderson, C.A. (1999). Attributional style, depression, and loneliness: A cross-cultural comparison of American and Chinese students. *Personality and Social Psychology Bulletin, 25*(4), 482–499.

Bond, M.H., & Hwang, K.K. (1990). The social psychology of Chinese people. In M.H. Bond (Ed.), *The psychology of the Chinese people* (4th ed.) (pp. 213–266). Hong Kong: Oxford University Press.

Chong, H, F., & Hung, Y.L. (2002). Indigenous counselling in the Chinese culture context: Experience transformed model. *Asian Journal of Counselling, 9*(1), 49–68.

Duan, C., Nilsson, J., Wang, C.C.D., Debernardi, N., Klevens, C., & Tallent, C. (2011). Internationalizing counselling: A Southeast Asian perspective. *Counselling Psychology Quarterly, 24*(1), 29–41.

Hsu, W.S., & Wang, C.D.C. (2011). Integrating Asian clients' filial piety beliefs into solution-focused brief therapy. *International Journal of Advanced Counselling, 33*(4), 322–334.

Kuo, B.C.H. (2004). Interdependent and relational tendencies among Asian clients: infusing collectivistic strategies into counselling. *Guidance and Counselling, 19*(4), 158–162.

Kuo, B.C.H., & Gingrich, L. (2005). Correlates of self-construals among Asian and Caucasian undergraduates in Canada: Cultural patterns and implications for counselling. *Guidance and Counselling, 20*(2), 78–88.

Moir-Bussy, A. (2014). Using SFBT in Hong Kong: Initiatives from Hong Kong master of counselling psychology students and implications for cultural contexts in Australia. *Journal of Solution-Focused Brief Therapy, 1*(1), 31–46.

Saner-Yiu, L., & Saner-Yiu R. (1985). Value dimensions in American counselling: A Taiwanese-American comparison. *International Journal for the Advancement of Counselling, 8*(2), 137–146.

Snider, P.D. (2005). Better meeting the counselling needs of ethnic Chinese international students: Exploring the relationship between cultural backgrounds and counselling expectations. In *Higher Education in a Changing World Sydney: Proceedings of the 2005 Annual International Conference of the Higher Education Research and Development Society of Australasia Inc. (HERDSA)*. Sydney, NSW: Higher Education Research and Development Society of Australasia. Retrieved from: http://conference.herdsa.org.au/2005/pdf/refer eed/paper_181.pdf.

Yip, K.S. (2008). Searching the Chinese cultural roots of the strengths perspective. In K.S.Yip (Ed.), *Strength-based perspective in working with clients with mental illness: A Chinese cultural articulation* (pp. 21–36). Hayppayge, NY: Nova Science Publishers, Inc.

Yuan, X. (2013). Face revisited – Negative face wants in Chinese culture. *China Media Research, 9*(1), 90–100

5

SOLUTION FOCUSED INTERVENTIONS IN ADDICTIONS TREATMENT IN ASIA

'Breaking the bonds of shame and isolation'

Andrew da Roza

In Asia, the shame of addictions and the cultural weight to keep personal issues inside the nuclear family make solution focused brief therapy (SFBT) an ideal intervention for recovery. SFBT validates and supports clients' values and allows the client to articulate the best outcome of therapy in their own cultural frame of reference. Importantly, SFBT invites clients to imagine a future free of their addiction. This chapter discusses how SFBT uniquely empowers addicts in Asia with a new hope, that they can free themselves from the bondage of their secrets and shame that are so powerfully forged by cultural norms.

Cultures in Asia

There are many ethnicities, cultures and races in Asia. Many people from Asia also travel abroad to study and work and they often adopt aspects of other cultures. Some people have grown up outside Asia and have returned to Asia to study and work. Finally, popular cultures have spread between Asian cities and between Asia and the West and have pervaded daily life since ships first started sailing. It may therefore appear dangerously reductionist to refer to 'Asian culture'.

Further, slicing and dicing the concept of 'culture'—measuring it and making comparisons—can be extraordinarily complex, as demonstrated by Minkov (2013). Minkov compared 27 cross-cultural studies, each methodology with their own conceptualisations, assumptions, methodologies and pitfalls. It can be hard to draw meaningful conclusions across the studies: as Minkov put it: '(C)ulture can be whatever a scholar decides it should be' (p. 9).

While comparisons across cultures can be difficult, there is empirical support for identifying basic values essential to Chinese culture, such as: 'tolerance, harmony with others, filial piety, having a sense of shame, protecting your "face", having few desires, moderation, and keeping oneself disinterested and pure' (Minkov, 2013, p. 219). Further, there appears to be an empirically derived Chinese culture of collectivism versus individuality (Hofstede, 2001). This is sometimes attributed to Confucianism in China, which values a focus on: the family unit rather than individuals; family and clan harmony; harmony and stability being based on unequal relationships (e.g., father and children and scholars and pupils); and saving face – with shame as an attendant and main social management tool (Bond, 2010).

The Analects of Confucius warn that:

> (I)f officials lead the people with administrative injunctions and put them in their place with penal law, they will avoid punishments but will be without a sense of shame. Lead them with excellence and put them in their place through roles and ritual practices, and in addition to developing a sense of shame, they will order themselves harmoniously.

It also advises us to: '. . . listen more to others' opinions and withhold questions and doubts . . .'; '. . . observe more what is happening around us . . .' and '. . . not take risks . . .' The ultimate goal is to rarely make mistakes in speech and rarely regret our actions (Confucius, & in Waley, 1938).

When harmony is at stake, there is great risk that any statement may cause offence. It therefore makes sense to only speak if: (a) one is sure how everyone else will react and (b) if what is said is certain to make a material difference.

Readers who assume that Communism crowded out Confucianism in China may be interested to read about the revival of Confucianism in contemporary China (Lin, 2012).

Culture and addictions

It is not hard to see how such tenets, if viscerally held, would nurture the precipitants and perpetuators of addictions: shame and isolation.

If 'harmony' is the watchword and if it is the ultimate responsibility of each person to maintain the 'face', dignity and prestige of the family – then the wreckage in the wake of an addict is not only heinously against the natural order of things – it is something to deny, avoid and bury deep.

More practically, if filial piety commands that the decision for the addict to seek outside help has to be surrendered to the head of the household (whether or not they may also be an addict), then the chances that secrets will be shared with strangers in the helping professions is slim to none.

It is no surprise therefore that in Asia, the first outside interjections may come from the police, judiciary and the prison service, where there is a focus on deterrence and punishment (and, therefore, shaming). This focus makes a poor bedfellow with effective recovery interventions.

Given the Confucian tenets, it is not surprising, in the author's experience, that doctors, psychiatrists and psychologists are venerated 'experts', called upon to 'cure' the addict once and for all. It is also no surprise to the author that interventions that vigorously dispute 'irrational' thoughts and doggedly break down 'resistance' and 'denial' go unchallenged by clients and their families. Nor is it a surprise to see that clients become demoralised, resentful and withdrawn as a result.

Alcoholics Anonymous (AA) and other recovery groups in Asia do provide a safe haven of non-judgmental connections. They abound with phrases from the United States such as: 'you are only as sick as your secrets'. However, if an Asian addict is not there in mind and body to hear it, then, like a tree falling in the wilderness, there is no sound.

The recovery 'rooms' are anathema to many aspects of Asian culture. The Alcoholics Anonymous Basic Text's (2001) – known informally as The Big Book – insistence that participants openly and regularly admit their addiction and articulate their darkest secrets to strangers provides poor comfort. Listening to others parade their own shame provides even less comfort.

Solution focused brief therapy and addictions in Asia

SFBT offers several intervention possibilities for working with people with addictions in Asia. No longer need the therapist pose as an 'elevated expert' in the Confucian tradition and start with a long and imperious list of shaming closed questions – proving to the client, that sharing with strangers is an inherently invasive and invalidating experience.

With SFBT, the first question from the therapist is addressed with the intention not of completing a bureaucratic 'form of shame' but of asking about a client's 'best hopes' in the moment. If the client is reluctant to disclose their addictions, SFBT allows the client to decide what they wish to talk about – what viscerally ails them – for which addiction may only be but one symptom (Berg & Miller, 1992; Berg & Reuss, 1998).

SFBT not only allows the therapist as much space as the client needs to establish trust, it exhorts therapists to stay 'one step behind' and to lead from that, 'not knowing' position (Pichot, 2009). This provides an important safety feature: invasion and intrusion are eliminated.

Instead of reinforcing the societal assumption of heinous mala fides or incorrigible weakness, SFBT allows the client to address the empowering question of what helped them be successful in the past (Berg & Reuss, 1998). Discussions about past victories, strengths and resources and the attendant compliments of the therapist are very powerful. With a fair 'wind in their sails', it can be a short journey for clients to contemplate how these strengths and resources can be applied to problems in the present moment.

The Asian client need not touch on the shameful past at all, since, in SFBT, the solutions and the process by which they are discovered bear no relationship to the wreckage of the past (De Jong & Berg, 2013; Pichot, 2009).

Steve de Shazer (1984) declared that SFBT was the 'Death of Resistance', and I extrapolate this to mean that SFBT liberates an addict from the bonds of toxic shame.

If the client is initially unwilling to share their inner world or the inner worlds of those they are honour-bound to protect (such as family members), then SFBT can invite the client to share their perceptions of the inner worlds of more distant and abstract 'others', such as Society and future bosses: 'What does Society want to see you do differently?'; 'What would you be doing that tells potential employers that they can count on you?'; 'What would others be doing when your problem goes away?'.

SFBT allows the client to drive the dialogue of recovery by being in the present moment and future centred. Free from the explorations of the trauma of the past, SFBT invites the client into the future, to articulate a vision, a goal and the next small, single step.

When SFBT allows a client to roam free in the wonderland of the miracle question, the author and other SFBT practitioners in addiction interventions have noted a marked change in clients (Korman & Soderquist, 1994; Pichot, 2009). The author has witnessed clients taken aback at being given permission to dream of a better tomorrow – believing that they are undeserving of such luxuries. Once they are able to articulate the aftermath of the miracle, they become animated, hopeful and open to taking responsibility for their recovery.

It takes time and persistence, but when the euphoria of endless possibilities descends on a client, trust blossoms and the therapist can, in that moment, become a member of the client's inner circle. It is as though the steel door that culture locked and bolted stays intact but a new window is opened next to it. From that window a breeze is allowed to enter – one of hope, openness and willingness. For some clients this may be the birth of a new spiritual experience, as the golden light of day illuminates the farthest and darkest corners of their lives.

Perhaps one of the most powerful features of SFBT is relationship questions. Relationships are the foundation on which culture rests. It is no wonder that the Analects of Confucius (Confucius, & in Waley, 1938) emphasise that virtue (rén or 仁) exists only in relationships.

In Asia, many clients wanting to explore solutions in recovery appear intuitively drawn to relationship questions. How a client's relative perceives abstinence and what a relative will do differently as a result hold infinitely more possibilities than questions about how the client will experience sobriety. It is by predicting the future world through the eyes of others that change becomes not only possible but likely.

In Asia, where an addict's deep sense of shame is forged in the furnaces of culture, nothing appears to weaken these shackles more than coping questions. Statements such as: 'I am amazed. With all the anger, criticism and disappointment shown by your family, how did you manage to cope?'; 'How do you get from one minute to the next?'; 'How did you wake up each morning and face another day?' Tears fall, as years of frustration are unlocked. As the coping dialogue progresses, the clients' tears are replaced by new tears – those of joy, at finally being accepted, understood and validated for who they are. There is no finer moment in therapy.

The value of SFBT with addicts in Asia was brought home to the author when he recently attended a course on smoking cessation at the Health Promotion Board, a Singapore Government body under the Ministry of Health. One of the primary interventions taught on the course was SFBT. The ethos of SFBT was taught ingeniously using the Chinese complex character (聽) 'tīng', meaning: 'to hear'.

聽

The upper left portion of the character is 'ear' – reminding therapists to paraphrase and summarise – key skills in SFBT. The lower left portion is 'king' – reminding the therapist that the client's perspective and language is front and centre, throughout the interaction – something that SFBT seeks to honour. The 'cross' at the top right of the character represents 'reception' – reminding the therapist to be attentive and in the present moment – an outcome that SFBT therapists pursue. The middle portion under the 'cross' is 'eye', reminding the therapist to observe the client carefully, notice their emotions and any disconnect between what they say and how they present. The bottom right portion represents 'one heart', exhorting therapists to work with compassion and reminding that the heart of compassion beats strongly in SFBT.

Hopes for the future

It is the author's hope that SFBT will become the leading intervention in addictions recovery in Asia – rending asunder the bonds of shame and isolation – making it possible for addicts to know a new freedom and new happiness.

Acknowledgements

I am indebted to Ms Susan Tan of ECI Consulting Holdings Pte. Ltd, trainer for the inspired teaching of SFBT during the Singapore Health Promotion Board's smoking cessation programme.

References

Alcoholics Anonymous. (2001). *The basic text for Alcoholics Anonymous* (4th ed.). New York, NY: Alcoholics Anonymous World Services, Inc.

Berg, I.S., & Miller, S.D. (1992). *Working with the problem drinker.* New York, NY: W.W. Norton & Company, Inc.

Berg, I.S., & Reuss, N.H. (1998). *Solutions step by step.* New York, NY: W.W. Norton & Company, Inc.

Bond, M.H. (2010). *The Oxford handbook of Chinese psychology.* New York, NY: Oxford University Press.

Confucius, & in Waley, A. (1938). *The analects of Confucius.* New York, NY: Random House.

De Jong, P., & Berg, I.K. (2013). *Interviewing for solutions* (4th ed.). Belmont CA: Brooks/Cole, Cengage Learning.

de Shazer, S. (1984). The death of resistance. *Family Process, 23,* 79–93.

Hofstede, G. (2001). *Culture's consequences – comparing values, behaviors, institutions and organizations across nations* (2nd ed.). Thousand Oaks, CA: Sage Publications, Inc.

Korman, H., & Soderquist, M. (1994). *'Talk about a miracle!' Co-operating with addicts and their networks.* Retrieved from: http://www.sikt.nu/publications/ (Originally published in Swedish: *Snacka om mirakel.* Stockholm, Sweden: Mareld).

Lin, D.Q. (2012). Working to be worthy – shame and the Confucian technology of governing. In A.B. Kipnis (Ed.), *Chinese modernity and the individual psyche.* New York, NY: Palgrave Macmillen.

Minkov, M. (2013). *Cross-cultural analysis – the art and science of comparing the world's modern societies and their cultures.* Thousand Oaks, CA: SAGE Publications, Inc.

Pichot, T. (2009). *Solution-focused substance abuse treatment.* New York, NY: Routledge Taylor & Francis Group.

6

THE UNSUNG HEROES AND HEROINES

Uncovering clients' hidden strengths and resources within a Singapore mental health setting

Eunice Limin Seah

Introduction

As a psychologist at The Institute of Mental Health (IMH), I work with adult clients with mental health issues (including those with intellectual disability [ID] and who may be on the autism spectrum) who are diagnosed and referred by psychiatrists for therapy. Just as in mental health settings elsewhere, the dominant medical model often limits clinicians' understanding of their clients to their respective psychiatric diagnoses. While diagnoses provide a universal short-hand system to guide treatment, clinicians run a risk of homogenising individuals with the same diagnoses (e.g., schizophrenia).

In the past, I used various forms of therapy that typically focused on symptom alleviation through specific techniques that were derived from pre-determined clinical models. While this provided instant access to many helpful techniques, operating from this paradigm implies a 'one-size-fits-all' assumption and undermines each client's unique experience of their mental health condition, their range of coping abilities and the larger picture of their envisioned life beyond symptoms.

Instead, I am employing solution-focused brief therapy (SFBT) as this enables clients to capitalise on their *unique* capabilities in living life and manage their mental health issues. Allowing us to amplify and reinforce what has been adaptive, each client's expertise then facilitates moving towards envisioned changes in their lives. Rather than targeting symptoms per se, SFBT redirects clients to work towards a more hopeful life situation, which often results in a concomitant reduction of symptoms.

SFBT has been shown to be effective in addressing a variety of mental health conditions (e.g., Gingerich & Peterson 2013). Given the dearth of research into its effectiveness in Asia, this chapter aims to contribute clinical evidence from individual case studies using SFBT in a Singapore mental health setting. The use of SFBT techniques with four clients is described to showcase the applicability of SFBT across a variety of mental health issues as well as highlighting the individuality of these clients. For each client, the particular techniques that were pivotal in their progress are described and reflected upon, including any cultural or other adaptations that were used.

Lili: 'Learning to walk again'

Lili, a 29-year-old Chinese female, presented to therapy with depressed mood.[1] Lili hoped to cope better with environmental cues that triggered memories of unpleasant interactions with her parents and how they purportedly controlled the kinds of emotions she should be experiencing. Lili's second therapy goal was to work towards communicating her emotions more adaptively and becoming more 'accepting' of them.

The *Elicit, Amplify, Reinforce and Start Again (EARS) process* increased Lili's confidence by reinforcing what she did well. Her social interactions subsequently increased, which provided opportunities for Lili to learn about the above-mentioned triggers and initiate more effective coping strategies.

Scaling questions were pivotal in driving Lili's progress. While scaling her communication abilities, Lili figured that to move from 2 to 2.5/10, she needed to communicate her emotions effectively across more situations but found it difficult to identify them as they were sometimes 'mixed'. I highlighted to Lili that she had successfully communicated her emotions to me without identifying any of her emotions! Upon further exploration, Lili discovered that she tended to analyse her emotions, which she wanted to stop as it did not help her communicate emotions effectively.

As if on cue, Lili's ability to cope with uncomfortable and intense emotions was tested across subsequent occasions. For example, when her good friend died, Lili allowed herself to feel upset and cry for a few days, contrary to her previous strategy of suppressing her emotions. Realising that she did not require others' permission to experience certain emotions, they lasted for a shorter time.

On another occasion, Lili also experienced intense emotions when the anniversary of her friend's death coincided with the hospital admission of another friend. Tapping on her strength in drawing, I invited her to draw something that represented her emotions. From that process, Lili realised that the drawing helped her view her emotions from an outside perspective and realise that grief was temporary, which made her 'hopeful'. Through these processes, Lili gradually learnt that her emotions were 'temporary states', which she allowed to 'flow through', eventually mastering an ability to 'sit with' her emotions.

Reflection. Unlike the other clients in this chapter, no cultural adaptations were required in my work with Lili. Her English-speaking abilities and understanding of abstract concepts made adaptations needless. Lili's story highlights that negotiating tiny steps of change through *scaling* is pivotal towards bigger, quicker, client-driven and sustained change.

Faith in hardiness

Faith, a 46-year-old Chinese female, was diagnosed with major depressive disorder. When Faith first presented to therapy, she was juggling complicated divorce proceedings, her diploma studies and managing her emotional well-being as well as her children's, and sometimes contemplated suicide. She wanted to work toward being more patient with her children who blamed her for various changes related to the divorce. Riding on Faith's dedication to her children and her 'hardiness', the SFBT technique *The Worst Case (Graveside or Crematorium) Scenario* (WCS) (Henden, 2008) was used to address Faith's suicidal ideations on one occasion and was pivotal in empowering Faith to handle future problems more confidently.

Faith was invited to 'fast-forward' to the future by supposing that she was attending her own funeral following a completed suicide and to visualise who might be present, what they might be doing and what she might say to them. This provided an opportunity for Faith to build fuller, future-oriented insights into the consequences of suicide.

Faith's 'eureka' moment came when she visualised herself telling her crying and 'traumatised' children, 'Sorry, I love you but I could not take it so I took a shortcut'. Immediately saying, 'Yeah, that's a shortcut, luckily I did not (attempt suicide) last night', Faith realised that her children would have perceived her as an 'irresponsible mom' if she had committed suicide. This realisation motivated her to complete her studies.

Faith revealed that my acknowledgement of her 'hardiness' (*amplification of strength*) increased her self-confidence, which helped her handle future challenges. One such challenge was attending a breast health examination, which she had delayed for fear of its outcome. The ensuing medical investigations, which indicated the disappearance of previous abnormalities, further strengthened Faith's self-confidence and religious faith to cope with further challenges. Together with her constant efforts to do things differently in order to update me on 'What has been better since the last session?' (*pre-suppositional question*), Faith's self-confidence motivated her to rise above her emotional issues and she continued pushing herself to do 'hardy' things such as seeking professional help for her children's emotional issues and continuing with her studies while maintaining a part-time job.

Reflection. Faith's dedication to her children was at the core of her therapeutic progress, while SFBT techniques (e.g., the WCS) elicited this belief and facilitated Faith to work towards it. To adapt the WCS to the Singapore context, I adapted the 'funeral' setting to allude to the 'wake' that was held before the cremation of the deceased. More importantly, as the topic of death is considered taboo by some Singaporeans, I was cautious in using the WCS with Faith and decided to do so only because of our strong rapport.

Ana: Shooting (and) busybody

Diagnosed with Asperger's syndrome when in school, Ana, a 20-year-old Malay female, presented with extended durations of hand washing and showering, which she called 'OCD'. Ana could express herself in simple English language but found it difficult to understand more complex concepts. Ana hoped to achieve a 'normal life' as a result of working on her OCD.

Ana struggled with answering more abstract SFBT questions about her preferred future (i.e., visualising a normal life). Consistent with the SFBT principle of *doing what works*, I therefore incorporated *externalisation* (not an SFBT technique) to help Ana visualise OCD (the problem) as a concrete entity by reframing OCD as a 'visitor' and asking Ana to name and describe its characteristics.

Naming OCD 'Busybody', Ana visualised OCD as an enormous object that extended beyond the room. Using exaggerated hand gestures and facial expressions, I gestured to indicate the times when enormous 'Busybody' became physically smaller (*eliciting exceptions*). A pivotal moment arose when Ana said that she would be continuing with rifle shooting classes when 'Busybody' was smaller. In subsequent sessions, Ana became increasingly proactive in preparing for shooting classes (e.g., booking the shooting range). Ana said that focusing on rifle shooting resulted in less frequent visits from 'Busybody' (fewer OCD symptoms). In the process of therapy, Ana also became more aware of the strategies she was already using to keep Busybody smaller (e.g., reading the Quran) and was encouraged to continue using them.

When Ana and her parents agreed to terminate therapy a few sessions later, Ana was still attending shooting classes and was even eligible to participate in a shooting competition!

Reflection. Ana's story highlights the importance of tailoring SFBT to the client's level of understanding. The therapist's creativity was challenged to think beyond the realms of specific SFBT techniques and incorporate non-SFBT techniques, to enhance the effectiveness of therapy. However, this was done in a considered way that stayed true to the philosophy of SFBT of doing what works. Working alongside Ana also attuned me to the role of her Islamic faith in her progress. Overall, Ana's story highlights that *exceptions* offered glimpses into slivers of her envisioned life, which motivated her to work hard towards it and reducing her OCD symptoms concomitantly.

Kate: 'Happy'

Kate, a 24-year-old Chinese female, was an individual with mild ID who could write and express herself verbally in simple English but had difficulties understanding complex concepts. She presented to the first therapy session with her mother, Suxian, who wanted to work on Kate's temper tantrums.

Eliciting exceptions during the initial sessions served to diffuse Suxian's frustration and critical comments towards Kate, which shifted their focus towards Kate's more desirable behaviours and also paved the way for *constructing a common project*. Equal turn-taking opportunities to hear and understand each other's perspectives empowered them to hear each other's viewpoints. For example, Kate's assistance with domestic chores made Suxian happy, which in turn made Kate happy. Capitalising on this, I explored how they would like to feel towards each other as a result of therapy by using happy- and unhappy-looking paper emoticons to concretise emotions for Kate. Unanimously choosing the happy-looking emoticon to indicate their desired relationship after therapy, Kate and Suxian derived a shared therapy direction for subsequent sessions.

Eliciting exceptions also revealed Kate's ability to generate solutions. For example, while Suxian was happy whenever Kate folded newspapers for her grandmother's market stall, Suxian disliked tidying up after Kate who left newspapers lying around. Upon exploring what could be done differently, Kate spontaneously generated a solution by asking her friends to telephone her at a later time so that she could complete her task and not leave the newspapers lying around.

Learning about what could be done differently about Kate's tantrums between sessions allowed for the co-construction of alternatives. For example, on one occasion, Kate started shouting after she was told that she had to miss therapy because her grandmother had taken ill. Kate revealed that she could not account for her absence from the sheltered workshop if she had missed therapy, so Suxian suggested that Kate could communicate her emotions through simple writing in future. As a result of these processes, Suxian reported that Kate demonstrated fewer anger outbursts and recovered faster from each episode.

Reflection. Kate's story highlights that using SFBT to *Construct a Common Project* provides one useful way to work with parent-child dyads, including people with ID (PWID) and their caregivers, when the child is often perceived as 'the problem'. Cultural sensitivity was also essential. For example, I translated the sessions into Mandarin as Suxian was dominantly Mandarin-speaking. Knowing that Suxian identified with most Asian clients who commonly perceive therapists as authority figures, I anticipated that engaging Suxian's joint therapy alliance could be overwhelming and be perceived as blaming Suxian for Kate's tantrums. Hence, I affirmed Suxian's parental expertise by listening non-judgementally to her efforts in managing Kate's behaviours, amplifying her successes. Using tangible assistive aids to concretise the session to enhance Kate's comprehension was also key.

Conclusions

Contrary to the popular belief that SFBT is limited only to English-speaking, well-schooled clients, the four case examples indicate that SFBT can be successfully applied to clients ranging from Mandarin-speaking clients through to PWID and working professionals. Attuning myself to each client, being culturally sensitive and tailoring SFBT to each client creatively as much as possible were key to enhancing the effectiveness of SFBT. These four clients' common hope of an envisioned life on which they have successfully embarked strongly attests to their individuality, capabilities and zest for life alongside their mental health issues. In closing, I hope these clients' stories will inspire other mental health professionals to use SFBT in Asian settings.

Acknowledgements

This chapter is dedicated to: the clients in this chapter; the two clients whose equally meaningful therapeutic journeys I could not include due to space constraints; Mr Ong Lue Ping; my partner, Mr Adrian Yeo: and Mrs Debbie Hogan.

Note

1 Lili's diagnosis was not accessible at the time of preparing this chapter. Lili and Faith were diagnosed by IMH psychiatrists, but their diagnoses were not the focus of therapy.

References

Gingerich, W.J., & Peterson, L.T. (2013). Effectiveness of solution-focused brief therapy: A systematic qualitative review of controlled outcome studies. *Research on Social Work Practice, 23*, 266–283.
Henden, J. (2008). The solution focused approach in working with the suicidal. In *Preventing suicide: The solution-focused approach* (pp. 144–145). West Sussex, England: John Wiley & Sons Ltd.

7

FROM HELPLESS AND HOPELESS TO EMPOWERMENT AND RECOVERY

Using solution-focused brief therapy with clients with psychosis

Jane Tuomola and Yi Ping Lee

Introduction

Many authors have written about how to apply solution-focused brief therapy (SFBT) with clients with psychosis (e.g. Hawkes, 2003; Macdonald, 2011; O'Hanlon & Rowan, 2003). This chapter takes a different focus and describes how SFBT has transformed the work of a group of case managers (CMs) who work with clients with psychosis in Singapore. An in-depth interview with one of the senior CMs highlights the power of SFBT to change practice. That her journey was no isolated example is supported by comments from the other CMs and the team leader. A case study illustrates the application of SFBT in this setting. Cultural factors related to using SFBT in Singapore are also discussed.

The setting and the start of SFBT in the team

The Early Psychosis Intervention Programme (EPIP) is based at the Institute of Mental Health, the only psychiatric hospital in Singapore. EPIP works with clients experiencing their first episode of or those at risk of developing psychosis. A multi-disciplinary team approach provides a comprehensive and personalised service anchored by case management. Each client is assigned a CM who functions as a central point of contact: providing supportive counselling and on-going psychoeducation, and linking them with community resources necessary for recovery.

In 2010, the team leader wanted to improve case management within the team. To facilitate clients' recovery, help them remain hopeful and increase their self-worth, she wanted CMs to focus more on clients' strengths and resources. She had been to an introduction-to-SFBT course and thought this model would be good to guide the CMs in their work. Indeed, SFBT has been indicated as a good way of operationalising strengths based case management (Greene et al., 2006). All the CMs then attended the introduction-to-SFBT course, which was followed up with group supervision.

An interview with a senior CM, Yi Ping Lee, illustrates how SFBT transformed her practice as a result.

My journey with solution-focused brief therapy

Q: Tell me about your work as a CM before training in SFBT.

A: I didn't have guidance from any theoretical framework. I offered 'supportive work', which included suggestions on how clients could better solve their 'problems'. Listening to clients' complaints was helpful to my clients, albeit not for long – but was very unhealthy for me. I had periods of burn-out and found myself avoiding clients. Helplessness was a common feeling, and I questioned my competency.

Q: What were your feelings about SFBT initially?

A: I didn't think SFBT would be useful. I thought that SFBT meant offering solutions to clients' problems and wondered what there was to learn about this.

Q: So what changed?

A: I realised my initial beliefs about SFBT had been utterly wrong. The turning point came when I was re-introduced to the guiding principles behind SFBT in supervision. During the introductory course in SFBT, I had been more interested in learning questions, and had not believed in the importance of learning the philosophy behind the framework.

Q: How was the philosophy helpful?

A: Applying SFBT principles like 'if something works, do more of it' in my personal tough moments shifted my mindset about my ability to overcome my problems. I picked myself up more quickly, by reflecting on past times when I had overcome a similar problem. By doing the things that helped in the past, I got similarly good results, and was able to sustain these by doing more of what worked. Having experienced the benefits of SFBT in my personal life, I was more interested in applying SFBT in my work.

Q: What else was helpful?

A: Reading about the medical model and problem solving as 'the paradigm of the helping professions' (De Jong & Berg, 2013, pp. 5–6), and the difference between this and solution building, helped anchor my belief that SFBT could guide me in my work.

Q: How did your work with clients change after using SFBT?

A: The shift in my mindset towards my clients was dramatic. I got excited about meeting clients. For the first time at EPIP, I was hopeful and confident. I talked less about what clients should do; instead I got curious. I got clients to talk about what had worked in the past. Even when clients appeared helpless and hopeless, I didn't feel stuck. I asked how they'd managed so far, and explored what qualities they had drawn on to cope. I was amazed to learn what my clients did to help themselves. Seeing clients smiling and becoming hopeful encouraged me. I could see I was being helpful, and this encouraged me to master my skills.

Q: How have you used SFBT since then?

A: I listen to my clients and caregivers from an 'SF' perspective: listening for strengths, exceptions and other opportunities to switch from problem-focus to solution building. Questions on coping, exceptions, scaling for hope and confidence, and giving compliments are common tools that I use.

Q: What did your clients notice you doing differently?

A: Many clients and their caregivers noted they liked the change in my style of engagement. As one caregiver told me: 'I noticed a change in the way you talked about my son. Thanks for helping me become more aware of his strengths. It helped change my perspective about him. Asking me about times my son was "better" was refreshing. I was reminded of how he is capable of taking care of himself and does a good job in completing the tasks we entrust him to do.'

Q: What are the main differences to your work since using SFBT?

A: 1. I view clients with a more positive frame of mind, instead of seeing them as 'resistant or difficult'.

2. I can engage clients better, regardless of the extent of their psychosocial concerns.

3. I am more helpful to clients. Clients have noted a change in their thinking patterns after sessions, for example, commenting that they were more aware of their strengths and abilities, and felt more hopeful about their situation.

4. I finally know how to help clients empower themselves.

5. I no longer prepare 'solutions' prior to sessions. Instead, I elicit past solutions that were useful, and which could give clues to address their current difficulties.

6. I end sessions with a positive note, which makes me and clients feel good. As a result, I find myself looking forward to sessions rather than feeling 'dread'.

7. SFBT principles have also helped me address my own difficulties more effectively in tough times. My own self-worth has improved significantly too.

Q: Tell me about a client with whom SFBT worked well.

A: I was working with a 40-year-old Chinese female, who was separated from her husband and was living with her daughter. Her diagnosis was treatment-resistant schizophrenia. She was stable on clozapine treatment, and her psychotic symptoms were in full remission. The client, however, experienced sleep problems: sleeping too much, from 11 p.m. to midday the next day. This worried her due to her wish to seek employment to help with her family's financial situation.

Sleep hygiene strategies had been discussed with her several times, but to no avail. Both her doctor and I felt stuck. The doctor was unable to reduce the clozapine any further, due to concerns over a potential relapse. Her sleeping problems posed a significant perpetuating factor to her illness, affecting her ability to seek employment, which reinforced her negative self-worth and financial worries.

I asked for exceptions of waking up earlier than midday. I was expecting she would tell me a time when she at least woke up at 10 a.m. To my surprise, she recalled a recent time where she had woken up at 4:30 a.m.! That coincided with a Chinese festival where she was required to wake early to pay respects at her ancestors' tombs. I got a rich description about how she managed to do this. What impressed me further was her ability to stay awake that day without taking a nap. We explored 'what worked' for that day, broken down into details. This helped the client feel more hopeful about her ability to make changes to her sleeping. I also arranged job training for her, to give her a reason to wake up early. This idea came about when the client shared that, besides having the family's help to wake her early that day, what was most helpful was her reminding herself several times before the festival: 'This is an important event for my family. I want to be a part of it. I need to wake at 4:30 a.m. this coming Saturday.' The session ended well, with both the client and I knowing she had the strategies to wake up early.

Yi Ping's experiences are not an isolated example of the impact of SFBT in the team. Themes from discussions with the other CMs about how SFBT made a difference to their clients included empowerment, fostering hope and inspiring change as illustrated by the following quotes:

- 'It gives the power back to the client. They begin to see themselves as the expert in their lives, which improves their confidence.'
- 'Exceptions give clients more possibilities and hope for change.'
- 'It is a positive model for clients to focus on their strengths.'
- 'Ironically, by slowing down and by "leading from one step behind", clients often take bigger steps than they or we thought possible.'

The CMs also talked about how it had helped them feel more positive and less burdened by their work, and how versatile the SFBT tools were:

- 'I can let go and trust clients to do more.'
- 'I no longer get into power struggles with clients.'
- 'I don't work harder than the client.'
- 'I can apply the tools to many different situations.'
- 'Not feeling the need to solve clients' problems has taken away a big burden.'
- 'It is versatile as we can also use it when contacting clients by phone or text.'

One of the challenges the CMs talked about in their work was how to work with the clients' goals, which often conflicted with the family's, team's or other agencies' goals for the client. After being trained in SFBT, they found it easier to develop and work on a common project (Korman, 2004), which led to better engagement and clients staying more in contact with the team.

The team leader also noticed changes in the CMs' work. As well as observing them using SFBT questions with clients and colleagues, she had noticed they were more confident, calmer and less stressed. They now had techniques to improve engagement and help clients work on their goals of recovery.

SFBT therefore had a positive impact on the CMs' work and the lives of their clients.

Cultural factors

The clients of EPIP reflect the society in Singapore: they come from a diverse range of cultures and backgrounds. Using the model in this context therefore required some adaptations. As three of the CMs explain:

> Similar to other Asian countries, most people in Singapore are brought up to be humble, instead of being proud or showy. As a result, giving and receiving compliments was initially challenging and uncomfortable. However, as we experienced compliments in our supervision, we gradually noticed that we felt more confident and learnt positive things about ourselves. Being on the receiving end allowed us to empathise more with clients. This helped us take things slowly and not be overly effusive, yet hold on to the notion that SFBT is a great opportunity for clients to learn about their strengths and successes, and to improve their confidence.

> Singapore is a country that is very focused on achievement. Clients often have high expectations of themselves or report that others have high expectations of them. Psychosis can significantly interfere with studying or working, which can lead to clients seeing themselves

as failures. SFBT is a useful tool to help expand their ideas of success, and to identify areas in their lives where they are still doing well and can build upon to move towards their goals.

In the Asian, and particularly Chinese, culture, there is a strong sense of hierarchy. Counsellors are seen as the experts. This can make it hard initially for clients: in SFBT, they are expected to come up with their own answers. It is important to acknowledge this struggle explicitly and explain the rationale behind the model.

Reflections

The CMs' stories and comments illustrate what a positive impact training and supervision in SFBT can have. These inspiring messages demonstrate that SFBT can make a difference to the case management approach with clients with psychosis and that it works well with Asian clients. We hope these experiences will encourage others to use SFBT in similar settings.

References

De Jong, P., & Berg, I.K. (2013). *Interviewing for solutions* (4th ed.). Belmont, CA: Brooks/Cole, Cengage Learning.

Greene, G.J., Kondrat, D.C., Lee, M.Y., Clement, J., Siebert, H., Mentzer, R.A., & Pinnell, S.R. (2006). A solution-focused approach to case management and recovery with consumers who have a severe mental illness. *Families in Society: The Journal of Contemporary Social Services, 87*, 339–350.

Hawkes, D. (2003). A solution focused approach to 'psychosis'. In B. O'Connell & S. Palmer (Eds.), *Handbook of solution-focused therapy* (pp. 146–155). London, UK: Sage.

Korman, H. (2004). *The common project.* Retrieved from www.sikt.nu/wp-content/uploads/2015/06/Creating-a-common-project.pdf

Macdonald, A. (2011). Solution-focused approaches to severe mental illness. In *Solution-focused therapy: Theory, research & practice* (pp. 145–167). London, UK: Sage.

O'Hanlon, B., & Rowan, T. (2003). *Solution oriented approaches to chronic and severe mental illness.* New York, NY: Norton.

8

SIMPLER AND SIMPLER!

The 10-minute solution building approach in a psychiatric setting

Kotaro Fujioka

It's simple but not easy.

(Insoo Kim Berg)

Introduction

In Japan, psychiatrists have to see many outpatients for several reasons, e.g., insurance limitations and the shortage of psychiatrists. I developed the 10-minute version of the solution building approach (SBA) as a result of the demands of my work. We Japanese have a tradition of making things compact, just like bonsai and haiku, distilling much content into a limited space. This 10-minute session may well be a product of my Japaneseness!

This chapter describes the method of practising the 10-minute SBA sessions along with eight key points. The six patterns of change shown by patients are explained, along with suitable interventions for each situation. These can help us to be mindful of subtle differences and to learn different focuses of the intervention. I also present a case example of a 10-minute session to demonstrate the 10-minute SBA in action.

How to practise the 10-minute SBA

In the first session, we have to collect patient information necessary not only for the SB session, but also for medical decisions. For the purpose of the SB session, we need to try to identify goals that are important for the patient. Therefore, we need at least 40 to 60 minutes.

Then we have to tell the patient that from the next session on we have only 10 minutes to talk and should ensure they agree. Finally, we give feedback, compliments and a task to the patient as in the standard SBA protocol.

The structure of following sessions is also similar to the standard SBA protocol. Just start with the question 'What's better?' and keep the solution talk going. In the standard protocol, we would take a break before feedback. However, in a 10-minute session, we do not take a break owing to limited time.

There are eight key points to remember about the 10-minute SBA, which are discussed below. These eight points are well known; however, they are more significant in shorter sessions.

Things to remember for the 10-minute SBA

1 Consider the setting of the session to identify the patient's goal

For inpatients, their goal point can be the time of discharge. For outpatients, it can be the time they finish treatment. The goal-setting is more significant for 10-minute sessions than the standard session to make the most of the limited time.

FIGURE 8.1 Establish where they're headed.
(Credit: Kotaro Fujioka)

2 Keeping the patient on track

We must discuss what is important for the patient. This is especially important in short sessions. When you do not understand what they want, just ask, 'How does it relate to what you want?' Then make sure to keep the conversation focused on their goal (see Figure 8.2).

3 Compliments are key!

Compliments encourage the patient to talk more easily. Compliments give the patient satisfaction despite the short session. When the session gets bogged down, more compliments can help to get it moving again.

FIGURE 8.2 Don't let them stray.
(Credit: Kotaro Fujioka)

4   Highlight the patient's achievements

In many cases, patients forget what they have achieved. They might remember when we ask and compliment them. Talking about the patient's recent achievements moves them forward. Furthermore, the conversation during this part of the session can be used to 'do more tasks'. It is an easier way to make up tasks in a short-time session than proposing new trials, and easier for the patient to work on.

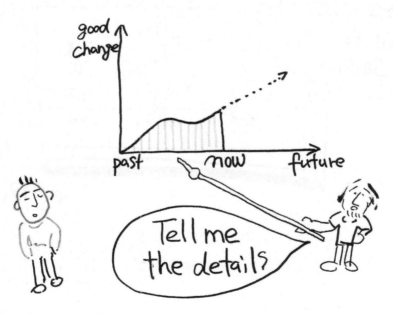

FIGURE 8.3 Remind them how far they've come.
(Credit: Kotaro Fujioka)

5 Go slow

I understand these words to mean, 'Don't push the patient'. A 10-minute session does not mean you have to find conclusions in a short time. Therefore, follow the patient from one step behind. Take time to talk about the important issues for the patient and help them to describe them concretely.

6 Catch and use KEYWORDS

'Keywords' are words that the patient uses repeatedly and often. They could connect with what they want or their values. Include these keywords in your questions, feedback and compliments.

7 Don't forget your schedule

Finish within the prearranged 10 minutes. It is not only for our sake, but for patients to develop the skill to talk about themselves in a limited time. It is similar to a boxer physically memorising 3-minute rounds. When you cannot find a solution, or a new issue comes up at the end of the session, say, 'We can talk about it in the next session.' You have to tell the patient you are not going to just stop talking, but intend to talk about the issue in the next session.

FIGURE 8.4 Stick to time limits.

(Credit: Kotaro Fujioka)

8   *All's well that ends well*

Finish the session with compliments, feedback on what they have achieved and tasks. Suggesting 'do more of what works' tasks is a quickly achievable message, even in a brief session, and it also encourages the patient. It looks like we are giving the patient a 'gift' that can help them until the next session.

The six patterns of change

We hear many different patients' stories. I have categorised these stories into six types, which are discussed and illustrated below. These categories are helpful for becoming mindful of change and acquiring the skill to make neat interventions. In the graphs below, the y-axis shows positive changes towards the goals, and the x-axis shows time. In reality, our life shows a complex combination of these patterns. Therefore, we should pay attention to changes between the previous and current sessions in order to simplify the conversation, especially in brief sessions.

1   *Improvement*

The patient reports positive changes and is getting closer to their goal. In such cases, simply ask: 'How did you do that?'

Of course, compliments and many other questions are used. We often ask: 'To maintain this progress, what do you need to keep doing?'

The answer can just be used for 'do more of what works' tasks. When you do not have enough time, 'highlight the patient's achievements'.

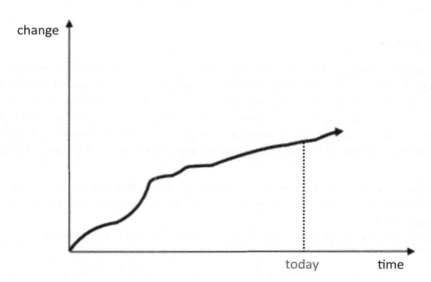

FIGURE 8.5 Improvement.

(Credit: Kotaro Fujioka)

2 Deterioration

In practice, we frequently come across this pattern. In such cases, we should be curious about how the patient has managed until today. Coping questions and the questions below are useful:

'What is better now than at the worst time?'
'How did you try to stop things from getting worse?'

When focusing on solution talk, the patient may often remember and report 'improvements'.

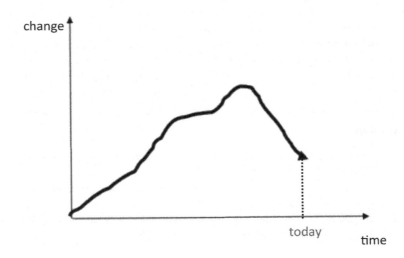

FIGURE 8.6 Deterioration.
(Credit: Kotaro Fujioka)

3 Stagnation

This is the hardest pattern for us. We often see this pattern in patients with social withdrawal, complicated post-traumatic stress disorder and serious chronic diseases. In such cases, we have to remind ourselves even more to 'go slow'. We often find patients unable to think about their future, much less their goal. Use coping questions, and find and talk about people, things and pets that support the patient even to a small degree. Then compliment the patient about their having good relations with their 'supporters'. I think these three assumptions are helpful to remind us to 'go slow' (Dolan, 2007).

- They may be experiencing suffering that is too severe to explain. Try to ask about this gently.
- For us, it might look like very slow progress. However, they might feel that the change is frighteningly quick.
- Regard the patient's attitude not as resistance or laziness, but as fear of failure.

In many cases, they cannot feel even the least hope. However, keep asking about the smallest changes and how to avoid getting worse. Always compliment them and wait patiently. Even if the conversation becomes repetitive, this is not a problem.

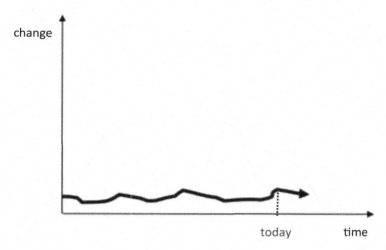

FIGURE 8.7 Stagnation.
(Credit: Kotaro Fujioka)

4   Instability

Sometimes a patient who could be diagnosed with 'borderline personality disorder' shows changes like this. They could demonstrate problematic behaviours and are sometimes seen as trying to manipulate us, e.g., by threatening suicide or unreasonable aggression. We need to fasten our seatbelts tightly and ride this rollercoaster. The seatbelt is 'keeping the patient on track'. When they challenge us, gently reconfirm the reason they are here:

'You said you wanted to "get a balance" in your life. Is that still important to you?'

When they say 'yes', continue with solution talk. Sometimes, they behave problematically, e.g., self-injury or overdosing. When we see such behaviours, exploring the 'good reason' for the behaviour is useful and it helps us to avoid negative feelings towards them.

5   Remission and stability

Many patients with chronic mental and physical diseases follow this pattern. We can understand their special needs when asking them their goals. I ask them the following questions:

'How have you prevented recurrence so far?'
'What do you still wish to change by coming here?'

Imagine a patient with substance dependency or gambling addiction. When they have been away from the problems and appear to be in this pattern, many changes might have occurred in their life, e.g., improvement of relationships with family and friends, or saving up money. When they talk about these changes, you will find the story is often pattern 1, Improvement.

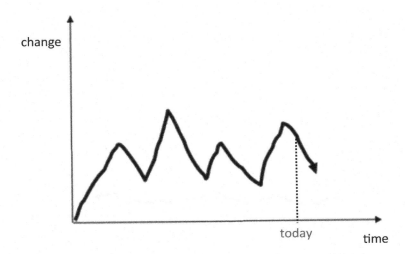

FIGURE 8.8 Instability.
(Credit: Kotaro Fujioka)

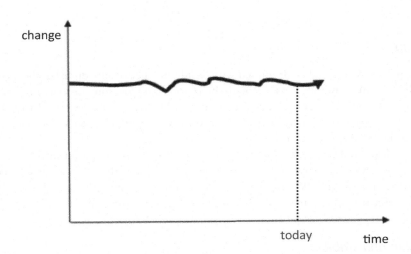

FIGURE 8.9 Remission and stability.
(Credit: Kotaro Fujioka)

6 Ending therapy

Finally, we have to discuss how to maintain their good state. The following questions are useful:

'What do you need to keep doing in order to maintain this state?'
'What may be the first tiny sign of relapse? If you notice it, what should you do?'
'How do you plan to use this experience in your life?'

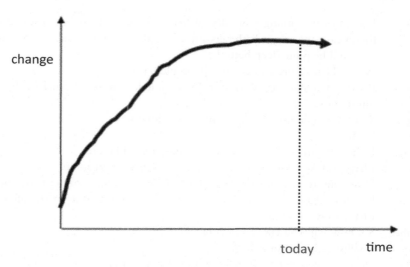

FIGURE 8.10 Ending the therapy.
(Credit: Kotaro Fujioka)

Now I would like to share a case example to demonstrate the 10-minute SBA in action.

Case example

Katsuko, a 30-year-old female office worker, was diagnosed with depression. She was in our hospital for three months then returned to her job three months ago. Her goal was: 'Being able to continue my job and have a stable private life. Then to reduce medication and get married and have children in the future'. She is a typical pattern 2 patient. (The words in [ ] [square brackets] below show the aim of each intervention).

Psychiatrist: Hi, Katsuko. What has changed even a little bit since we met before? [Exploring change]

Katsuko: For two weeks, we had much more work than usual. I felt terribly tired and sleepy every morning. I'm worried about recurrence.

Psychiatrist: That sounds so hard for you. Katsuko, tell me what has not got worse in your life. [Exploring exceptions]

Katsuko: I can go to work every day. Once I start working, I forget my tiredness, and time passes quickly. At my worst time, I couldn't work at all.

Psychiatrist: That's really important for you, right? [Compliment and affirm by agreeing with the goal] What else?

Katsuko: Even at the weekend, I get up at the same time as weekdays. And I take a nap in the afternoon. That helps.

Psychiatrist: Yes. You said you needed to get up at the same time every day and to rest enough, didn't you?

Katsuko: Yes, and taking a bath every day. I know it's easy for most people.

Psychiatrist: How significant is it for you? [Knowing the value of her behaviour]

Katsuko:	I used to hate bathing every day. When I was badly depressed, it was worse. But my friend gave me aroma bath salts and I love them! They reduce back pain and tiredness, and help me sleep better!
Psychiatrist:	Wow! That's a great discovery! [Compliment]
Katsuko:	Besides, I bought a waterproof TV to watch a music channel in the bath. I love music shows!
Psychiatrist:	What a wonderful idea! You tried something new!
Katsuko:	Yeah.
Psychiatrist:	Is there anything else needed to maintain this situation?
Katsuko:	I have to take a lunch break. It's hard to stop work at noon.
Psychiatrist:	How important is that for you? [Knowing the meaning of her behaviour]
Katsuko:	If I don't have one, I feel sleepy and lose concentration in the afternoon. Then I have to work late.
Psychiatrist:	So, how will you take a lunch break?
Katsuko:	I will switch off from work.
Psychiatrist:	How will you switch off from work? [Keywords]
Katsuko:	I need to turn my PC to sleep mode and leave my office. Yes! I don't have to stay at the office and keep working! I'll go to the park with lunch or to a cafe and read books. Yes, that's what I need.
Psychiatrist:	That's a great idea! You need to leave your office at lunchtime.
Katsuko:	Yes, I think, there's no alternative!
Psychiatrist:	Katsuko, you have got through two tough weeks without absence in spite of your condition. I'm amazed at your effort and your clever ideas. You know taking a bath with aroma bath salts and music refreshes you wonderfully! What a great idea! What a smart person you are! And you need to take a lunch break and leave your office. It's important to keep your concentration and to go home on time, right? [Feedback]
Katsuko:	Yes, right.
Psychiatrist:	Keep doing the things that keep your condition good and you know well. Of course, you can try anything new that seems helpful and see how it goes. [Tasks] I don't think we need to change the prescription now, right?
Katsuko:	Yeah, I agree.
Psychiatrist:	So, do more of what works, and see you in two weeks.
Katsuko:	Thank you. See you!

Conclusions

Ten minutes are short. If you use the time for just listening, it flashes by. However, by structuring the conversation carefully, you can help to effectively build solutions for your clients even in the short time. The essential things are the minimum structure, the eight key-points and goal setting as outlined above. I believe this can help all therapists working in settings where time is limited.

Reference

Dolan, Y.M. (2007, October). Workshop. Workshop conducted by Solution Works, Fukuoka, Japan.

9

BEING BILINGUAL

Cheryl Ng

Introduction

For speech-language therapists (SLT) working in hospital settings, the use of problem-focused language is common. While we possess clinical expertise, we are not experts on our clients' lives. Problem-focused language alone may be ineffective in supporting change beyond the impairment level. This chapter illustrates how solution-focused (SF) language can be a useful adjunct to problem-focused language in speech-language therapy. It can help clients cope with their sudden change in ability, increase insight into what works and recognise progress. Case examples and personal reflections on how the SF approach may be adapted to the Singapore context will be shared.

Problem-focused language

As an SLT in a hospital setting, I see adult clients with acquired communication disorders such as aphasia, cognitive-communication disorder and dysarthria. These may be secondary to neurological disorders such as stroke, traumatic brain injury and Parkinson's disease.

In hospital settings, the use of the medical approach and its associated problem-focused language is common (McAllister, 2010). There is a tendency to perceive clients in terms of their deficits as clinicians seek to investigate root causes and solve clients' problems. Problem-focused language has utility in many situations such as when diagnosing, prescribing treatments and providing information. However, when it comes to engaging or motivating change in clients, problem-focused language may be inadequate or counter-productive.

For example, when working with a client with speech impairment within a problem-focused framework, the SLT would investigate the impairment: when it is worse, the cause and the extent of the impairment. The SLT may also be directive with therapy goals and treatment.

Limitations to the use of problem-focused language, however, include reinforcing SLTs as the 'experts'. Clients may feel disempowered and lack ownership for treatment goals and solutions. As these goals and solutions originate from the therapists' point of reference (and not the clients'), the therapeutic alliance is impacted and the relationship is no longer collaborative.

Solution-focused language

Using SF language does not mean that we stop being SLTs with our knowledge and skills. We still need to fulfil our professional responsibility and recognise when using problem-focused language is helpful (Burns, 2006). However, we are by no means experts on our clients' lives. SF language facilitates communication when we wish to support our clients beyond the impairment level. It enables exploration of clients' viewpoints of their impairment, competence and coping strategies. Acknowledging these means that we can be less directive and follow the clients' lead.

Being bilingual

Being bilingual in both problem-focused and solution-focused language provides SLTs with the flexibility to *code-switch* depending on what best serves our clients. Two case examples will illustrate how SF language may be weaved into speech-language therapy.

Jim's story

Jim is a stroke survivor in his 50s, whose mild cognitive-communication disorder was causing a significant functional impact. Jim had recently found a job that had become a great source of stress. During our first session, he quickly delved into extensive details about his problems. I listened while picking out key words that indicated resources and competence. After complimenting him, I clarified the common platform for our work.

Cheryl: How would you like things to be different?
Jim: I want to be better in my memory . . . So I can be more independent at work.
Cheryl: What needs to happen today for you to say that it was useful?
Jim: Help me to be better at remembering things . . . like the instructions that my boss and colleagues give me. Because of my terrible memory, it's making things difficult for me at work.
Cheryl: I'm impressed by how responsible you are with your work. So you want to be better at remembering instructions at work?
Jim: Yes. The other day, my boss was upset with me because I forgot to tell his instructions to my colleagues.
Cheryl: Tell me what have you tried that works. What helps you to remember better?

By being curious about what helped, I hoped to discover what Jim's resources were. Once those resources were established, they were used to construct a solution.

Jim: Writing down helps. Sometimes I write in a notebook or post-it note. I don't know why I stopped doing that.
Cheryl: So writing down stuff helps . . . What else?
Jim: I keep telling myself what I need to remember by saying it over and over again in my head. Rest also helps. After the stroke, I get tired easily and my brain doesn't work well.
Cheryl: Saying things over and over again and having enough rest help. You seem to understand your body well. What gave you the idea saying things over and over in your head helps?

Jim: I don't know . . . I do that when I need to buy groceries. I just repeat the things I need to buy in my head.

Cheryl: Anything else that helps?

Jim: The most important thing is that I need to stay positive. I'm too hard on myself. I tell myself this is my adjustment and to give myself more time.

I complimented him on how well he knew himself and what he needed to do to improve his memory. I assured him that how he felt was normal after a stroke. I noted his memory strategies and encouraged him to do more of them. I also asked him how useful today's session had been.

Jim: [Smiling] I like how you let me tell you what I need . . . My thoughts are confused . . . You point back to me. I realise I can handle my wrong thoughts.

Jim taught me that listening to what our clients want and recognising their competence are both important in building our therapeutic alliance. By maintaining a not-knowing stance, Jim articulated solutions from *his* frame of reference. As such, the solutions had a higher chance of fitting naturally in his life and would be more effective.

Liz's story

Liz, a 65-year-old, came to the clinic with her helper[1], Maria. Liz had Parkinson's disease and presented with moderate dysarthria characterised by a soft voice and mildly imprecise articulation. Her speech intelligibility was about 60 per cent. Liz expressed that she wanted to improve her interaction with Maria. I explored what realisation of this goal would look like.

Cheryl: What would you notice when it's easier for you to interact together?

Liz: Maria would be able to understand me. It'd be less tiring, as I don't have to keep repeating.

Cheryl: When communication is less tiring, what would it be instead?

Liz: Easier . . . smoother.

Cheryl: You'd like communication to be easier and smoother. How about you, Maria? When you're talking well with Liz, how would you know?

Maria: Ma'am [will] not be angry with me. I want Ma'am [to] be happy with me. I want [to] understand Ma'am but sometime[s it's] hard for me.

Cheryl: Both of you want communication to be happier, easier and smoother. Let's say, '10' equals happy, easier and smoother communication; Liz gets her message across and doesn't need to repeat herself. And '1' equals unsuccessful, tiring communication; Liz's message doesn't get across at all. Liz, where would you put your interactions with Maria right now?

Liz: Maybe '6'.

Cheryl: What makes it '6' and not '1'?

Liz: She can understand me sometimes. I use my loud voice and pronounce words more clearly. I spell. Maria encourages me to speak louder.

Cheryl: It's nice to hear that Maria has been encouraging and that helps. Tell me more about the spelling. How does that work?

Liz: If Maria doesn't understand what I say, I spell it out.

Cheryl: How effective is that?

Liz: Quite effective.

Cheryl: Sounds useful. What else brings it to a '6'?

Liz: When she uses a normal tone of voice when talking . . . and not be impatient.

Cheryl: So it helps when you spell, use a loud voice and articulate clearly. It also helps when Maria encourages you and uses a normal or patient tone of voice. Anything else?

Liz: That's all.

Cheryl: How about you, Maria? What number would you put down . . . about how well you can understand Liz?

Maria: '7'.

Cheryl: Tell me more?

Maria: When Ma'am speak louder and slow[ly], [it is] easier for me. When she spell[s] out, [it is] also better. [It is] Important [that] Ma'am speak simple English. Sometime[s] I no [don't] understand what Ma'am say because I don't know [the] word.

Cheryl: So spelling and speaking slowly and loudly help. And simple English helps. Liz, did you know this?

Liz: No, I didn't.

Cheryl: What are your thoughts about what Maria said?

Liz: I'm surprised because I thought my English is simple enough. Maybe I need to simplify more.

I continued the discussion about what 1 point up the scale would look like from each of their perspectives. We explored what would be something small that each would like the other person to do in order to move 1 point up on the scale. At the end of the session, we listed all the helpful strategies and identified two strategies to try. I affirmed their strengths. They shared with me that the session was useful because it 'cleared the air' between them and gave them concrete steps forward.

Rating scales serve as concrete visualisations for therapy baseline and outcome measures, as well as for plotting small steps forward. When used with a dyad, differences between their ratings and perspectives can be insightful and enable meaningful dialogue.

Personal reflections on using the SF approach in Singapore

In the next segment, I would like to share some thoughts on how the SF approach can be adapted to the Singapore context. Singapore is an ethnically diverse country with many languages, religions and cultures. Most Singaporeans are of Asian descent, comprising mainly Chinese, Malays and Indians. While younger Singaporeans may be influenced by Western culture, many from the older generation still lean towards Asian culture and values. Some adaptations may be required when using the SF approach in this context:

1   Clients who do not have English as their first language or are less educated

While English is the working language in Singapore, it may not be the first language for all Singaporeans. This is particularly true for some elderly clients who received limited or no formal education. Many of them have Malay, Mandarin or dialects as their dominant language.

I have attempted SF questions in Mandarin and Hokkien, which I speak at a basic conversational level. Due to my limited competence in those languages, conversational fluency is affected, and I am less able at capturing and expressing nuances in meaning. As such, I enlist the help of carers or therapy assistants to aid in translation.

Some clients may have no or limited formal schooling. My experience is they might find some SF questions such as the miracle question too abstract or complex to comprehend. In such scenarios, I adapt my language to one that is familiar to them by simplifying my SF language, explaining the questions, or using Singlish.[2] I also attempt more concrete questions such as scaling. In situations where SF questions are still too difficult for clients, I may use them with carers instead.

If my clients are truly unaware of any possible solutions or if clients specifically request advice, I may offer ideas. This will be done tentatively to avoid assumptions that my solutions will be useful. I usually end the session by suggesting that clients and carers observe when things are better and notice what helps.

2   Giving compliments

According to Manes (1983), the speech event of compliments and their responses is a mirror of cultural values. I have noticed that some Singaporean clients appear embarrassed or uncomfortable when complimented. Many, particularly those who are older, may deny or reject compliments. This might be because they are unaccustomed to receiving compliments. The literature attributes such responses to modesty, a value which is of utmost importance in Chinese politeness (Gu, 1990; Chen, 1993). Compliments appear better accepted when:

- They focus on effort and process, instead of personal attributes (e.g., 'You've thought hard about this' vs. 'You are such a kind person').
- They are self-compliments.
- They are given strategically rather than too frequently.
- They highlight change that has already been noticed and accepted by the client.

Conclusion

As an SF practitioner, I have adapted its use across a variety of contexts – therapy, clinical education and leadership. The SF approach is not a totally new or different therapy. Emphasis on efficiency and clear goals is something that all clinical specialities will recognise. What may be different is the stance and kinds of questions asked. What is suggested here is that SF language can be a useful adjunct to problem-focused language. *Being bilingual* enables SLTs to pay attention to what truly matters to clients.

Notes

1 'Helper' refers to a domestic worker who works and lives within the employer's household. Helpers may clean, cook and provide care for children and elderly dependents. English is often not their first language. Hence, they may not speak fluently.
2 Singlish is the English-based creole spoken colloquially in Singapore. It has its unique slang, intonation and syntax. Singlish is more pronounced in informal speech.

References

Burns, K. (2006). *Focus on solutions: A health professional's guide.* Chichester, UK: John Wiley & Sons.

Chen, R. (1993). Responding to compliments: A contrastive study of politeness strategies between American English and Chinese speakers. *Journal of Pragmatics, 20,* 49–75.

Gu, Y. (1990). Politeness phenomena in modern Chinese. *Journal of Pragmatics, 14*(2), 237–257.

Manes, J. (1983). Compliments: A mirror of cultural values. In N. Wolfson & E. Judds (Eds.), *Sociolinguistics and language acquisition* (pp. 96–102). Rowley, MA: Newbury House, Rowley.

McAllister, M. (2010). Solution focused nursing: A fitting model for mental health nurses working in a public health paradigm. *Contemporary Nurse, 34*(2), 149–157.

10

A PERFECT MATCH

Petra Maierhöfer

Introduction

I moved from Germany to Manila in the Philippines in 2006 and then trained in solution focused brief therapy (SFBT) in 2009. From the very first day of training I felt that SFBT had a significant impact on me, not only professionally but personally. I am an occupational therapist by training and now also do counselling. SFBT fits very well with the occupational therapy (OT) model. SFBT also suits the cultural and economic conditions I have observed in the Philippines. In this chapter I will share how SFBT integrates into the OT philosophy and how I use it with clients in the Philippines, and illustrate this with case examples.

First encounters

Soon after starting training in SFBT, I shared an evening with a friend and her younger son. She started complaining about her older adolescent son. Usually I would have listened politely, not knowing how to turn it into a more fruitful encounter. Because of the SFBT training, I felt inspired to ask my friend about the occasions she enjoyed most with her son. Silence. Her eyes widened. I was taught to identify cues like eye movements showing that people are thinking and to wait patiently for their replies. More silence. After a few moments she told me, with a smile on her face, about the times she appreciated most with her son.

Then her younger boy talked about his training in Aikido. I kept asking more details with genuine interest, keeping my focus on the boy. Later the mother admitted how surprised she was at how much her son had to share. I complimented my friend for just listening to him and said how impressed I was seeing her several times holding back a comment.

It was a pleasant evening for all of us. I enjoyed hearing that there are sides of her older son my friend really appreciates. She seemed to be happy identifying and sharing pleasant memories about him and pleased that the younger one had talked so much about himself. He stayed all the time with us at the table, listening attentively to what his mother had to say about the positive qualities of his brother and kept on passionately answering my questions about Aikido.

Being able to change the course of a conversation with minor interventions was so satisfying that I knew SFBT was right for me and could be useful in my profession as an occupational therapist.

Why SFBT suits occupational therapy

As an occupational therapist I have worked in a variety of psychiatric, paediatric, geriatric and neurological fields. I worked in hospitals, centres for rehabilitation, child care institutions, schools, homes for the elderly and private clinics.

OT is prescribed when people's motor, intellectual, emotional or mental functions are affected or disabled, to name a few. OT is client-centred and seeks to activate clients' own resources. Assessing the clients' situation, identifying realistic goals, and how to achieve them are essential parts of the therapy. Creative materials, daily life activities and specific therapeutic techniques and materials are used. Occupational therapists often collaborate with clients' family members or partners, and with medical doctors, psychologists, therapists, educators and health workers.

Both OT and SFBT are based on identifying clients' strengths and manageable goals. Both help clients to figure out an individual, realistic and doable way to work on their goals. OT brings in knowledge about motoric, sensorial, intellectual, emotional and mental functions. SFBT offers a detailed guideline and framework to communicate with clients. Its structure allows the therapist to navigate effectively and supportively through a session with a client. SFBT tools can be useful in many encounters. A particularly helpful aspect for me is how SFBT turns conversations from complaints into fruitful meetings and helps the client pay attention to the smallest steps in the desired direction.

My workplace in Manila

Currently I work in Manila at In Touch Community Services. In Touch is a non-profit organisation and has a multi-professional, multi-national and multi-lingual team. It provides counselling, coaching, consulting and therapy for local and international clients; runs a telephone crisis line; and provides employee assistance programs (EAP) for companies as well as holding various trainings and seminars.

I started working at In Touch Community Services after starting my training in SFBT. Enabled and encouraged by the training, I shifted to counselling and extended my services to new clientele such as adolescents and couples. However, I still keep my OT knowledge in mind. Below, I will share some of the barriers to seeking help in the Philippines and how SFBT helps address some of these.

Barriers to seeking therapy and counselling in the Philippines

Seeking therapy or counselling in the Philippines is not common. There are many reasons why it can be difficult for people to access therapy, which are listed below.

Keeping face. As in many Asian cultures, keeping face is important to the Filipino people. The anticipated view of family, friends and colleagues about you is very important. People are often afraid that if others know that they can't cope, they may lose face or be disgraced and stigmatised. In addition, people often avoid talking about something that might make themselves and others feel uncomfortable. It is of value in this culture to remain emotionally balanced. Thus, many people avoid displaying distress openly (Bulatao, 1964; Weggel, 1994).

Lack of accessibility. The people of the Philippine islands face a lot of natural and human disasters, poverty and unemployment. These can lead to people experiencing trauma and emotional distress, in addition to physical hardships. However, there are very few mental health services in the country, especially in rural areas. Sometimes clients have to fly to Manila or travel many hours by bus to attend sessions.

Costs. The rate for one hour's counselling is around four times the minimum daily wage or more. Counselling sessions are not covered by health insurance so most clients have to pay for counselling from their own pockets unless services offer subsidies.

SFBT and the Philippines – A perfect match

Multiple reasons prevent people from accessing therapy, and even when they do seek help they often come for only a few sessions. Interventions are therefore ideally short, affordable, effective and discreet.

The SFBT approach does not require clients to share the history or details of their problems. This prevents clients feeling uncomfortable, since the approach focuses on people's strengths rather than their deficits. Several clients admitted that they were nervous before the first session expecting to be asked 'nasty' questions and that they were relieved that I didn't focus on their failures.

In the Philippines it is often the case that clients cancel appointments and don't show up anymore. SFBT assumes each session might be the last opportunity to meet the client and so focuses quickly on revealing strengths and resources and tries to leave the client with an idea of how to cope with a difficult situation or how to move on and to facilitate change.

These aspects make efficient use of what little time there is and people are more comfortable – as they save face, money and time. In this context I find SFBT tools very suitable.

This case example illustrates how helpful even a single session can be. A university student came to see me, obviously very tense and agitated. He had failed an exam and was anxious about losing his parents' support, and he had argued with his girlfriend. When asked what had helped him to cope, he came up with a whole list of what had kept him going. We explored these in detail and he developed a clear plan how to move on. In the next session he answered my question about what could be helpful for him today with: 'Nothing. I don't need a session anymore. I just came in to let you know that I'm doing very well.'

Useful tools

Some of the specific SFBT tools I have found most useful in this cultural context are described below and illustrated with case examples.

Highlighting strengths and exceptions. SFBT focuses on what is going well in people's lives. This sets a tone of hope and is key to figuring out solutions.

A couple wanted to improve their relationship. When asked about their love story they remembered the fascination with each other when they first met. When answering questions about times when their relationship was a little better, and what helped them to stay together, they described their good intentions and efforts to keep the relationship alive. Tears were rolling when their mutual bids to reach out to each other were acknowledged.

Children's faces brighten up when I ask them 'What are you good at?' and the parents light up alike when answering 'What do you like about your child?'

A boy always became noisy when his parents started complaining about him. One day, he just listened for half a minute. My immediate comment was, 'Wow, I'm impressed. You were able to keep quiet and listening even when it must be hard for you to hear your dad complaining about you.' The boy was obviously proud and in follow-up sessions he was able to listen longer. 'Oh, this time you were even able to listen for more than two minutes. Look at your parents' smiling faces. It seems they are pleased about your listening.'

A 5-year-old had anger issues and banged doors wherever she could. Once it was a little softer and I commented, 'How were you able to close the door so softly? My ears really liked it.' This remark led her to strive for closing doors without any sound.

It is a mutually moving moment when a strength of a person emerges and is highlighted. I am often surprised how quickly clients are able to change as a result.

Compliments. I noticed differences in how people perceive compliments in different cultures. For some, judging remarks like 'fantastic', 'great', 'wow' are acceptable, whereas for others they sound exaggerated. For them a gently surprised look could be more appropriate. In this context, it seems to work better to relate compliments to an action and wrap them in questions or give them indirectly: 'How did you know a calming environment is important when talking to your employee?', 'I wonder if your intentions to save the company have ever been acknowledged.' 'What were the effects of you being able to say clearly what outcome you prefer?'

Scaling. If I could select just one SFBT tool as the most useful, it would be scaling. Scaling is an extremely flexible tool and is almost a microcosm of the whole SFBT model. I choose what to put on each end based on the clients' preferred outcomes and explore how they got to the chosen position and their manageable next steps.

A young student suffered from panic attacks, was worried about her future, had lost appetite, cried a lot and felt very tired. She wanted to be happy again with laughter, talking, going out, being able to clearly think and stay calm. The 10 of the scale included this description and also that the problem might still exist but on a manageable level. The student rated herself at a 4. She had noticed that there were fewer panic attacks in the last two weeks and remembered that she felt strong the previous year. We created a scaling chart displaying trends over time. She inserted her line over the past few months. It bounced up and down but after a major drop from the initial peak it showed a general upward tendency. We meticulously explored what had helped her to move up. It became obvious that enough sleep, focusing on present activities and opening up to friends were crucial for her wellbeing.

End of session feedback. The surprised look on clients' faces when I start the feedback announcing 'I'm very impressed about you' is always a delight for me. By summarising their challenges, clients told me that made them feel heard and seen in their struggles. It contrasts to and prepares the ground for what impresses me about the client. By then the client is almost eager to absorb what has been noticed about their intentions and efforts.

Assignments can be tailored to each client and their readiness for change. Specifically when clients come in for one or a few sessions only, I find it helpful for myself as well as for the client when they leave with a self-help tool like scaling. 'At what point am I today?' or 'What can I do to make my situation right now a little better?' are helpful questions.

Conclusions

SFBT has changed my professional life. I find it so convincing that I shifted from pure OT to counselling. Its efficient and flexible structure and simple tools fit very well with OT as both SFBT and OT focus on steps towards desired outcomes and clients' resources. Adding SFBT techniques into OT training would be wonderful!

I also observed that the SFBT model matches perfectly to the cultural and economic conditions of the Philippine people. SFBT helps clients reach their goals in a way that respects their cultural beliefs and also saves them face, time and money!

Acknowledgements

My sincere gratitude goes to the training and input of Jelly Virata, Debbie Hogan, Dave Hogan, Therese Steiner, John Henden, Yvonne Dolan, Terry Trepper, Gunther Schmidt and Kirsten Dierolf and to my local SFBT group in Manila. Each practitioner enriches SFBT with their own background, and I have been inspired by each of them.

References

Bulatao, J.C. (1964). Hiya. *Philippine Studies*, *12*(3), 424–438.
Weggel, O. (1994). *Die Asiaten*. Munich, Germany: Deutscher Taschenbuch Verlag.

11

SOLUTION-FOCUSED PLAY THERAPY

Working with children in the Philippines

Maria Aurora Assumpta D. Catipon

Introduction

A client's readiness to engage and verbally express themselves presents a challenge when working with children, who are usually referred by others. Expressing and engaging with strangers usually takes time for many children, especially Asian children, whose parents tend to be more restrictive and directive than their Western counterparts (Chao & Tseng, 2002; Kagitçibasi, 2007). Keeping a deliberate awareness of the child's readiness to engage, by entering their world of play, has been exhorted among therapists working with children in the Filipino culture (Carandang, 2009).

This chapter shares the case examples of two children referred by their school to a community-based centre for assessment and counselling in Metro Manila, Philippines. These case examples, children with school refusal and anxiety, illustrate how solution-focused brief therapy (SFBT) can be combined with play therapy to be effective and address cultural issues in this setting.

Pikachu draws the preferred future

This story shows a process with a child who communicated with her family differently in this single session.

Katrina was a 7-year-old girl who had returned with her family to the Philippines from abroad. Beginning her first year in her new school was marked by weeks of struggle, including a refusal to speak. Her anxiety was disruptive as the teacher had to search for her when she disappeared from class, calm her down and wait for her to be ready to re-join the class.

Arriving at the centre with her parents and sister, Katrina initially refused to go into the therapy room, and did not speak a word throughout the session. She did, however, speak to her sister in a whisper when I invited her into the room. After a few minutes of playing, I prompted the girls that in a while, we would be talking together with their parents.

Problem-free conversation naming strengths and resources. I left Katrina and her sister playing while I spoke to their parents who were within view and earshot. I asked about Katrina's strengths, and her parents said that she was a very good student in her previous school and was also very organised at home. Mum also said that Katrina and her sister were very close to each other. I commented how impressed I was with both sisters, i.e., how nicely they played together, how carefully they moved about and how neatly they returned the toys. I also noted that the relationship the girls had with each other said a lot about the quality of care and attention their parents gave them.

Imagining the preferred future. After 15–20 minutes, I invited the girls to come and sit with us. I asked Mum and Dad's wishes for Katrina. Mum said she would like Katrina 'to be happy and ready to stay in school'. I asked Katrina, 'I wonder what Katrina wishes can be better?' As Katrina remained quiet, I opened the curtain hiding the puppets and asked aloud, 'Hmm . . . I wonder who here knows Katrina and about being ready for school?' Katrina then slowly walked to the puppet corner and took out Pikachu, the yellow mouselike creature from Pokémon. I had a conversation with Pikachu, e.g., guessing what colour 'he' liked and what 'his' favourite snack was in school, to which he responded by 'shaking' and 'nodding.' I asked Pikachu for help, as Katrina needed to be ready for school. I asked 'him': 'I wonder what being ready for school means? What would that day look like? Can you draw it for me?'

Pikachu then expertly drew on the whiteboard. 'He' drew the layout of Katrina's school: the playground, the cafeteria, and her classroom. Pikachu pointed with the marker at the cafeteria. I asked who the human figures 'he' drew were. Pikachu pointed to Mum and to herself (Katrina). I asked, 'When Katrina is ready for school, she and Mum will be in the cafeteria?' Mum clarified that she usually brought Katrina to the classroom and waited outside the door. I asked, 'Where will Mum be when Katrina is ready to go to school?' Pikachu drew dotted lines from the class-room to the cafeteria then struck the cafeteria with the marker. 'Mum will be staying in the caf-eteria?' Katrina vigorously nodded. Mum, excitedly took a picture of the drawing and said she'd like to send it to Katrina's teacher.

Scaling. I asked how ready Katrina was to go back to school. I drew three faces on the white-board. A frown meant she was not yet ready, a straight face meant that she was a bit ready and would probably go to school, while the happy face meant that she was ready and happy to go to school. Katrina thought carefully. She pointed to the straight face. Mum asked, 'If Katrina is at the straight face, where will Mum be?' Katrina pointed to Mum in the cafeteria. I asked, 'How about when Katrina is at the smiling face?' Katrina pointed to outside of the school campus and drew a car. I asked, 'How could the smiley face happen?' Katrina sat quietly for a long time. I responded, 'That must be something Pikachu needs to think about.'

What's better? While Katrina didn't magically go back to school every day after the session, Mum did get to sit in the cafeteria for the first time while Katrina braved her way to classroom. However, she reverted back to not attending school after two days. By the week's end, Mum and teacher decided to ease the struggle with school by assuring Katrina that she could come back to school anytime she was ready. After all, it had just been a few months since the family repatriated to the Philippines. They also had to deal with Katrina's father being away from the family for the first time, since his work was still overseas.

Mum gave me updates on what had been better. She sent Katrina's drawings via email of her doing school work, playing with her sister or talking on the phone with her father. Mum relaxed about her staying at home until one day, Mum sent a message that Katrina had gone back to school on her own. To date, Katrina has been going to school every day. Mum sent a message saying Katrina was 'vibrant, happy and doing very, very well in school.'

The next story demonstrates the story of a boy who was more comfortable expressing himself and much readier to engage verbally.

Modified 'Truth or Dare'

Javier was a smart, articulate 10-year-old boy whose parents were separated. His father was concerned about his recurrent skin allergy, which his doctors attributed to stress. Javier had to deal with unsettling circumstances that included having to live alternately between both parents' homes every two weeks. Javier's dad expressed concern and wanted to understand what his son was going through to help him cope.

Javier was expressive, articulate and very engaged. Given the high level of involvement of his father, I asked Dad and Javier to the first session and to play two games. I invited them to pick out figures that represented the other and talk about what made them choose them. I then asked them to play a modified game of 'Truth or Dare'. Each took turns picking out questions from a jar for the other to answer as a 'challenge' to see how much they knew about each other. If each answered correctly, they received a block to build a tower. If the answer was wrong or unknown or if they didn't feel like answering, they could pick out a 'dare' from another jar. These were fun, playful tasks that both Dad and Javier enjoyed doing, e.g., singing a silly song, or doing a goofy dance. In addition, if a question was answered wrong, the other could share the answer.

Such questions asked in a playful way were used to facilitate a solution-focused conversation between child and parent. These questions elicited strengths, resources, goals and also exceptions in the face of difficulty and included:

- Who is/was my hero? Fictional or real?
- What makes me happy? What do I say or do when I am happy?
- What was my greatest challenge? How did I overcome this?
- What wishes of mine have come true? How did it come true?
- What do I do to make myself feel better?
- What is was school like for me?
- What do/did I do to cope with school?
- What do you think I appreciate most about you?
- What do I wish for you?

Through this game-like exchange, Javier told his father that he wished he did not have to keep transferring homes. What emerged was an understanding of the stress in having to move between both parents and how Dad could help him.

The same games were done with Mum in a separate session. What stood out was Javier being able to express how he liked how Mum could really listen to him. Javier also expressed, with a significant amount of emotion, his need for more physical presence from her, e.g., at dinner time. Through the use of scaling and exception questions, Mum listened and understood what Javier needed from her.

Javier's parents later gave feedback about what was better. As Mum decided to spend quality time by being physically present at dinner time, she said Javier managed to open up and feel listened to. The parents talked about synchronizing schedules in the two homes, which helped Javier adjust and cope. His father also noted that his skin allergies were gone, and he also did excellently in school and managed to negotiate effectively with his parents when he needed a change in his routine.

Reflections

Although parents seeking help for their children is now a more acceptable practice in the Philippines, it is still considered the last resort after exhausting support from family, teachers and the school counsellor. There is still stigma associated with seeing an external practitioner, and the cost makes it unaffordable to many. In a culture where individual achievements and failings reflect on the family as a whole (Chao & Tseng, 2002), having to seek outside help is viewed as a sign of failure that leads to feelings of shame. The solution-focused philosophy, however, views clients as competent and capable. Focusing on strengths and reinforcing these with parents and the children avoids any feelings of shame and makes it possible to move forward more quickly.

Recognising the underlying values behind the still-held attitudes toward therapy, *pakiramdaman*, or the process of feeling one's way around with the child and his parents as a way of regarding them with utmost respect via a nondirective approach, remains a core skill strongly emphasised among Filipino child therapists (Dey, Catipon, Garcia, & Tarroja, 2015). Thus, combining a nondirective play phase with the philosophy of SFBT is important in addressing the cultural discomfort with therapy. SFBT also lends itself well to addressing the cost issue, as the approach aims to be brief. Given these factors, two processes, enabled by combining a nondirective play phase and SFBT, are salient for me:

1   Giving the child permission to express themselves freely in their own way, i.e., through 'play'

In the nondirective phase, the therapist is able to get to know the child and have an intuitive feel of their needs and resources, including how and when they are ready to work with their parents. A therapist's initial response could include an invitation to the child to explore the different toys in the playroom, alert silence, nonverbal exchanges, creative play with clay, sand tray or free drawing, or direct conversation. While being nondirective is not always necessary as Filipino children vary with the changes associated with urbanisation and globalisation, the initial stance of allowing the child to take the lead remains a valued trait among local therapists.

2   Establishing safety through a structure that allows a child to communicate their needs with the therapist, and allows effective communication with parents

Safety is partly provided by the elements and structure of SFBT that reinforce unconditional positive regard with strengths-based assumptions about the child and parent (Berg & Steiner, 2003). A feeling of safety is also made possible, with the fun ways of working with both children and their parents together allowing children and parents to communicate their needs and wishes to each other. Thus, after allowing the child to take the lead in the playroom so they feel comfortable, I can begin to thread in SFBT questions either directly or through a game.

Beginning with a nondirective play therapy phase, then moving to SFBT, has allowed me to work more efficiently, while still heeding the central value guiding Filipino social behaviour, i.e., the quality of respect, rooted in a regard for the other as '*not* different,' or as one's equal (Bulatao, 1998). The most rewarding of all is the benefit of immediate feedback about the growing confidence of the child and in their parents' ability to journey with them toward their preferred future.

References

Berg, I.K., & Steiner, T. (2003). *Children's solution work*. New York, NY: W.W. Norton and Company, Inc.

Bulatao, J.C. (1998) *Phenomena and their interpretation: Landmark essays 1957–1989*. Quezon City: Ateneo de Manila University Press.

Carandang, M.L.A. (2009). *Magic of play*. Manila, Philippines: Anvil.

Chao, R., & Tseng, V. (2002). Parenting of Asians. In M.H. Bornstein (Ed.), *Handbook of parenting. Vol. 4. Social conditions and applied parenting* (2nd ed.) (pp. 59–93). Mahwah, NJ: Erlbaum.

Dey, L.T., Catipon, M.A., Garcia, W.G., & Tarroja, C. (2015). *Play therapy in the Philippines*. Manuscript in preparation.

Kagitçibasi, Ç. (2007). *Family, self, and human development across cultures: Theory and applications* (2nd ed.). Hillsdale, NJ: Lawrence Erlbaum.

12

THE SOLUTION BALLOON

An effective tool for applying SFBT with children and families

David Blakely

Two concepts inform my work using solution-focused brief therapy (SFBT). The first is a clear understanding that I am striving towards *awareness* and not *commitment* with clients. SFBT is goal-driven and resource-based, with a natural movement toward positive change action. It can become very natural to focus on and encourage behavioural change. My personal focus is on developing awareness with my clients of possible positive actions: e.g., I get clients to talk about small simple actions they might take, encouraging them to remain aware of the good possibilities.

However, I do not ask the client to do the potential actions they describe. The growth of awareness opens the door of possibilities, whereas requesting a specific action of the client creates the risk of failure if the task is not completed.

The second concept is that families and children seem to have greater clarity and longer lasting memories when the issues discussed are expressed in pictorial form. This is especially true when focusing on increasing their awareness of helpful behaviour, rather than following through on the behaviour. That means that during almost every session I will write or draw something meaningful from our conversation on the whiteboard in my office. At the end of the session I will take photographs and either print the photos or email them to the clients. This allows the clients to remain aware of the conversation, and is hopefully a natural process towards taking one or more of the simple steps mentioned.

The Solution Balloon is a picture metaphor suggested by M. L. Chong (personal communication, 2012), which effectively encapsulates the SFBT concepts outlined above. In this chapter I will share this tool and make the experience as practical as possible. I will illustrate its use in the context of the eight counselling sessions I had with a family.

Case example

The family is a reconstituted family consisting of a mother, a father and three children. Theresa (8 years old) was born during the mother's first marriage. The youngest two children were born during her present marriage.

A key step for me in working with young children is to meet the parents first, which affords an opportunity to form an alliance with the parents, and set a clear agenda before meeting the children. The mother and stepfather, therefore, attended the first meeting.

The session began with the discussion of the strengths and resources of the family. This focus on strengths allowed both individuals to feel engaged and part of a united team. The mother and stepfather identified the following resources: the stepfather was engaging with all three children, Theresa enjoyed drawing and dancing, the parents communicated well with open-ended questions and expressed difficult topics in neutral terms, and the family liked adventure.

The mother and stepfather raised two concerns. The first was that Theresa was displaying signs of anxiety that included bed-wetting and becoming quieter than normal. The second was to discuss whether it was an appropriate time for them to discuss with Theresa about having her stepfather adopt her.

The session ended with the couple deciding now was not a good time to discuss adoption, considering Theresa's anxiety problems. Instead, they were going to focus on a continued effort to discuss feelings with Theresa instead and maintain the positive actions they already had in place.

Session two occurred two weeks later. Theresa and her mother were present. This is the session in which I introduced the Solution Balloon, which I use as a structure for helping both adult and child in identifying solution-focused (SF) goals and resources.

I drew the Solution Balloon on the white board and explained that the balloon rises because of hot air put in to it. In the same way a family rises and gets stronger by all the good things they do. I asked Theresa and her mother to tell me all the good things about themselves as individuals and their family. These are illustrated in Figure 12.1.

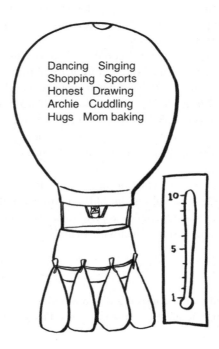

FIGURE 12.1 Theresa's family response on a sample Solution Balloon.
(Credit: Naomi Blakely)

It is important to take your time when doing this phase. Make sure you hear stories that feature positive emotions and behaviours found in daily life.

Once we had filled the balloon, I explained to the family that each hot air balloon has ballasts that weigh the balloon down. In the same way each family has challenges that make it hard for them to be at their best. I asked the family to tell me three burdens they faced. They were only allowed three and so it was important to choose the difficulties that truly mattered most to them. The purpose is to limit, without denying, the pains or burdens the family faces. As the family told me their challenges, I wrote them on the ballasts. The mother said one burden was for Theresa to be able to talk directly to her father. Theresa said she was sad when her sister scratched her, and finally that she was scared when her mother scolded her.

Now comes an important transition, as this is the time where we develop SF goals that guide the remainder of counselling. I asked the family to choose one word for what they hoped would change because of our counselling session. In keeping to the core SF beliefs, the focus is making sure each session is self-contained. That means this goal could be for only the one session, or may become an ongoing goal throughout therapy.

Theresa and her mother hoped for more courage. I drew a 'brave meter' on the left side of the white board (see Figure 12.2). The two red marks on the brave meter visually identified where Theresa and her mother were on the scale, so as to begin focusing on small changes.

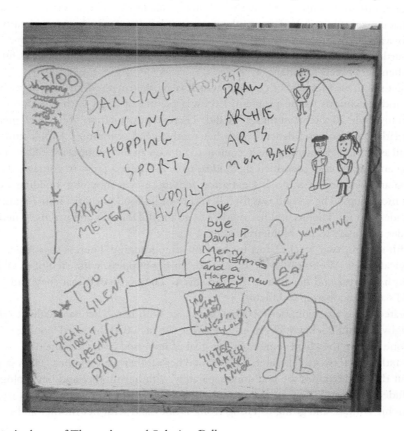

FIGURE 12.2 A photo of Theresa's actual Solution Balloon.
(Photo credit: David Blakely)

The Solution Balloon at the end of this chapter has a 1 to 10 scale on the right side of the balloon. This can be used to measure progress towards the family's goal and named in any way that is helpful for the family.

Theresa and her mother then shared that hugs, cuddles, art, sports and shopping would all help Theresa's brave meter grow. Theresa shared that going shopping after counselling would be the most helpful. I ended the session encouraging Mum and Theresa to do more of the things that helped them be brave, and to review their position on the brave meter each week.

The third session was two weeks later, and was attended by the mother and stepfather. The meeting had three goals. The first was to decide how to respond to possible legal complaints from Theresa's biological father. The second was to strengthen the mother's coping. The third goal was to continue to incorporate Theresa into the reconstituted family. We discussed the couple's positive resources, which included support, honesty, unity, balance of life, and communication.

This session remained focused on the core of SFBT by strengthening the clients' goals with the resources they possessed as a couple.

We ended the session with four suggestions. The first was to maintain the good actions they had done as a couple. The second was for the couple to start discussing couple and family goals for the coming year. The third suggestion was for the couple to consider a romantic date. Finally, I encouraged the mother to write what good things about herself she has kept since her divorce. These suggestions are examples of how the solutions a client identifies often don't seem to relate to the initial concerns raised. It is part of the process of how we trust clients to identify meaningful steps forward.

The fourth session was one week later, attended by Theresa and her mother. Our focus was on strengthening Theresa's courage.

We discussed their 'presents' of courage, which is another method for helping a child express resources and exceptions to the problem. I drew a picture of a gift with a bow on, and asked Theresa to highlight all the brave things she did. Theresa drew pictures of having a meal with her biological father, singing and dancing with her mother, and swimming. I took time to hear as much detail as possible, allowing these resources to take on an increasing sense of life and strength.

Theresa and her mother identified three ideas to help Theresa grow in courage. The first was for Theresa and her mother to do one extra fun activity such as shopping, building a doll house, or sharing more hugs. The second was for Theresa to order food once in a non-English language. The third idea was for Theresa and her mother to go to McDonald's and practise Theresa sharing what she desired to say to her biological father.

The fifth session, two weeks later, focused on strengthening Theresa's courage to speak to her biological father. We role-played the scenario, using puppets, with each of us taking on the roles of both Theresa and her father. We did this as Theresa shared that they had practised at McDonald's and described it as difficult.

We created a courage reminder for Theresa to take with her. Theresa decided to draw a basketball, rugby ball and hockey stick. In each drawing she included the word 'courage'. The drawing was done to help the client remember her goal of increased courage longer.

In the sixth session two weeks later, Theresa and her mother were present. Theresa was able to share about the fun activities she had done separately with her mother and her biological father. They included playing air hockey and monopoly with her father, dressing up as a true princess, reading Archie comics, and going to Hong Kong Disneyland with her mother and reconstituted family.

As Theresa still struggled to share her concerns with her biological father, we created a list of fun activities Theresa could complete with her family while practising speaking up to her biological father. These included swimming, going to the playground, dressing up, shopping, arts and crafts, playing with toys, dancing and singing, eating ice and acting out characters from Archie.

Sessions seven and eight were both attended by Theresa, her mother and her stepfather. Both sessions were a time to process their experience in court, as Theresa's biological father had made a court application with regards to access to Theresa. The focus of the sessions was Theresa having her feelings acknowledged, and the family reaffirming their strengths and resources. The eighth session was our final session as the family felt confident they had the knowledge and resources to move forward and remain positive.

Reflections as a therapist

This chapter was written to demonstrate a specific technique, the Solution Balloon. The Solution Balloon was key in two ways. The first was the establishment of the theme of courage that remained part of their goals throughout the eight sessions. The second was the family's expectation that change will happen through a focus on their strengths. This technique may make a meaningful contribution to a self-contained single session, or set the context for continuing an effective counselling relationship.

In my 19 years of work as a counsellor in Singapore, I have been struck by the melding of both Eastern and Western ideals within society. This has been especially true in the evolving look of families in Singapore. When I first moved to Singapore, mixed cultural marriages like my own seemed few and far between. Nowadays, I see many more family units that are from different cultural backgrounds, including remarriages and re-constituted families. It is in this light that I see my work in this case study as a reflection of what works within the evolving reality of Singapore.

There are two reflections of Singapore society that blend well with the SFBT concepts represented in the Solution Balloon. The first reflection is that the Singaporean culture appreciates practical ideas that can be put in to action quickly. The second reflection is that Singaporean culture holds a reservation about publicly discussing personal family flaws. The use of the Solution Balloon helped the couple identify meaningful changes needed, without having to dwell on their personal flaws, and then take practical steps that family members had confidence taking as the ideas came from them.

It is my hope and encouragement that some of our readers will find joy just as I have in the use of this tool and the SFBT approach.

Acknowledgements

I want to give a special mention to Ms Chong Ming Li, who first gave me the suggestion of using a hot air balloon as an effective metaphor for bringing solution-focused ideas alive.

I am deeply grateful for the family permitting me to use their story to help this chapter come to life.

A sample Solution Balloon is included on the final page of this chapter (see Figure 12.3). Please feel free to make copies and use it with your clients. If the Solution Balloon is used in any presentation, please give appropriate credit.

A special thank-you to Naomi Blakely, who provided the artwork for the chapter.

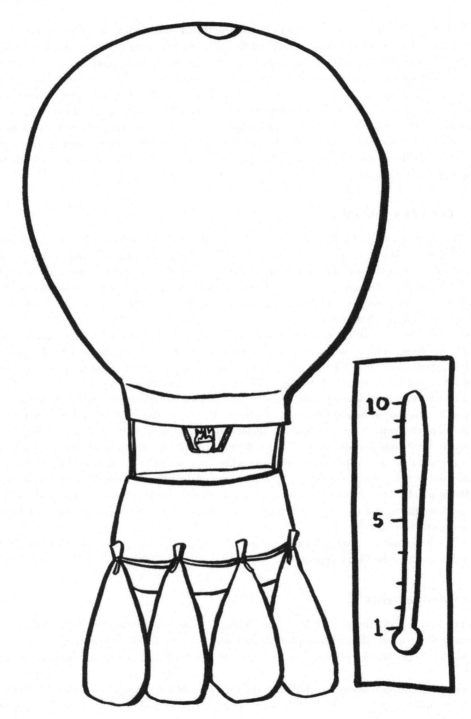

FIGURE 12.3 The Solution Balloon.

(Credit: Naomi Blakely)

13

WORKING WITH TAIWANESE MOTHER-DAUGHTER RELATIONAL CONFLICT USING THE SOLUTION-FOCUSED BRIEF THERAPY FRAMEWORK

A practice-based reflection

Wei-Su Hsu and Ben C. H. Kuo

The mother–daughter dyad within Chinese society is a particularly close-knit relationship. This is due to the fact that a Chinese mother typically plays the 'giver' role within the traditional family system – the individual who makes the most sacrifices for family, especially for the children. This relationship is heightened by the similar gender role the daughters share with their mothers, such as getting married and bearing children in an expected and timely manner (Liu, 2000). In this chapter we illustrate the ways in which solution-focused brief therapy (SFBT) can be applied to reduce and manage Taiwanese mother-daughter conflicts. We highlight effective and culturally responsive intervention strategies when working with this dyadic relationship. The 'counsellor' in both cases refers to the first author of this chapter.

Striking a balance between pursuing personal autonomy and parental approval

In our years of counselling female adult clients in Taiwan we have observed a common theme – a struggle towards pursuing one's personal independence and autonomy within the family. The following case example of a 28-year-old woman named 'Mei-Ling' provides such an illustration.

Mei-Ling had a strong longing for independence, which included wishing to choose her own career, her work location, and her dating and marriage partner. These personal aspirations conflicted with the wishes of Mei-Ling's mother, who wanted her to move back to her hometown, live at home, and share the workload for their family business. Mei-Ling's mother disapproved of her relationship with her boyfriend and insisted on finding a man more compatible with the social status and background of her family.

Mei-Ling's distress at this juncture was prompted by several external pressures entrenched in Taiwanese cultural values and gender expectations. There is a traditional belief that women's marriageability (i.e., to find an optimal suitor) and childbearing years are best before 30 years of age. Mei-Ling's single status at age 28 was making both herself and her mother highly anxious and was heightening the tension between them. Feeling confused and stressed, Mei-Ling sought counselling.

While Mei-Ling wished to please her mother because of the many sacrifices her mother had made for her and her family, she was nevertheless infuriated with her mother's constant interference with her independence. Despite the resentment, Mei-Ling, like most Taiwanese daughters, still strived to live up to her mother's expectations. The inability to measure up and to reconcile the differences between the mother and the daughter put Mei-Ling in a deep quandary.

In responding to the miracle question, Taiwanese female clients often envision their mothers' full endorsement of their needs for independence. Some clients can begin to discover small steps towards influencing their mothers. Others respond by stating that things are simply 'never going to happen' and then revert back to despair and hopelessness. In a culturally responsive manner, the counsellor helped Mei-Ling reframe her struggle by pointing out her thoughtfulness in considering the needs and perspectives of her significant others and her broad respect and deference to them – an inherent quality of Chinese collectivism (Kuo, 2004).

The counsellor affirmed Mei-Ling's intentions to 'simultaneously' strive for autonomy and also seek out her mother's approval. The authors' experiences suggest that focusing on one goal to the exclusion of the other would be detrimental for Taiwanese daughters. In working with Mei-Ling, several avenues were taken. First, Mei-Ling was helped to clarify the personal significance of choosing her career and the work location, and her rationale for being in her current relationship. Second, Mei-Ling was guided to ascertain her views about her mother's expectations by using relationship questions. Finally, she arrived at a reasonable compromise. She realised she could find a job in the area near her family, and be closer to her mother. She would be involved in her family business only if her present job and long-term career plan did not pan out. Mei-Ling also made minor concessions by giving herself more time to assess the long-term prospect of her current romantic relationship and explore the boyfriend's willingness to relocate with her. With this compromise, Mei-Ling was able to pursue her own dreams while also attend to her mother's wishes.

By exploring positive communication strategies that Mei-Ling had used successfully in the past with her mother (i.e., exception experiences), she discovered she could effectively communicate with her mother without hurting or upsetting her in the process.

In some cases there are unforeseeable obstacles in this process that a client will have to prepare for. For instance, the client may experience anger and frustration in the process of communicating and confronting her mother face-to-face.

Through realising the good intention behind her mother's expectations for her (i.e., a genuine desire for her daughter to have a secure marriage and a prosperous life), Mei-Ling's negative emotions diminished. Relationship questions prompted Mei-Ling to consider how her mother would be affected if she knew that Mei-Ling's insistence on pursuing her dreams was also motivated by the same strong desire for a secure and prosperous life. She realised they shared a common goal. Following this, Mei-Ling came up with a more amiable approach that balanced meeting her own and her mother's wishes. This prompted the mother to be more open to letting go of Mei-Ling and to allow Mei-Ling more room to make her own career and relationship decisions.

Scaling was then used, with 10 representing interacting with the mother in a mutual and amicable manner and 1 representing a direct confrontation with her. This encouraged Mei-Ling to carefully explore the strategies she could engage in communicating to her mother.

Mei-Ling decided she needed to refrain from discussing her romantic relationship with her mother for the time being, to avoid aggravating the situation. Instead, she was supported to quietly enhance and build up her personal successes on her own. With increasing successes and achievements over time, Mei-Ling was in a stronger position to persuade her mother to support her views and to garner her acceptance. Mei–Ling also wanted to master the skills of responding and coping with her mother's worry and frequent nagging. This was achieved by identifying the positive 'exceptions' from her past. Mei–Ling identified being successful with resolving conflicts with her mother on several occasions by minimising and avoiding direct confrontation with her mother. Mei–Ling noted that listening to her mother, refraining from talking back to her, remaining calm and keeping quiet had helped calm her mother in past conflicts.

The timely use of praise is very important when working with Taiwanese clients. The counsellor affirmed Mei–Ling's sensitivity and thoughtfulness towards her mother's opinions and wishes. This type of praise is especially impactful for Taiwanese clients, as it reflects a respect for filial piety – one of the utmost values within the traditional Chinese familism and the Confucian code of ethics (Kuo, Hsu & Lai, 2011).

Re-establishing the boundary between personal autonomy and the mother-daughter relationship

Within the typical Taiwanese family nowadays, it is not unusual to find that mothers place excessive demands on their children that exceed their children's ability to manage. In situations like this, Taiwanese daughters may end up experiencing a significant amount of guilt and self-blame. The following case of 25-year-old 'Hong-Fei' exemplifies such a dynamic.

Hong-Fei came to counselling to address her self-injurious behaviours. After the counsellor probed the reasons for Hong-Fei's self-injurious acts, Hong-Fei disclosed that her father had been an alcoholic for many years and often acted unpredictably towards her and her family. Ever since she was a young girl it had always been the expectation of her mother that Hong-Fei would be able to bring about changes in her father because Hong-Fei had always had a closer relationship with her father than did her mother. Considering the amount of pain and suffering her mother had endured, Hong-Fei was motivated to submit to her mother's wish. Recently, Hong-Fei completed her master's degree and landed a new job. Hong-Fei's mother began to blame her for being overly selfish as she pursued her own goals and future at the expense of helping her father with his problems. Hong-Fei concurred with her mother's disappointment and resentment, and began to dismiss her own accomplishments, as they represented her 'selfishness'.

Coping questions served to facilitate Hong-Fei in rediscovering and identifying many of her personal strengths over varying stages of her life. For example, the counsellor asked: 'How did you manage to cope and grow up under such a hard family circumstance?' And 'How did you find the resources to achieve a master's degree and obtain a good job with little support from your family?' These questions helped Hong-Fei to save face (from an otherwise shameful situation with her father), as well as discern adaptive coping strategies she had utilised in dealing with difficult situations and emotions in the past. Despite all the hardships, Hong-Fei found ways to support herself through her graduate study and secured a job. The coping questions helped Hong-Fei to experience increased self-compassion, self-empathy and self-acceptance. Hong-Fei explored concrete coping strategies she could use to tackle anticipated challenges and soothe her current emotional distress. As a consequence, her self-injurious behaviours diminished.

Learning to distinguish and accept what is and is not within a client's control is another critical element of the SFBT intervention. For example the counsellor's praise prompted Hong-Fei to discern what she could or could not do at the moment. The use of scaling questions encouraged Hong-Fei to recount and evaluate the efforts she had made in assisting her father thus far and the likelihood of seeing changes in him in the future. These questions gradually softened Hong-Fei's rigid insistence on changing her father's behaviours through her own efforts.

In general, acts of self-injury may reflect a Taiwanese daughter's deep-seated emotional distress and conflict, stemming from her inability to hold her ground and to placate her mother's negative emotions. These behaviours may represent the unspoken reactions a daughter feels in having her individuality and her voice drowned out by the domineering force of her mother.

Through SFBT interventions Hong-Fei was supported to reconsider ways to affect her mother, increase the mother's understanding of her, and realistically consider the likelihood of her father changing. When Hong-Fei responded in frustration about the immoveable position her mother would be in, as a reframe the counsellor pointed out to Hong-Fei the specific meaning behind her emotions. That is, her emotions signalled her increasing realisation of the unchangeable nature of her mother and the disparity between her own position and that of her mother. As a consequence, Hong-Fei began to experience increasing appreciation and acceptance of her own individuality and the divergence between her perspective and her mother's. Within the Taiwanese context, while the presence of a daughter's self-injury may halt a mother's interference momentarily, it does not mean that this behaviour will bring about the mother's true understanding of the daughter's intents.

After Hong-Fei took the courage to directly disclose to her mother about her emotional conflicts, her mother reacted with disgruntlement and lamented that she could no longer place any expectations on her daughter. This caught Hong-Fei by surprise and set her back to a state of self-blame. In response, the counsellor asked: 'How do you help your mother in seeking improvement in the current situation while accepting the present reality?' The discussion surrounding how to help her mother reinvigorated Hong-Fei, as she regained additional strengths from this intervention process. As Hong-Fei continued to cope with the unfolding situation, she was able to refocus on the successful coping methods she used in the past, to draw upon her knowledge of her mother, and to remind herself regularly of her mother's love for her. The exchange further enabled Hong-Fei to delimit a clearer mother-daughter boundary and to re-define the way in which she would interact and maintain her relationship with her mother. By so doing, Hong-Fei was able to gradually reassert her individuality through transforming herself from the role of being a 'daughter' to her mother, to a full-grown, independent person.

Conclusion

The above two cases demonstrate that SFBT can effectively support Taiwanese female clients in better defining their plans of action amidst struggles and conflicts. By simultaneously ascribing importance to the mother's needs, the daughter's goals and their relationship, counselling can move forward with minimal negative impact on either party. A critical lesson for Taiwanese female clients to learn through an SFBT intervention is to rise above the overpowering influences of their mothers and to assert their individuality within the complex, culturally conditioned Taiwanese relational dynamic (Kuo, et al., 2011). Once a client has gained clarity about the goals for herself, the mother and their relationship, the client's own position will become firmer and more enduring. The main task of the counsellor is to skilfully assist the client in solidifying and affirming her position and voice without being obscured by the expectations and demands of the mother. Such a process exemplifies an enhanced capacity for 'self-determination' on the part of the client – a therapeutic goal that coincides with one of the core principles of SFBT (De Jong & Berg, 2013).

References

De Jong, P., & Berg, I.K. (2013). *Interviewing for solutions* (4th ed.). Belmont CA: Brooks/Cole, Cengage Learning.

Kuo, B.C.H. (2004). Interdependent and relational tendencies among Asian clients: Infusing collectivistic strategies into counselling. *Guidance and Counselling, 19*, 158–162.

Kuo, B.C.H., Hsu, W.S., & Lai, N.H. (2011). Indigenous crisis counselling in Taiwan: An exploratory qualitative case study of an expert therapist. *International Journal for the Advancement of Counselling, 33*, 1–21.

Liu, W. (2000). Motherhood: A social constructive perspective. *Research in Applied Psychology, 6*, 97–130.

14

'THERE WERE SO MANY LITTLE THINGS'

Working creatively with clients

Amanda Jewitt

Introduction

In this chapter, I will share stories of two clients from my practice in Singapore who found creative and unique solutions through therapy: one case of severe anxiety and the other relating to
the devastation over the break-up of a long-term relationship. They demonstrate how significant
it is to uncover details of clients' lives, not only to give context to solution building but also to
ensure the client's preferred outcome remains at the centre of the therapy. The ways in which
the solution-focused (SF) approach of gathering details remains respectful of and adaptable to the
Asian cultural context will also be discussed.

Relocation and relationships

My practice in Singapore draws mainly from the expatriate community and includes clients from
many cultures and countries, including many parts of Asia. A common feature of all the expatriate
clients in my practice was that the problems they were experiencing were further complicated by
being away from their usual support networks. The effort needed to build support networks in
a completely new environment complicated by culture shock, (many having never lived in Asia
before) was often a significant factor raised by clients. The SF therapist's 'not knowing stance' and
curiosity were essential in building trust and remaining respectful towards the client's own culture
and their adopted one.

Often, re-locating to another country does not work out the way you planned. This was the
case in the first client's story. This client had relocated to Singapore to be with her long-term
partner. She had a job she loved in her home country and she had been able to transfer to the
Singapore office with her company. She had been due to get married to her partner, but shortly
after she arrived, he suddenly ended their relationship. The client was understandably shocked and
confused. She came to therapy wanting to develop coping strategies to help her adjust to life in
Singapore, build a new network of relationships and, specifically, cope with unexpectedly being
single. Her preferred outcome was to feel better about herself and her behaviour and to develop
an acceptance of her 'single self'.

The client's miracle picture was that she would be happy to get through her weekends as a single person: she would be looking forward to planning what to do with her free time and would be efficient when at work. She would feel independent and free to do what she wanted with her time and able to trust others. She mentioned many colleagues and friends who would notice the difference.

On the scale, where 10 was she felt confident in enjoying free time and 0 was the opposite, she felt she was at a 3 as she was able to plan some activities and get some enjoyment from the weekends. She thought if she could begin to trust others again it might help her move up the scale. She mentioned that people had been trying to involve her in their plans from time to time, but she had not been open to this because she was feeling a lack of trust. I was very curious about this so I asked her what these people saw to make them keep trying. She paused for a long time, and then stated that she was unsure but felt they might think she was worth trying to reconnect with. I asked her what it would take for her to be open to these attempts to connect, and she said she felt she must 'just try it', as what she was doing was not working for her.

We discussed whom she might make a small start with. She said she was willing to try with a particular friend who had been attempting to engage her in conversation the previous day about going out together. This friend had been persistent in trying to connect and she had 'rejected' her each time. She said she had not really acknowledged this before. She decided to try being more open to reconnecting with her friend the next day as she thought trying this would move her at least 1 point up on the scale. I asked her to notice what difference this made and note any attempts to connect with her by other friends or colleagues and to observe what difference these interactions made to her.

The client emailed between sessions. She said opening up to her persistent friend went very well and they were spending more time together, which made her feel less isolated and lonely. She had also made her own attempts to connect with colleagues, which led to her entering a sporting event with them. She felt that making that small effort with her friend had precipitated a series of events that had served to help her see she could still trust people and enjoy herself whilst being single. I encouraged the client to continue what she was doing to maintain all her hard work.

In a follow-up session the client reported things were much better. Although she still had 'down times', she was enjoying her free time more and wanted to plan to further expand her current sporting and social activities to ensure she did not experience the isolation again. The most significant moment for this client appeared to be when she was asked what others around her saw to make them want to keep trying to connect with her. She paused for a very long time, and eventually answered 'I don't know', but what she followed up with was that she was rejecting people now, whereas before this crisis she was fun to be around and lived life to the fullest. Her friends wanted her back and she said that she had been 'shutting them down'.

From the next session her attitude and mood changed significantly. She had stopped all contact with her ex-partner and had plans to do new things to rebuild a healthy social life. This one small detail about her friend trying to re-connect led to a conversation about what it was that made people keep trying to connect with her and made the client think about herself from the perspective of other people who knew her. This highlighted that to move towards her preferred future, she would need to be open to connecting with others more. The client has contacted me since we ended therapy and is continuing to thrive.

Although it wasn't an issue for the client above, many Western clients I worked with came to therapy to try to manage their behaviour in ways more 'appropriate' to their Asian environment.

A few mentioned that they had difficulties connecting and forming strong relationships with their Asian work colleagues, with some saying these colleagues commented on their 'volatile' emotions. Exploring details about how clients can show more appropriate behaviour that respects the culture where they work and live, yet at the same time helps them move towards their own goals, can be very helpful.

More details . . .

The second story is that of a client suffering with agoraphobia and anxiety. She described how she had been trying to motivate herself to leave her home but every time she did, she would experience an anxiety attack and have to return immediately. It had become so debilitating that she stopped trying to go out unless it was absolutely essential. It emerged, when she was describing the details of her week, that when it was essential, she was able to force herself to go out, despite her anxiety. I was very curious about how she had been able to manage her anxiety on these rare occasions. She described one occasion when she had to pick up her pet from the vet: she had no choice but to get on with it as the animal needed treatment. She had a very difficult time but she was able to cope with the anxiety, complete the task and get home. We looked more closely at the client's day-to-day routine. Apart from the exception already described, she had also fostered a dog, and whilst he was staying with her she took him for a 3-km run every day; she said she could only do this if she remained close to home. These two details revealed important exceptions to her usual experience of anxiety and agoraphobia, and significant clues to what this client was capable of. I complimented her on managing to cope with her anxiety in order to take care of her pets.

I asked her how she coped on the rare occasions she was out. It emerged that although she would still feel the anxiety, she pushed through it using tools learned in our sessions and managed her feelings because there was no choice. These rare exceptions provided useful details of what she did to cope, examples of strengths the client was not acknowledging, and a platform for examining how she could use this to help herself every time she felt similar symptoms. She believed this new understanding and knowledge could help her to 'kick the anxiety out of her life'. She mentioned that maybe, if she was challenged, she might be able to do more: she said she wanted to be 'kicked in the backside'. She was very explicit about what her preferred outcome from therapy was from this point: she wanted a plan with action steps and challenges to get her motivated to go out more. The client's sense of clear goals and the details of times she managed her anxiety helped to build a picture of what she wanted and also what she was capable of. She experimented with different tools we had explored during sessions to help her cope whilst out.

Her achievements were significant: she began to feel more confident to go out by herself and could complete the challenges she set herself, re-join her social network and even put together a support group for other anxiety sufferers. This was a very important achievement for her as she had been unable initially to find other anxiety sufferers who were willing to talk about their problems. Support groups do not seem to be as popular in Singapore as they are in Europe, possibly because it is not as acceptable to share feelings and emotions publicly in Asia. She now has a robust group of over 80 members, however, which may indicate that the stigma around seeking help for mental health problems in Asia is slowly changing.

She said in feedback three months after the end of therapy: 'It feels a lot easier now.' Listening to the finer details of the client's daily life uncovered some revealing exceptions. These led to her acknowledging strengths she had forgotten and led to some key understanding of what she was capable of coping with in terms of anxiety.

'. . . There were so many little things . . .'

When listening to clients' stories we are always on the lookout for the small clues hidden amongst the problem talk that will provide us with evidence of previously unacknowledged exceptions to their current difficulties. This feedback (from the first client above) says so much about how amazingly unobtrusive the SF process can be for clients. The SF approach is unobtrusive because the process works closely within the context of the client's life, which can be particularly helpful when the therapist and client are from different cultures.

In many Asian cultures, seeking help for and sharing problems are perceived as things that will result in a loss of respect and dignity in front of their family or community. Even once someone has overcome this stigma and sought help, many problem-focused therapies can compound feelings of shame by asking clients for details about their problems and revealing clients' weaknesses and deficits in the process. The SF approach to gathering details is very different and focuses on asking for details about clients' strengths, resources, exceptions and preferred futures. The SF principles of curiosity and not making assumptions underline that the therapist believes the client is competent and the expert in their own lives, and this can build confidence in clients.

Final reflections

I often attempt to work out what really happened during a session that made the difference for the client: my reflections have so far led me to the conclusion that it is different with every client. Clients are unique and so is their path to a solution. Two things that are always really important with all clients are: sticking with what the client says they want and getting details through SF questioning. It does not matter how small, 'boring' or mundane the clients feel these details are, they can often reveal very important competencies, resources and exceptions to the problem that the client has not acknowledged for a long time, if ever. These two cases show that when clients share the details of their lives, therapists discover that they have wonderful resources. These are often 'forgotten' by clients' conscious minds, and finding new and different ways for them to remember and acknowledge these becomes a creative collaboration between the therapist and client.

While the SF approach gives the structure for gathering details for solution building, the actual details are unique to each client and give precious clues to the client's unique solution. The details always come from the client, who is the expert in their own life and no assumptions are made by the therapist about what the solutions should look like. As such, paying attention to and being respectful of the cultural context the client comes from as well as the one they currently live in should be an inherent part of the SF approach and is crucial in building the specific solutions that will work for each client.

SECTION 2

Solution focused practice in supervision in Asia

15

INTRODUCTION TO SOLUTION FOCUSED PRACTICE IN SUPERVISION IN ASIA

Alan K. L. Yeo

Introduction

Supervision is an integral part of a therapist's professional development. With the growth of solution focused brief therapy (SFBT) in Asia, the need for SF supervision will most likely increase. It is hard to imagine any professional not appreciating supervision as a form of on-going support and training, especially given the oft-cited quote of Insoo Kim Berg, 'easy to learn but hard to do' (Connie & Metcalf, 2009, p. 179).

An example of the growth of SF supervision in Asia comes from Singapore. A peer supervision group was formed after completing the inaugural graduate diploma course in SFBT in 2001 and continued for five years. As the SF community continued to grow, a new peer supervision group was formed in 2008 and has expanded into two groups. The groups meet monthly to present cases, using the Norman (2003) reflecting team format, and share success stories or new ideas.

Some people trained in SFBT may choose to seek out SF supervision to support them in their choice to use the approach with their clients. For others, supervision holds the key to embracing the SF approach after training, as my own journey shows.

My background in psychology, and studies in the UK and USA, paved the way for a mid-career switch to doing therapy. Therapy is not a common aspiration among Asians, though that view has been changing over the past 20 years, with an increasing number of counselling and therapy courses at the diploma, degree and Master's level. After learning SF in 2001, I did not immediately embrace it as my therapeutic approach of choice. I was inspired by Insoo and her team when they came to Singapore to run the inaugural SFBT programme, mostly because there was not an iota of intent to inspire. They might have delighted in the successes of the approach, but never of themselves. I was in awe, overwhelmed by their radical content and captivating delivery. Alas, when trying to put the ideas into practice, I was sometimes disheartened. 'Simple but not easy' became my motto, which provided some comfort that I was not alone. I only embraced SFBT over time through the kindness, patience and generous sharing of my SF supervisors. I still used an eclectic/integrative approach then, so I was also exposed to other supervision modalities. While all my supervisors 'conspired' to make me a better therapist, I found only SF supervision made me a better person as well. Although all therapy models I know originated in the West, I suspect the influence of Eastern philosophies in the early days of SF development (de Shazer & Dolan, 2007, Chap. 1) might have had a part to play. As a third-generation Singaporean Chinese, I grew up among relatives spewing Chinese proverbs and repeating classic Chinese parables. Many of these words of wisdom have their parallels among SF tenets.

In this chapter I will share the key issues concerning SF supervision and research into the effectiveness of SF supervision, and will specifically highlight its applications in Asia. This will be followed by brief descriptions of the contributions by the authors to this section.

Uniqueness of SF supervision

Thomas's (2013) seminal book on SF supervision is based on SF practices and research, and his inductive observation of his own and others' supervision. Thomas' book is precious as it includes many personal insights into the minds and work of the founders of SFBT. Many of the themes raised in the book are echoed by our SF supervision stories in this section. Common themes raised and expounded in the Thomas book include:

- Supervision is qualitatively different from therapy; though there are similar competencies, perhaps more competencies are needed to offer SF supervision.
- SF supervision, being inductively guided by its applications, is different from traditional supervision, which is mostly theory-driven.
- Thomas prefers the term 'therapist' over 'supervisee' to acknowledge the non-hierarchical stance he embraces. Berg also suggested the term 'super-visor' be questioned as it denotes an 'expert' stance (Thomas, 2013, Chap. 3, p. 59). The posture of co-learning, 'leading from one step behind', deemphasising hierarchy, is further expounded in the chapter devoted to Insoo Kim Berg's approach to supervision.
- Unlike Yeo (2014), who made a distinction between teaching/education and supervision, advocating that the former be kept to a minor role in supervision, SF treats teaching as essential to supervision (Thomas, 2013, p. 65). Both agree that it is more effective without a top-down approach, which can detract from the supportive ambience effective supervisors aim to create.
- Tentative language, sometimes termed 'hedging' (e.g., 'I'm not sure', 'suppose you do know'), promotes a sense of healthy and supportive curiosity that encourages self-discovery. This stance does not negate the times when a more directive approach is required (e.g., a violation of an ethical code) (Thomas, 2013, p. 68).
- SF supervision, based on systemic thinking (emphasising dynamic and holistic inter-relationships among its component parts such as members of a family, an organisation or a community), naturally avails itself to cultural adaptation. This quality is particularly pertinent for this book and this section focusing on SF supervision in Asia.
- While isomorphism (match between a supervisee's and supervisor's therapeutic model) is often helpful in providing a common vocabulary, SF supervision does not depend on isomorphism.

Other authors writing on the topic of SF supervision (Pichot & Dolan, 2003, Chap. 8) have suggested several principles to enhance SF supervision in agency settings: go slow, make making mistakes safe, avoid defending SF, ask for feedback even when it hurts, listen, don't react, among others.

While these principles, taken individually, are not unique to SF supervision, Pichot and Dolan put them together to create and reinforce the spirit and tenets of SF philosophy. Many of our contributors applied or adapted these supervision ideas in their organisations in Asia with positive results.

Research on SF supervision

There is some research into the effectiveness of SF supervision, which is outlined below.

Rudes (1992) and Rudes, Shilts and Berg (1997), cited in Thomas (2013), used a recursive frame analysis to analyse semantic shifts in SF dialogue. With Insoo as the supervisor, they found that supervisees highlighted aspects of supervision that they found helpful. Among these were: a less hierarchical supervisor-supervisee relationship, focus on supervisees' strengths and resources as opposed to correction of deficits, and the collaborative use of language towards a more useful reconceptualisation of the case, including SF techniques such as looking for exceptions, complimenting, etc.

Triantafillou (2007, cited in Thomas, 2013, p. 167) found that therapists who were supervised using SF approaches reported greater job satisfaction, compared with administrative supervision alone. SF supervision also contributed to the therapists' clients in a residential treatment facility reporting decreased use of psychotropic medication, compared with the control group, who received only administrative supervision. In this study, the prescribing psychiatrists were blind to the supervision study. It would be encouraging to see if similar findings can be replicated with Asian populations.

There is also some research relating to SF supervision in Asia. For example, in Taiwan, Hsu and Tsai (2008, 2011), adapting Norman's (2003) reflecting team method, explored their supervisees' (who were school counsellors) experiences of SF supervision using a qualitative approach. They noted improvements in their supervisees, including enhanced ability and professional efficacy in providing counselling to difficult involuntary clients, and positive development and growth such as awareness of own emotions and a more positive attitude about their interpersonal relationships. The supervisees were more effective in applying SFBT, and reported an increase in confidence in doing so. Pertinent to the school context, the supervisees were also better in relating with the students, their parents and the teachers.

Hsu (2009), using videotaped role-play counselling sessions, studied what was helpful about SF supervision for six school counsellors in Taiwan. The respondents found the following helpful: identifying concrete and constructive supervisory goals, and evaluating and identifying supervisees' growth and changes over time, among others. The author then trained the counsellors on the identified aspects, incorporated SF principles, and had them practise these aspects in role plays. The improvements from addressing these elements, and honing the SF skills associated with them, were reflected in increased positive and constructive reframing, and a decrease in punitive and disapproving responses when addressing parents or teachers who sought their assistance.

Many of our contributors also found that the success of their supervision extended beyond the therapy room. Sometimes the success was in the context of their work, such as in organisations or schools, and sometimes the success had a bearing on them as a person – for example, their confidence, way of thinking, or even lifestyle changes. This may be explained by the likelihood that one cannot advocate respect in our relationship with our clients or supervisees and not be congruent in valuing and applying this outside of therapy.

Cultural adaptations of SF supervision

Some cultural adaptations of Norman's (2003) reflecting team model have been found to be helpful. Hsu and Kuo (2013) found that to address the awkwardness among Taiwanese supervisees over being praised directly, the case presenter in their 'team case conference' was asked to sit outside the group, but within ear-shot of the affirmations. The presenters are spared the need to address these compliments head on, which is culturally uncomfortable given their high values placed on modesty and humbleness. Also, when it comes to giving feedback, in line with the cultural view of a supervisor as an expert who provides information on what to do (as opposed to exploring with an emphasis on the supervisee's resources and self-discovery), some amount of direction by the supervisor seemed to be better received. However, as supervisees become more competent and familiar with the SF tenets and approach, directiveness was curtailed.

It would be interesting to see how the findings of the above studies and adaptations impinge on stereotypic notions of some Asian cultures preferring direction from supervisors, or that compliments have limited effect on supervisees because these are culturally unfamiliar. Positive client outcomes as a result of SF supervision would also contribute significantly to increasing use of SF in mental health or school settings. The contributors in this section collectively seem to suggest that perhaps the cultural differences may not be that great, and it is likely that the SF approach can be adapted to overcome these differences consistent with the published studies cited.

Contributions by authors

Seven authors from Singapore, Hong Kong and Korea share their successes in using SF supervision. They cover a wide range of settings such as mental health institution, hospital, university, international school, government project and private practice. Several types of issues are addressed – case management, speech therapy interns, graduate interns in post-graduate Counselling or Psychology programmes, staff development in schools, group, peer and individual supervision, supervisors in corporations and in private practice.

The strengths of SF supervision and its contributions are highlighted in a piece on case managers in a mental health facility in Singapore. In a culture where recognising one's strength does not come naturally, Jane Tuomola used SF supervision to build confidence for the team, and describes the ripple effect on other aspects of their performance in this challenging, problem-focused hospital context.

A speech therapist intern on the verge of giving up his university programme in Singapore was encouraged when his 'bilingual' supervisor, Valerie Lim, used SF language in supervision to help him reach his goals with zest.

SF supervision continues to be an integral part of learning for a group of Chinese Master in Counselling Psychology students in a Hong Kong university. Using SF conversations, Ann Moir-Bussy helped students navigate the intricacies of cross-cultural differences towards compliments (giving and receiving) and grasp the miracle question, with apparent ease.

In a large International School in Hong Kong, Natalie Broderick made a significant change in mind-set from the problem-focused, cause-and-effect approach to an efficacy and purpose orientation. Working with an SF supervision approach, she and her team 'converted' the establishment of administrators and faculty to a strength-based perspective with lasting impact.

A project empowering Korean women who are the heads of lower income families started with five agencies. With the impressive outcomes of both the team of SF-trained supervisors and the families, the project has since been expanded nationwide over the last 10 years, and continues to expand. Adapting to different cultural values and attitudes towards the SF approach, Yunjoo Kim and her team inspire with the number of lives in which they have made a difference.

Supervising supervisors is often more demanding because of their more advanced knowledge and skill sets, and their added responsibilities in organisations. Lilian Ing shares the smooth flow of supervision that comes with using the solution circle model across varied corporate settings in Singapore. Contrary to stereotypes of Asians (e.g., wanting to be told what to do by an expert), Lilian found that when clients were treated with respect and goals were set from their frame of reference, SF could be transported across continents with minimal modifications.

Inspired by his supervisor, and by how SF has in part been influenced by Eastern philosophies, Alan Yeo shares anecdotes of how Chinese idioms not only can enhance the learning of SF tenets during supervision, but can be a turning point during supervision or therapy. Idioms are, after all, a reflection of the supervisee's or client's frame of reference, and as such could be applied to other languages and cultures.

Conclusions

Reflecting on the contributions of the authors in this supervision section, it is clear that differences in cultures and values need to be addressed. The authors demonstrated the relative ease that the SF platform brings to this process. The widespread use of the Internet often brings cultures closer together. People travel more widely, for further studies, pleasure or job opportunities. Yet, in therapy, differences in values, including social and cultural practices, are often at the core of the clients' struggles. The SF approach of 'working at the surface' can be effective in therapy and supervision, judging from this modest collection of 'what works'.

The authors shared their hopes that the effectiveness of SF supervision would encourage more therapists to try this approach in Asia.

References

Connie, E., & Metcalf, L. (2009). *The art of solution focused therapy*. New York, NY: Springer.

de Shazer, S., & Dolan, Y. (2007). *More than miracles: The state of the art of solution-focused brief therapy*. New York, NY: Routledge/ Taylor & Francis.

Hsu, W. (2009). The components of solution-focused supervision. *Bulletin of Educational Psychology, 41*(2), 475–496.

Hsu, W.S., & Kuo, B.C.H. (2013). Solution-focused supervision with school counsellors in Taiwan. In F. Thomas (Ed.), *Solution-focused supervision: a resource-oriented approach to developing clinical expertise* (pp. 197–204). New York, NY: Springer.

Hsu, W.S., & Tsai, S. (2008). The effects of solution-focused group supervision on school counselors. *Bulletin of Educational Psychology, 39*(4), 603–622.

Hsu, W.S., & Tsai, S.L. (2011). The effect of learning of solution-focused brief therapy for junior high school counselors (in Chinese). *Global Mental Health E-Journal, 2*(1), 1–19.

Norman, H. (2003). Solution-focused reflecting teams. In B. O'Connell & S. Palmer (Eds.), *Handbook of solution-focused therapy* (pp. 156–167). London: Sage.

Pichot, T., & Dolan, Y. (2003). *Solution-focused brief therapy: Its effective use in agency settings*. New York, NY: The Haworth Press.

Thomas, F.N. (2013). *Solution-focused supervision: A resource-oriented approach to developing clinical expertise*. Fort Worth, TX: Springer.

Yeo, A. (2014). Clinical supervision for counselling practice. In C. Lim & E. Sim (Eds.), *Clinical supervision clinicians' perspectives and practices: Towards professionalising counselling* (pp. 1–18). Singapore: Counselling & Care Centre.

16

FROM THE BLIND LEADING THE BLIND TO LEADING FROM ONE STEP BEHIND

Experiences with running a solution-focused supervision group for case managers

Jane Tuomola

Introduction

In 2011 the case managers (CM) at the Early Psychosis Intervention Programme (EPIP) at the Institute of Mental Health in Singapore (a large psychiatric hospital) attended an introduction to solution-focused (SF) therapy course. To build on this training and help the CMs put the skills learnt into practice, I was asked by the team manager to start an SF supervision group.

Starting an SF supervision group was an exciting proposition as my own training in SF therapy had completely changed my mind-set as a practising psychologist in working with clients. I was excited about sharing this approach with others. However, it was very daunting; while I had several years of experience as a supervisor, I was relatively new to the SF model. I initially felt like it would be the blind leading the blind. However, through my experiences over the last four years, I would now say I am confidently 'leading from one step behind': a sentiment that relates to how to work with supervisees when using this approach (Pichot & Dolan, 2003; Thomas, 2013).

There are many excellent resources on how to do SF supervision (e.g., Thomas, 2013; Wheeler, 2007). In this chapter I will share some of the key techniques used in the group, some challenges to implementing them in this cultural setting and the learning that took place for both me and my supervisees.

Structure of the group

Initially, there was one supervision group of four CMs meeting monthly for 3 hours. This has expanded to two groups of four CMs, meeting monthly for 2 hours. The CMs have professional backgrounds including psychology, social work and nursing. Prior to their SF training, they used different models of therapy (e.g., cognitive behavioural and psychodynamic). The cultural background of the CMs reflected the ethnic groups represented in Singapore and included Chinese, Malay and Indian.

Case presentations

During supervision the CMs took turns discussing clients.

We used the solution-focused reflecting team format (see, e.g., Norman, 2003). The steps included: *preparing,* i.e., the CM presents a specific question or need regarding a case, with which they want help; *presenting* information about the client and interventions implemented thus far; and then *clarifying* any questions from the other group members. The fourth step is *affirming,* where team members give the presenter compliments on what they have done well so far. This is followed by team members sharing *reflections,* which may include suggestions or recommendations about what to do next. Finally, the presenter *responds* to these reflections and sets a goal for their next steps with the client.

My role was to facilitate this process. What I found liberating was that it was not up to me to be the expert and be the only one offering suggestions. All the team members contributed equally, and each person offered wonderful ideas based on their own experience. I often felt I was learning more than I was offering! This was especially helpful in the beginning when I felt quite daunted supervising in a different model.

One of the CMs shares their experience of the reflecting team and how this made a difference to them and their clients.

A CM's experience of the reflecting team. I was apprehensive the first time I shared a client in group supervision using the reflecting team format. I worried about how to present the case and how my colleagues would see me.

I shared a client where there were numerous issues faced by the whole family, and the client was hard to engage. I blamed myself for not doing enough and was overwhelmed by their problems.

To my surprise, sharing this case gave a huge sense of relief. It was very encouraging when I started receiving compliments about what I had done well so far. I received positive feedback, which initially I didn't think I deserved. It felt strange to be complimented, but at the same time I felt good about myself. I stopped beating myself up for all the things that I could or should have done. Hearing feedback from different people was also more uplifting than hearing from just one supervisor. I felt the compliments laid the foundation for the feedback on what I could do next.

Another good thing was that I could listen to all the suggestions shared by the group about what might be useful and feasible. It gave me a sense of empowerment that I did not have to do *everything* that was recommended. The onus was still with me to decide what to do since I knew the client best. This was unlike previous supervision, where I often felt that I had overlooked numerous areas and had 1,001 things that I *had* to follow up.

It felt good to realise that I was already doing a lot, and I became hopeful that things would get better. Overall, the reflecting team gave me positive feedback that has kept me going when things feel difficult and invaluable useful and practical ideas. I felt good about myself, and think that my clients could also sense this.

For example, another client I worked with had a severe eating disorder and self-harmed frequently. My previous approach had been very problem focused. However, after the reflecting team session, things changed. Or rather, I changed. I truly started to believe in my client's strengths to manage her problems. We began to talk more about her studies, drawing and other interests and less about her symptoms. Surprisingly, her symptoms began to decrease. Before her discharge, we discussed the possible reasons things were better, and she said she didn't know. But what she knew was that she enjoyed my support and sessions more than before. She said I looked less worried and concerned.

My reflections. What stands out for me is how this CM went from feeling apprehension to relief and empowerment after only one session of SF supervision. Even more impressive was the tangible difference the clients experienced.

Another reflection is how difficult it was for the CMs initially being complimented. After a few sessions of supervision we discussed this. They shared that within many Asian cultures, people are brought up with the Confucian values of being humble and modest. Therefore, giving and receiving direct compliments is difficult. This has been written about in other accounts of SF supervision in Asia (e.g., Hsu & Kuo, 2013). In my experience with the group, this discomfort was gradually overcome by using more indirect compliments and using the supervisees' specific words as evidence rather than making general statements.

Asians are not alone in finding compliments difficult. Being from England, I could also relate to their discomfort. Typical responses in our culture range from a self-effacing qualification of a compliment to complete denial or self-denigration. Otherwise, this is seen as impolite, unfriendly and arrogant – as if you are boasting (Fox, 2004). In my own SF supervision, I also found it hard to receive compliments. Over time, however, I found this helpful in boosting my confidence with the SF model. This helped me explicitly empathise with the CMs, which in turn helped them empathise that their clients might also find compliments difficult. However, it also helped them understand the value of compliments and continue to use the technique.

The dual process of learning skills and experiencing the techniques themselves was another helpful aspect of supervision. As one CM said:

> The difference I found between SF and other models of supervision is that the SF supervision uses the same technique of SF therapy in supervision itself. . . . this is very crucial for a novice like me in learning practical skills and acquiring the knowledge base.

The fact that compliments preceded the suggestions in the reflecting team approach helped the CMs see the suggestions as positive options they could take, rather than feeling like a failure because they had overlooked them. This is particularly important in Asia, where highlighting deficits in public can lead to a sense of losing face. After moving to Singapore, I had been warned by other expatriate psychologists to choose my supervisees carefully, as supervisees were often reticent about sharing mistakes and did not want to reflect on them in order to learn and improve. However, all the CMs were very motivated to reflect on and improve their work, probably facilitated by the SF model. As one CM nicely summed it up: 'It creates a positive aura of learning from mistakes without any shame in order to enhance our skills.'

'Real plays'

We also used role plays to practise particular SF techniques. I asked the supervisees to choose a real problem in which they would like help. This was also my experience during my own SF therapy training. Prior to my SF training, all role plays I had done when learning other models of therapy were created scenarios from a client's perspective. While this has value, what changed me from being very sceptical of SF therapy to being an SF therapy convert was the chance to experience the model as a real client with a real issue and the difference it can make in your own life. One of the CMs coined this process a 'real play', which I love!

From a cultural perspective, airing problems in public in many Asian countries is frowned upon due to a loss of face and respect for the person and the family. Therefore, it is very important that the supervisor establish an atmosphere of trust and clear boundaries regarding confidentiality and that this only be introduced after trust and safety has been established. The CMs were also asked to choose only situations that they felt comfortable sharing.

Therefore, the model itself counteracts the cultural discomfort about sharing problems and flaws as it focuses on sharing more positive aspects of the person and situation. Only a brief description of the problem is necessary before moving on to highlight strengths and resources, exceptions and the picture of life without the problem.

Another positive effect of these 'real plays' was how the CMs' bond among themselves and with the supervisor improved: 'Hearing the group members share their challenges and their coping encouraged and prompted us to help each other in times of need. Our supervision becomes an enriching experience.' I also developed much more respect for and admiration of the CMs through learning about many of their life struggles and the strengths and qualities they had used to cope with and overcome them.

Readings

We often discussed various articles related to SF techniques or working with specific client groups. Previously, I would be very stressed, preparing my role as expert in order to impart the knowledge to my supervisees.

Now I approach this very differently, structuring the conversation using SF questions:

- What would you like to come out of our supervision discussion on this topic today so that it is helpful for you?
- What do you already know about this topic?
- What do you already do well in this area?
- On a scale of 1–10, how confident are you in this area?
- How will you know when you are one point higher on this scale?
- What will your clients/colleagues notice you doing differently?

After we discussed the material we had read, I asked some reflective questions:

- What did you learn? What was helpful from the reading/discussion?
- What questions do you still have? (If these could be answered by the group, we did; otherwise we discussed how they would find the answers.)
- What are your next small steps to take in this area so you can move up your scale?

Leading from behind, I highlighted areas of competence that the CMs already had. As Pichot and Dolan state: 'The role of the solution focused supervisor is to pull the wisdom from the therapists rather than tell them what to do' (2003, p. 173).

This was initially hard for the supervisees, who were expecting me to conform to the cultural stereotype of the wise expert and tell them what to do. Over time, it led to an increase in their own confidence in their skills and knowledge, and taking responsibility for their own learning.

It was also important for me to clarify the myth that solution-focused supervisors do not give direction:

> Especially in the beginning, staff members need specific information and ideas about how to apply the solution focused approach. Supervisor. . . . needs to be available to answer questions about the specific interventions and the purpose behind the methods used. Effective

supervisors must acquire the ability to determine when they need to provide information and when simply listening to the staff members will be more productive.

(Pichot & Dolan, 2003, p. 171)

For me, this was learning to balance highlighting the CMs existing skills and knowledge but also knowing when to share my own expertise.

Final thoughts

My journey of SF supervision over the last 4 years has been a fascinating process. I have learnt how to adapt the SF process from therapy to supervision and feel I can confidently lead others 'from one step behind'. The SF model lends itself very well to addressing many of the cultural challenges to the supervision process in Asia with only minor adaptations needed. It has been wonderful watching my supervisees gain in skills and confidence and hear from their clients how these in turn have benefitted them.

I will end with a quote from a supervisee:

> Inviting feedback not only on our successes but also on our short comings in an encouraging way has made it pleasant to continue with our work. Whatever pressures one has at work, SF supervision makes our day energised and we always look forward to another session.

As a supervisor there is not much more you could ask for – but I have to thank the SF model for that.

References

Fox, K. (2004). *Watching the English: The hidden rules of English behaviour*. London, UK: Hodder and Stoughton.

Hsu, W-S., & Kuo, B.C.H. (2013). Solution-focused supervision with school counsellors in Taiwan. In F.N. Thomas (Ed.), *Solution-focused supervision: A resource-oriented approach to developing clinical expertise* (pp. 197–204). New York, NY: Springer.

Norman, H. (2003). Solution focused reflecting teams. In W. O'Connell & S. Palmer (Eds.), *Handbook of solution-focused therapy* (pp. 156–167). London, UK: Sage Publications.

Pichot, T., & Dolan, Y.M. (2003). Solution focused supervision: Leading from one step behind. *Solution-focused brief therapy: Its effective use in agency settings* (pp. 159–179). New York, NY: The Haworth Press Inc.

Thomas, F.N. (2013). *Solution-focused supervision: A resource oriented approach to developing clinical expertise*. New York, NY: Springer.

Wheeler, J. (2007). Solution focused supervision. In T.S Nelson & F.N. Thomas (Eds.), *Handbook of solution-focused brief therapy: Clinical applications* (pp. 343–370). New York, NY: Haworth Press.

17

I'VE DONE IT BEFORE; I CAN DO IT AGAIN

Words of wisdom from a speech therapist supervisee

Valerie P. C. Lim

Introduction

Speech therapists or speech pathologists are allied health professionals who 'assess and treat speech, swallowing, language or communication problems in people of all ages to enable them to communicate to the best of their ability. They may also work with people who have eating and swallowing problems' (Ministry of Health, 2013). As part of our professional job scope, speech therapists are also involved in clinical supervision. This includes supervising student and practising speech therapists with the aim of helping them develop professional and clinical competencies that meet the standards of the COMPASS: Competency Assessment for Speech Pathology (McAllister, Lincoln, Ferguson & McAllister, 2006). As a speech therapist with 22 years of experience, I have had the pleasure of supervising and teaching over 150 students and supervisees, both locally in Singapore and overseas. I have always tried to find new ways to motivate and teach my supervisees. Amongst all the techniques that I have used, I have found solution focused brief therapy (SFBT) to be one of the most useful tools in my supervisory toolbox.

I was introduced to the world of SFBT about two years ago by a speech therapist friend and colleague in our department. She gave a few in-service presentations for our team, showed us some videos, and provided us with some solution focused questions to try. I was initially very sceptical about its application to my practice. I wondered how local Singaporean patients would take to this comparatively 'softer approach' and how it would fit into the medical model in which we were trained in. In times of illness, surely our patients would want something more than what appeared to be 'just counselling and affirmation'! However, as I was more exposed to it, I found it to be effective not only in my clinical work with patients, but also with my team mates and colleagues that I supervise and mentor. It has been such an inspirational mind-set change for me that I decided to undergo formal SFBT certification training.

This chapter provides a personal account of my experience with SFBT in clinical supervision.

In the next section, an example with a student clinician will be introduced. While referring to this case, I will provide an account of my pre-SFBT clinical supervisory practice, followed by a description of the positive changes in my supervisory practice since undergoing SFBT training. I will conclude with some views about the potential use of SFBT in clinical education in Singapore.

Case example

Ming Jian came to our department for his first six-week clinical placement. His university supervisors noted that Ming Jian was a good student with strong theoretical knowledge. However, the experience of being in an acute hospital environment was new, and it overwhelmed him. He started to exhibit some difficulties in translating his theoretical knowledge to clinical practice. In particular, Ming Jian was not able to perform the required oromotor examination (OME) consistently, and this inhibited his progress in his training. The OME is an assessment of tongue, lip, jaw and palate function. By the time I was called in to assist, Ming Jian knew he was about four weeks behind schedule. He was developing self-doubt, feeling disheartened, and wondering if he would ever meet the standard.

Clinical education practice before SFBT

Before my SFBT training, I would have relied on my skills and experience using the medical model, and undertaken a problem solving approach in the supervisory process. I would have asked myself the following questions: a) What was the Ming Jian's problem? b) When did it start? c) What was causing it? d) Where was the breakdown occurring and what was holding him back? and e) What could I do to help fix the issues he was facing?

This problem focused approach uses questions and language that focus on the problem and its causes and highlights the inadequacies and what is wrong with the supervisee, or what is NOT working. As a supervisor, I needed to have the answers to these questions as I would have felt that I had to properly diagnose Ming Jian's problem before intervening or finding a solution.

The problem-focused approach is commonly used in the health care setting. In fact, such problem-focused questions may be necessary when diagnosing a disorder, and when deciding on the most appropriate course of treatment. However, in my experience as a clinical supervisor, the problem-focused approach could never quite help me to facilitate greater engagement in my supervisees, or increase the motivation of my supervisees to initiate the changes that were necessary for them to progress in their professional training. This usually left me feeling frustrated, anxious and unaccomplished as an educator, especially when attempts to help the supervisee were unsuccessful.

Clinical education practice after SFBT

Following my SFBT training, I found myself using a different language and asking a different set of questions instead. For example, the questions that came to mind were: a) What is one thing Ming Jian could do differently? b) What difference would it make if he did? c) What would be a small sign that things are better? d) What is one small strength he has that I could build upon?

Learning SFBT taught me that by changing the questions we ask, we can reframe the scenario so that we can find a way to look beyond the immediate concerns and search for potential resolutions.

The use of the solution focused approach in clinical and peer supervision is not new (Burns, 2005; 2008). In particular, Burns (2008) discussed how solution focused conversations between the supervisor and supervisee may be short, yet more effective in helping supervisees clarify what they hope to achieve. These conversations can help develop clinical practice by building on the supervisee's existing therapeutic knowledge and skills, without reliance on supervisor cues, and acknowledge their own progress through their awareness of achieved positive changes.

For Ming Jian, who needed a lot of support, the solution focused approach was an appropriate tool to use. The following is a dialogue I had with Ming Jian in my supervisory role, and illustrates how a solution focused conversation was used to recognise his existing resources, focus on his strengths and competencies, and explore exceptions and the preferred future. Scaling questions were also applied to clarify Ming Jian's goals, determine his progress, and identify what was working for him and his next steps forward.

Supervisor:	You know, Ming Jian, the last few weeks must have been really difficult for you. But despite everything, you still show up at work every day on time, ready to go . . . how come?
Ming Jian:	*(looking surprised)* Oh . . . er . . . I need to be here . . . I have to try to get through this.
Supervisor:	You are not the type who gives up easily eh?
Ming Jian:	Ya . . . I guess so. Been like that since young. But, this has been tough, it's been quite stressful.
Supervisor:	Instead of being stressed, what do you want to feel instead?
Ming Jian:	Feel more calm, I guess
Supervisor:	Ok . . . suppose you were to feel calmer, what difference would that make?
Ming Jian:	I can think better.
Supervisor:	And when you think better, what happens?
Ming Jian:	I can remember what I know, I won't freeze.
Supervisor:	What helps you normally to feel calmer, even if it's a tiny bit?
Ming Jian:	Just focus on one thing at a time, because if I think too much, I start to feel too overwhelmed.
Supervisor:	OK. So, what is one thing you would like to focus on for your session today?
Ming Jian:	My OME. It would be good to do a full OME without stuffing up.
Supervisor:	*(I drew a scale on a piece of paper).* Suppose this was a scale for your OME. 10 is when you were calm and able to do a full OME. Suppose you were to be at 10, what would you notice yourself doing?
Ming Jian:	I would be doing the OME without any hiccups.
Supervisor:	Tell me what that means?
Ming Jian:	Well, I would be accurate in my assessment. I would remember all the steps without prompts. I would interpret observations accurately, and be able to step up and down smoothly in my instructions to the patient . . . oh, and . . . I would also link what I saw with the patient's case history.
Supervisor:	Suppose you were to achieve a 10, how would that change things for you?
Ming Jian:	I would be so relieved because it means I can move on. It will give me a boost.
Supervisor:	OK great, so where would you put yourself on the scale now?
Ming Jian:	Er . . . maybe a 7?
Supervisor:	A 7! Just wondering . . . why did you say a 7 and not 6?
Ming Jian:	*(Long pause)* Er . . . for OME only? Well, I think my instructions to the patient are not bad, and . . . and . . . I am accurate most of the time. Yesterday, I could step up and step down if the patient didn't understand. But, but . . . I think, it's not smooth . . . I'm still slow . . . I keep missing steps, and I still get confused about links to case history.

Supervisor:	So, can I ask . . . how will you know when you have reached an 8? What's one thing that you would be doing differently?
Ming Jian:	Oh . . . I'd be faster . . . and, and . . . I will be more consistent in remembering all the steps in the OME.
Supervisor:	OK, so you have been consistent before . . . that's great! When you did remember the steps before, what helped you?
Ming Jian:	Oh . . . *(smiling)*, I tell myself to calm down, and tell myself to use my strategy and to move from front to back.
Supervisor:	Tell me a bit more?
Ming Jian:	Oh . . . you know, start with the lips and move backwards in sequence . . . lips, jaw, tongue, soft palate.
Supervisor:	Sounds like a good strategy. OK let's go and see the client now. Just curious though, what's one thing you can tell yourself so you remember to be calm and is mindful of your strategy?
Ming Jian:	*(looks at me with a strange look, but smiling)* I don't know . . . maybe . . . I've done it before, I can do this again.

Ming Jian was able to complete his OME, and progressed to the next stage of his training. He reported that although he found the conversations awkward in the beginning, he found them to be useful in helping him get past the layers of thoughts in his head that were overwhelming him. He reported that he was surprised at my appreciation of his struggles in the last 4 weeks, something that no one had acknowledged before. The conversation we had, made him realise how much he wanted to complete his training, and that he should not give up. He has since graduated and is now working in London.

Conclusions

When helping supervisees to learn or refine a clinical skill, we often demonstrate and then observe them in action, or guide them step by step. However, there have been many times in the past where the same method was used with my supervisees, yet there was limited success in harnessing their full potential. Einstein said 'the significant problems we face cannot be solved at the same level of thinking we used when we created them' (as cited in Calaprice, 2000, p. 317). I have learnt through my solution focused journey that if something is not working, we should do something different. Using the solution focused approach, I have learnt that I can direct the conversation rather than the person, facilitate rather than insist on change, and use the supervisee's existing strengths to build confidence. This way of thinking is so different from a typical Asian supervisory experience, where the supervisor would assume a more 'expert' role, deliver advice in a top-down manner, and highlight mistakes rather than affirm any successes. The expectation of supervisees with an Asian upbringing is to respect their elders, and do what they are told to do. While respect for authority and honouring those in a senior position are paramount in the Asian culture, there is an expectation that they also know 'the right way' to do things and that the learner does not have the competence. The difference with the solution focused approach is that there is also a high respect for the learner and an acknowledgement of existing competencies.

With solution focused skills in my supervisory tool box, I feel that I can now be 'bilingual', and have two sets of languages at my disposal. I can use my problem focused language set to teach and help a supervisee diagnose a disorder, or I can switch over to use my newly found solution focused language if I need to.

What difference has the solution focused approach made for me? It has been valuable to me as a clinical supervisor because I find myself enjoying the supervisory process more. I feel less burdened knowing that I can help supervisees tap into their own resources instead of mine, and I believe that my supervision and mentorship practice is now more effective.

Feedback from my supervisees suggests that the solution focused approach has a place in our local clinical education scene. In our fast-paced environment in a Singapore hospital setting, where there are significant time constraints and performance-related stress and anxiety, my supervisees like the solution focused approach because it is affirming and collaborative. It makes them stop, think, process and consolidate their thoughts on the relevant issues in a novel and constructive manner. While it is not uncommon for clinical educators to have some initial scepticism about the use of the solution focused approach in our supervisory practice either with students, new graduates or even our team mates, it is my best hope that, given time and exposure, more educators will start to realise its potential and incorporate solution focused practice in their supervisory work.

References

Burns, K. (2005). Solution focused approaches to speech therapy and the health service. *Solution News*, *1*, 6–8.

Burns, K. (2008). Ten minute talk: Using a solution focused approach in supervision. *Solution News*, *3*, 8–12.

Calaprice, A. (Ed.). (2000). *The expanded quotable Einstein*. Princeton, NJ: Princeton University Press.

McAllister, S., Lincoln, M., Ferguson, A., & McAllister, L. (2006). *COMPASS: Competency assessment in speech pathology*. Melbourne, Australia: Speech Pathology Association of Australia.

Ministry of Health (2013, October 9). *Speech therapists*. Retrieved from https://www.moh.gov.sg/content/moh_web/healthprofessionalsportal/alliedhealthprofessionals/career_practice/allied_health_professions/speech_therapists.html.

18

SOLUTION FOCUSED SUPERVISION WITH HONG KONG COUNSELLING STUDENTS

Ann Moir-Bussy

Introduction

Solution focused supervision in counselling offers both a simple and a profound set of concepts for the relationship between supervisor and student. Solution focused supervision presupposes that the students have the answers within themselves, and hence the approach has an empowering effect on their learning and practice. Using solution focused techniques provides many options for the students to improve their practice. Central to solution focused supervision is the concept of conversation. This includes an attitude of mutual respect as together the search is for solutions rather than focusing on the problems. As Gubrium and Holstein noted, this conversation is a collaborative venture, making 'audible and visible the phenomenal depths of the individual subject' (2003, p. 29). I had the privilege of working with six students in Hong Kong as they studied and implemented solution focused therapy while on their internship. Their work within our group supervision sessions was inspiring and creative. In this chapter I will outline some of the methods and techniques we employed with the students and how they integrated their Chinese philosophy into their work with children.

Supervising internship students

Students learning to be therapists can often be their own worst critics. Because they feel less experienced they are often prone to self-deprecation, and create anxieties about becoming competent therapists (Briggs & Miller, 2005). In order to construct a sense of confidence the focus must be on the things the student does well rather than on the problem. Central to this happening is the development of an 'I-thou' relationship with the students, which suggests a more equal relationship, more depth and informality. Such a relationship is one of reciprocity, and for the supervisor, a stance of not-knowing allows the students to explore together the way forward. Using solution focused supervision, the supervisor becomes a facilitator who works with the students to identify and amplify the students' competencies. This is the opposite of the traditional hierarchical and managerial role that many supervisors adopt. Guilar cites Bill Isaacs from his book *The Art of Dialogue and Thinking Together* (1999): 'To respect someone is to look for the springs that feed their pool of experience' (2006, p. 10). This was the aim in supervising the Chinese students on their internship in Hong Kong. Such respect also supported the value of self-in-relationship, which is a central component of Chinese philosophy. Chinese relationships in the traditional sense are structured around a concept known as *gōu tōng*, which is a process of understanding others and then endeavouring to be understood by them (Gao, Ting-Tommey & Gudykunst, 1996).

Chinese Master of Counselling Psychology students

Six students studying for the Master of Counselling Psychology opted to complete the solution focused clinical practicum and use this model in their internship. As Sun noted in her book *Chinese Themes in Psychology:* 'It is most likely not an exaggeration to say that all persons of Chinese heritage have been influenced by Confucianism to a certain extent, and may in fact pay homage to Confucian values and beliefs' (2008, p. 2). In addition, the great traditions of Taoism and Buddhism influence the thinking of Chinese students. These students had been exposed to a variety of traditions, including the local traditions of their parents and the influences of Western tradition and globalisation, especially in the time that the British controlled Hong Kong. As they absorbed and practised the philosophy and techniques of solution focused therapy with their clients, they also came upon aspects of their heritage that did not always sit well with their cultural values, and they were challenged to explore these issues in supervision in a dialogic way. As the students engaged in this personal and professional development through solution focused supervision and dialogue, they were embracing both the practice of solution focused therapy and solution focused supervision. As Hermans (2004) notes, any new situation in a person's life leads to a new positioning for themselves. This new positioning takes place best within a dialogic encounter, which is at the heart of solution focused supervision. The students also had to engage in external dialogue (dialogue with the socio-cultural context in which they find themselves) and internal dialogue (between the many selves they have developed through their life) (Moir-Bussy, 2008). Solution focused supervision is a means of transformative learning.

The Chinese philosopher Wu (1997, p. 132) speaks of the 'hidden "I" in interpersonal relations' and regards this hiddenness as a process of becoming empty so that one can 'room' the other person, or 'a wombing forth of the other'. Adopting a solution focused stand with the students enabled this wombing forth to take place as the students discovered new ideas and solutions for themselves. A final point before giving examples from our sessions is the concept of strengths-based *wú wéi* supervision, developed by Edwards and Chen (1999). *Wú* means 'not' or 'non' and *wéi* means 'action', 'making', 'striving', 'straining', 'busyness'. So *wú wéi* supervision is not about striving but rather about 'side [stepping] hierarchy in favour of co-constructing ideas with those supervised' (Edwards & Chen, 1999, p. 351).

This is similar to solution focused supervision as it focuses on strengths rather than deficits, competencies rather than problems, potential rather than constraints, future possibilities rather than past problems and multiple perspectives rather than universal truths.

Solution focused supervision with the intern students

We held a group supervision session each week of the semester in which the students were practising solution focused therapy with their clients. Students took turns presenting a case, and the whole group would enter into a collaborative conversation around it. Some examples of these conversations follow.

In one case presentation an intern found it difficult to use compliments with his Chinese clients, both children and adults. In the group supervision, he was asked how he reacted to compliments. He became aware that he himself had difficulty accepting compliments. He began to wonder if it was an effective solution focused technique to use with Chinese clients. He was encouraged to explore the meaning of the word 'compliment' – 'a speech or act which explicitly and implicitly attributes credit to someone other than the speaker, usually the one addressed' (Holmes, 1986, p. 485). He also found from his research that the value of compliments could have a different meaning in some cultures. The response of the group was 'Wow! You did a lot of research around that – what else did you learn?' Interestingly, he blushed as they complimented him, and they immediately asked him if he felt comfortable receiving that compliment, and he realised he did not. He said this was because he had been taught not to appear proud. Exploring more about his cultural values and reading more research, he found from Lin (2008) that the Chinese are taught to obey modesty maxims and so maintain their response to a compliment in a humble way or even deny it. Using solution focused questions, he was invited to think about how he would like to be in giving compliments, particularly to special needs children who had worked hard and shown improvement. He wanted to be able to compliment in the correct cultural way, and he discovered that his clients were more willing to accept the compliment if it was given for their group contribution or for personal qualities like kindness and patience rather than personal compliments.

This approach to the supervision session left him feeling empowered and ready to work more easily with the use of compliments.

Another intern student phrased questions in a way that would match Chinese thinking and Chinese people's strong value of being a 'self-in-relation'. He came up with questions such as: What will be the first sign for you and others that things are moving in the right direction? How will other people know you need help?

When it came to using scaling questions, all of the group became very creative, designing scales that matched the age and need of their clients. An example was the scale designed to catch the Angry Bird for a boy who loved this mobile phone game icon. Another was a scale drawn on a Sprite bottle for a girl who loved Sprite. In particular, some of the interns were working with children with special needs, and in supervision it was clear to see how they used the principles and techniques of solution focused therapy to enable these children to become empowered and find their own solutions.

Their support of each other in supervision was also very powerful. 'Wow' was 'Wah!' for them, and it became common within our sessions for them to say 'Wah! That's great, how did you do that?', or use similar expressions to support and encourage each other on their solution focused journey.

Another example was from two other interns who found that when working with children who had special needs or learning difficulties, the parents would negate the work or achievements of the children. So, they invited the parents to join the session, modelling how to encourage and strengthen the child's self-esteem and how to compliment when their child achieved. They asked the question of one mother: 'What is it that you want most for your child?' The response was that she wanted her daughter to learn to be compliant and proactive in her work. The intern responded, 'Wah! That is exactly what your daughter told me – she really understands you so well – how did you help her to do that?' This was both building on their relationship and at the same time drawing the mother into her success of helping her daughter.

Parents' expectations were often very high, and comparisons with other children often led the weaker student to feel deflated or labelled and blamed. The interns began to help the parents rephrase negative statements such as 'She is lazy and naughty and does not get her homework completed' to 'She really wants to please you, how do you think we can show her that you are happy with the little things she has done?' Such work resulted in both child and parent working better together and a marked improvement in the child's learning.

The interns themselves examined the miracle question, wondering about the appropriateness of the word 'miracle' as either it was not understood by many Chinese people or it seemed to be related to religion, and in this case it couldn't happen to you as an individual. A discussion of 'What can you use in its place?' led to several creative ways of helping a person to find their preferred outcome. One example was of using films – 'We've seen the film you have made that tells us how you have been and what has been happening for you – now you are going to direct a new movie about you. What would you like to be different about this movie? Now imagine you are on the set and you begin with the old you – imagine it's finished and what are you doing now and who is noticing.' Incorporating local scenarios, another intern instructed, 'Imagine you are in the Wong Tai Sin temple and something wonderful happens. It is the place where a change occurs and you have all the answers . . .' In other words, using local knowledge and places enabled the clients to engage in the dialogue more readily.

Other questions used in supervision after the team had watched one of their colleagues present a case also helped them to use a solution focused approach. The questions focused on their strengths in the therapy and the positive feedback from the group reflections.

With this focus on developing the strengths of the student interns, the interns' learning grew from strength to strength. They became more confident, and their clinical work more successful. The more traditional supervision approach tends to focus on the therapist's problems. Focusing on a success–enhancing orientation to supervision also allowed the interns to see there are many alternative approaches that can be used, including building on their own style and strengths. In addition, sharing resources with each other gave each a sense of being a valuable contributor.

Conclusion

Watching the students develop personally and professionally as they used solution focused therapy and engaged in solution focused supervision was indeed a transformative learning experience, both for them and for me as a supervisor. Their learning was so powerful that at the end of the course they went as a group to Singapore and presented at the Solution Focused Brief Therapy Conference in 2012. I was just about to leave Hong Kong to return to Australia so could not go with them. They returned the day we were leaving and presented me with a wonderful memento – an Oscar for the World's Greatest Teacher. In reality, they were the world's greatest students! I came to call them 'the fabulous six', and it is encouraging to know they still use solution focused therapy in their work as counselling psychologists

References

Briggs, J., & Miller, G. (2005). Success enhancing supervision. *Journal of Family Psychotherapy, 16*(1–2), 199–220.

Edwards, J., & Chen, M-W. (1999). Strengths-based supervision: Frameworks, current practice and future directions – A Wu-Wei method. *The Family Journal: Counseling and Therapy for Couples and Families, 4*, 349–357.

Gao, G., Ting-Tommey, S., & Gudykunst, W. (1996). Chinese communication processes. In M. Bond (Ed.), *The handbook of Chinese psychology* (pp. 280–308). Hong Kong: Oxford University Press.

Gubrium, J., & Holstein, J. (Eds). (2003) *Inside interviewing – New lenses, new concerns.* Thousand Oaks, CA: Sage Publications.

Guilar, J. (2006). Intersubjectivity and dialogic instruction. *Radical Pedagogy, 8*(1) 1. Retrieved from: http://www.radicalpedagogy.org/radicalpedagogy/Intersubjectivity_and_Dialogic_Instruction.html.

Hermans, H. (2004). Introduction: The dialogical self in a global and digital age. *Identity: An International Journal of Theory and Research, 4,* 297–320.

Holmes, J. (1986). Compliment and compliment responses. *New Zealand Journal of Anthropological Linguistics, 28,* 485–508.

Lin, A. (2008). On English and Chinese compliments. *US-China Foreign Language, 6*(1), 65–68.

Moir-Bussy, A. (2008). The counselling education and supervision process: Dialogue and transformation. *Counselling, Psychotherapy and Health, 4*(1), 1–16.

Sun, T-L C. (2008). *Themes in Chinese psychology.* Singapore: Cengage Learning Asia Pty Ltd.

Wu, K-M. (1997). *On the "logic" of togetherness – A cultural hermeneutic.* Leiden, The Netherlands: Brill.

19

FROM SOLVING PROBLEMS TO FINDING SOLUTIONS

A change in perspective for consultation and supervision in an international school in Hong Kong

Natalie Broderick

Introduction

Primary and secondary education has witnessed a proliferation of ways to address problems: learning problems, behaviour problems, personnel problems and school climate problems. A great deal of energy is spent considering how to motivate reluctant students, how to intervene in learning problems, ways to provide quality professional development for faculty and, most importantly, how to ensure quality of instruction through teacher appraisal systems. Although well intended, such approaches rest on the assumption that in order to effect positive change, the problem itself must be described and analysed to determine causality, define outcomes and determine the best actions to fix what is perceived as broken. This is no clearer than in a large international school in Hong Kong where issues ranging from parental pressure for increasingly higher academic achievement to the evaluation and supervision of teachers and school counsellors are keenly focused on identifying areas for improvement.

The desire to improve, to grow, to learn, to become better at one's practice is certainly not unique to this school or to Hong Kong. At the macro level, school improvement plans are commonplace and a requisite part of maintaining accredited status. At an individual level, school professionals are encouraged to formulate SMART goals; goals that are specific, measurable, attainable, results-focused and time-bound. In theory the articulation of these goals should be the foundation for enriched professional conversations as teachers, counsellors and administrative supervisors work together to reflect on and increase knowledge and develop skills. In practice, too often goal-setting become an isolated exercise in and of itself with little application to the daily experience of teachers and counsellors. School administrators are charged with monitoring faculty goals often through routine beginning and end-of-year supervisory conferences.

Supervision in schools has an inherent tension. School administrators are caught between the need be educational leaders and ensure quality teaching while supporting individual faculty progress toward improved practice. They balance management and accountability for the overall quality of service provided to students with the responsibility to help teachers and school counsellors grow professionally. Mirroring the Asian context where authority figures are expected to be experts and givers of advice (Lam & Yuen, 2008), teachers and school counsellors tend to look to their supervising administrator to provide answers and guidance, knowing full well that their supervisor is also monitoring their performance. Many administrators wrestle with ways to maintain a consultative stance and build alliances with individual faculty members while being caught in what is essentially an evaluative dynamic. As a result, the supervision of classroom teachers, special educators and school counsellors often reflects a problem solving orientation with administrators identifying and documenting areas for growth that need remediation.

At the same time, classroom teachers, in their efforts to serve students who present with various learning and behavioural challenges, rely on consultation with counsellors and special educators in determining ways to solve classroom problems. In our roles as consultants and supervisors, we have similar aims: to assist the professionals in improving their practice in order to better serve students. By shifting perspective to a solution focused approach, we have the opportunity to support and affirm professional competence in a way that recognises strengths and energises toward positive outcomes. The SF approach also allows supervising administrators to better integrate a coaching/mentoring framework into their supervision. In this chapter, I discuss the application of a solution focused approach in consultation with and supervision of teachers and counsellors and give examples of a language that orients toward solutions and strengths.

Consultation

Special educators and school counsellors are masters at identifying and describing challenges and difficulties that students and faculty face. These professionals are on the frontlines when problems and issues arise and are a natural fit for re-orientation toward a solution focus by learning ways to convey empathy for teachers through active listening to uncover and build on strengths and exceptions. In my experience, faculty with a more teacher-centred classroom orientation, similar to that found in traditional Asian classrooms, bring detailed accounts of problems when seeking consultation and assistance with classroom management or with students who are not meeting achievement expectations. They are eager to look for antecedents to misbehaviour and rely on orchestrating consequences for control of classroom behaviour. They are particularly sensitive to their role in ensuring students reach grade-level, parental and administrator expectations. Thus teachers solicit both suggestions for classroom behaviour management and support for students who appear to be struggling with the curriculum.

I found that when working with teachers, it can be tempting to offer solutions – after all, that is what most teachers are seeking when they come with a concern. I observed that suggesting solutions comes with its own minefields, often coming across as pejorative and discounting the many attempts teachers may already have made to deal with a concern. I found the shift, from being seen as an expert with the answer, to be particularly difficult in this Hong Kong school where expertise is highly valued and often unquestioned. Adopting Murphy's (2008, p. 47) 'beginners mind-set', my team members now start from a position of genuine curiosity. Through tone of voice, selection of words and positive presuppositions they convey professional respect and the belief that the person that comes with a problem is also the person who has significant pathways toward solutions.

I begin by setting the tone for a positive and collaborative experience. 'What would you like to come away with from our meeting?' or 'What are your best hopes for this conversation?' or 'What needs to happen here for you to think this has been helpful for you?' frames the meeting or conversation in a way that firstly assumes the experience will be helpful and then invites the teacher to articulate a desired outcome rather than remain stuck in a problem. In this environment of high expectations, teachers are pressured to ensure they do everything right in supporting student achievement. Emphasising that the teacher is concerned enough to bring the issue to the table recognises their investment in providing adequate support for a student who is struggling and reduces the fear of parental and/or administrative criticism for not doing enough. In these situations, I use SF reflective questions:

> You have been working really hard with this student for a few weeks now so I know that you want some more support for her. What is working well already? What have you tried? Suppose things improved, just a little bit, what small differences would you notice? What kind of support would help? What would you do that you're not doing now?

In a highly competitive environment like Hong Kong, where high student performance is expected, teachers often push these students even further. Using SF consultation helps them slow down and reflect on what they are already doing in support of student learning and not focus only on achievement benchmarks.

Careful listening throughout is clearly needed in order to capitalise on opportunities to high-light strengths and exceptions. Along with listening for positives, we have realised it is crucial to convey an understanding of the perceived challenge, affirm the teacher's competence and look for resources. This takes a balance of affirming statements combined with gentle questioning used judiciously in the spirit of curiosity to avoid a sense that the specialists are grilling the teacher. A barrage of questions does not convey a sense of trust in the teacher's competence! At the same time, forced positivity and attempts to make light of a given situation can evoke the defensive 'You don't know what it's like'.

Creating and maintaining an alliance with teachers while maintaining a positive and supportive stance takes practice. At times it is undeniably easier to fall toward the examining of a problem in all its complexity. Generous use of targeted affirmations helps encourage teachers to explore and exploit their own strengths. I find giving evidence-based affirmations quite powerful, as the teachers are less likely to argue with 'evidence'. 'I really respect how you speak with such quiet authority'; 'I noticed how you get right down to his eye level when you are talking'. Gentle questions that orient toward strengths affirm what the teacher is doing well. 'The students are able to connect new information with previous learning . . . how did you manage to provide for all levels of their understanding?' Intentional use of strength-based language allows counsellors and special educations to raise the level of abstraction with better potential for transfer and generalisation to other situations 'You are really drawing on your curiosity in trying to figure that out'; 'I admire your perseverance in working this through'; 'Wow, your creativity and your love of learning really helped'. Through these conversations, teachers have tended to share more of the knowledge, skills and successes that they have available for solutions. I find they are more creative and likely to try something different, less likely to expect someone else to take over the problem and more likely to come for further supportive consultation.

At times teachers who come with problems and issues are so focused on describing what's wrong that I find it difficult to change their orientation. When terms like 'never' and 'always' and 'constantly' pepper the conversation, we ask teachers, 'May I invite you to try an experiment? Please notice for the next two or three days when the problem is not happening or is happening a bit less and make a mental note of those times. Notice when the student gets started within a few minutes', 'Notice when she is sitting quietly', 'Take note of when he participates in the small group discussion'. Suggesting that the teacher try something different can also lead to an experiment. 'I wonder what might happen if you gave just one direction and then were just silent.' Follow-up conversations are important to expand and explore a positive trajectory to increase the desired change. Teachers find these kinds of suggestions very useful as they allow them a chance to experiment and explore what will work for them, instead of being told how to solve the immediate situation. One teacher was pleasantly surprised when she tried a different approach with a student who talked during silent reading time, recognising with quiet affirmation when he was silently reading, which led to the teacher being more observant about exceptions for not only that student but others as well.

From consultation to supervision

Improving instructional quality is a worthwhile goal and pay for performance systems have become the latest effort to reward teachers for what they know and do. Such systems have the unfortunate possibility of remaining administrator-driven without ways to encourage the strengths and autonomy of individual teachers in growing their practice. Drawing from the tenets of solution focused work, supervision in our school is beginning to mirror consultation in spite of the evaluative component. Administrators approach supervision sessions from a stance of genuine curiosity that mitigates the power differential often experienced in traditional school structures and fully supports individual professional growth. At the same time, supervising administrators thoughtfully use language to set expectations and highlight specific areas of practice that are important to encourage. For example, instead of the directive 'Consider ways to involve all students', a question of 'What are you doing when all students are involved?' presupposes that there are times when all students are involved, leads the teacher to recognise that as an important area on which to focus and encourages reflection on personal efficacy in making that happen. Modelled after the consultation conversation, the supervising administrator carefully and intentionally listens and names the resources, skills and strengths that emerge. Judicious use of questions has led the supervisee to acknowledge resources or imagine a preferred state, for example, 'What will you be doing differently when students are working together more collaboratively?' or 'What will it look and sound like when you are able to explain this concept so she understands it?' Responses from teachers such as 'I see myself as a coach managing this group of learners who are excitedly sharing their own ideas' or 'I can break this down by using a simple story as a way to show the similarities' demonstrate the ownership teachers begin to feel in creating a desired future, a hallmark of the SF approach.

With judicious use of questions and listening for glimpses of previous successes, administrators as supervisors are able to guide a diverse group of professionals to recognise their strengths in developing solutions toward improved practice. For example, in most school situations, supervision of school counsellors is generally managed by school administrators. Most school administrators, however, have little or no experience in clinical supervision and are not able to offer traditional guidance in honing counselling practice. With a solution focused orientation, supervision sessions encourage counsellors to deepen their practice and feel successful in their work through intentional dialogue without the assumption that the supervisor has more wisdom or more experience. School counsellors identify their own professional goals and monitor the impact on their work with students, faculty and families. The supervisor is well versed in the process of solution focused supervision and not necessarily equipped with deeper knowledge of the specialised work of a counsellor. Supervision has a different flavour with scaling questions ('With 10 meaning you felt really positive about the goal, where would you put yourself? What would you be doing differently if you moved up a number?'); questions that seek strengths and solutions ('What kinds of questions did you use to get him to think differently about that situation?'); or statements/ questions that affirm ('It sounds like you have that family really talking. How did you get them to talk to each other and not just to you?').

Final thoughts

Seeking exceptions, finding ways to highlight strengths and harnessing small improvements is a welcome alternative to examining problems and diagnosing weaknesses. The shift in perspective from problem solving to one of focusing not on the problem but on a solution is far more than a subtle change in language. It requires perseverance and encouragement for those 'in the trenches'. In our large international school, subtle influences of Asian deference to expertise rest in those with positional power. Using SF principles in consultation and supervision has been a refreshing means to promote professional growth. For lasting change to take hold, we are finding ways to take advantage of multiple pathways and small pockets of influence. Formal and informal collegial dialogue is beginning to listen for strengths, skills, and attitudes that can be highlighted and harnessed toward the preferred future. We are encouraging each other to remember that change is constant and inevitable, that small changes can have big impacts, and, most importantly, that people, including those being supervised, have the resources to grow, change and help themselves. Evidence from our school's experience supports other research findings that solution focused supervision is well received (Koob, 2002; Hsu, 2007) and has great potential to enrich teacher and school counsellor supervision.

References

Hsu, W. (2007). Effects of solution-focused supervision. *Bulletin of Educational Psychology, 38*(3), 331–354.

Koob, J.J. (2002). The effects of solution-focused supervision on the perceived self-efficacy of therapists in training. *The Clinical Supervisor, 21*(2), 161–183.

Lam, C., & Yuen, M. (2008). Applying solution focused questions with primary school pupils: A Hong Kong teacher's reflections. *Pastoral Care in Education: An International Journal of Personal, Social and Emotional Development, 26*(2), 103–110.

Murphy, J.J. (2008). *Solution-focused counseling in the schools* (2nd ed.). Alexandria, VA: American Counseling Association.

20

THE UTILISATION OF A SOLUTION FOCUSED APPROACH IN THE SUPERVISION OF A GOVERNMENT WELFARE PROJECT IN SOUTH KOREA

Yunjoo Kim

Introduction

In January 2004, I was contacted by the Policy of Women Team, Ministry of Health and Welfare to consult with them with regards to the trial Case Management of the Matriarchal Low-Income Families Project. I proposed a solution focused (SF) approach that would effectively utilise the strengths of social workers, clients and communities for the project. It was the first time that a welfare project of the government in South Korea allowed and approved the practice of one model! The Solution Center was assigned supervisory roles for this project. This chapter describes how we used the SF approach during supervision during this project and the results of the research for this project.

Beginnings

The Case Management for the Matriarchal Low-Income Families Project started with three practice agencies in April 2004 and two more in 2005. In 2007, the Korean Institute for Health Family (previously a state-run agency of the Ministry of Women and Families) re-named the project 'Case Management for Single-Parent Families'. Since 2010, this project has been expanded to 30 agencies across the country.

From 2004 to 2009, the Solution Center provided supervision for this project. In 2008, follow-up research (Solution Center, 2008) on 329 cases who had completed the counselling between 6 months to 3 years before showed significant and promising improvements in many of the clients' lives: 79.6 per cent of the cases responded that their lives became better after the SF intervention, with 19 cases being no longer considered 'welfare', while only14.6 per cent did not experience any significant change from the project.

Basic course of SF approach

We trained practitioners in the basic SF approach in a 10-hour program, instead of the usual 20-hour program due to time constraints. Two new agencies were then trained in 2005. The previously trained practitioners were our co-trainers as this approach helped them to build up their confidence in using SF, as well as inspiring the newer learners. In 2006, five agencies requested further SF training to enhance their work with other agencies. We trained social workers from agencies in the same area.

Supervision of the SF approach

When my colleagues and I supervised the practitioners, we always reminded ourselves:

- Supervisees know their clients and their situation well – they are the experts.
- If something works in supervision, do more of it. But if it does not work, do something different. In doing this we always asked and listened to what was working from the supervisees' perspective.

On-site supervision

On-site supervision allowed us to better monitor each practitioner's progress, and to notice small changes, given their different work contexts. It also gave the practitioners more time to work with their clients.

We started each supervision with, 'What can I do to help you today?' The practitioners would typically ask us for help with their clients. Occasionally they raised some personal issues, which allowed us to influence them in other positive ways such that they would, in turn, relate with their clients more effectively. To instil confidence, we would ask: 'How did you do that to help your client?' or 'What would your client say about how you have helped them?'

In 2006, some practitioners requested a live supervisor with their most 'difficult' clients. We visited the clients' homes as a team. I shared that I was very impressed with the practitioners and complimented them on their hard work so as to boost their confidence. One common piece of feedback from them was, 'I learned a lot from you and we appreciate your support. I think that live supervision was particularly helpful.'

Supervision with special themes

As our project was nearing its third year, the practitioners, from different agencies, brought up some interesting issues. Using a format where by a practitioner led the group, some of the following suggestions emerged:

- To cooperate more effectively with involuntary clients
- To ask and follow up the miracle question in more detail

The team leaders also wanted to enhance their leadership skills, so the supervision team decided to counsel them separately. The team leaders felt they held a huge burden to satisfy the practitioners' and teams' expectations, almost being like a father in the Korean family culture. The team leaders, being new to SF, initially complimented their staff too much. As a result the staff frequently tended to overthink this and became suspicious of ulterior meanings. In order to come up with better ideas on complimenting their practitioners, every leader was given some time to search for his or her experiences as a successful leader. They began to recognise that 'too much is as bad as too little' when complimenting their staff. Through supervision, the team leaders shared their successful experiences and received positive feedback from us and each other, and started gaining more confidence as leaders and picked up ideas on how to improve themselves.

Writing the manual for practitioners

At the time of the start of the project, there were several theoretical books on case management in Korea but none on actually how to do case management using the SF approach. I therefore wrote a manual focusing on what the targeted practitioners were curious about and tried to create a useful guide for them. I reviewed questions frequently asked by practitioners and also provided some interview extracts as models of a good SF approach. The manual, *Strengths Perspective Solution Focused Case Management* (Kim & Hwang, 2006) has been widely read by practitioners in many fields. My colleague Helen Noh and I have recently edited and published a new book to expand on this, *The Strength Based Solution Focused Case Management* (Noh & Kim, 2014).

Reporting on their SF practice

We also wanted our practitioners to understand SF principles and acquire SF skills through another method: reporting. We asked the practitioners to report to us, monthly for the first year, what they felt they did well and what they would change in the future because we wanted them to familiarise themselves with the SF approach. As they became more accomplished with the SF approach, the reports were requested quarterly. After they wrote their reports, they shared them in supervision.

The questions on the report form were:

- What has your team done well for the last month (or three months)?
- What has helped your team to do these things well?
- What new things has your team tried for the last month (or three months)?
- What helped your team to be able to try these new things?
- What will your team want help for during the next supervision session?
- What will your team want to share with practitioners in other agencies?

The respondents gained self-confidence as they talked about what they did well. My colleagues and I thought it was important that the practitioners spend time focusing on positive things and complimenting each other. By frequently writing a report, the practitioners were able to have some time to think about the processes, especially on how they were able to succeed. This practice allowed the practitioners to communicate more easily and effectively with their clients and at the same time realise the exceptions, when things were going well with their clients, which they might have overlooked before.

Below is a summary of the quantitative and qualitative research data we gathered about the project's effectiveness.

Summary of quantitative research

Questionnaires were given at intake and again as each case was closed. Of the 128 women who participated in both pre- and post-tests, their overall life satisfaction rate increased by 7.8 per cent. Different types of changes were detected based on the different needs expressed by the clients at pre-test. For example, 89 clients who responded to having financial difficulties had an 8.3 per cent increase in their income at post-test. Furthermore, 34 clients who had responded to having mental health issues at pre-test showed a 7.8 per cent decrease in depression and a 10.2 per cent decrease in stress (Noh, You & Park, 2006).

The satisfaction rate of clients toward their practitioners was relatively high. On a 4-point scale, the total average rating was 3.1 on nine items. The items that had the highest scores were, 'I would recommend this agency to other people' and 'It was easy to contact my practitioner' with the average rating of 3.4, followed by the question, 'I will contact my practitioner if I need further help', with the average rating of 3.3.

For the 15 practitioners who participated in both pre-test and post-tests, there was an increase of 6.6 per cent in their job performance and an increase of 8.6 per cent in self-esteem. With respect to their attitude towards poverty, the practitioners' attitude increased by 11 per cent in positive ways: they started to view the poor families more as hard working, challenging and constantly pursuing ways to survive. There also was an increase of 12.5 per cent in the practitioners' view of 'clients as experts of their lives.'

Although the SF supervision project was not aimed at eradicating poverty, we observed that clients could change aspects of their perceptions and attitudes towards their low-income situations in a short time when their practitioners respected and trusted them.

Summary of the qualitative research

Further detailed information on the clients' perceptions were collected through qualitative interviews with the clients (Noh, You & Park, 2006). From these extracts, which are representative of the general feedback, we could see the effectiveness of the intervention and supervision from the clients' perspectives.

> Client 1: 'When I met the case manager of this agency, I thought that she would just tell me what to do. But she did not. Instead, she always listened to me and respected my opinion. She always asked me, *"What do you think about this?"* or *"What can I do to help you?"* I know she respects me deeply.'
>
> Client 2: 'I had met social workers before when I had problems. Those social workers seemed to know everything and took care of all my problems by themselves. So I just accepted their services. But I knew they wouldn't be able to take care of my problems forever. My recent case manager helped me to find the solutions relying more on myself. This was very different from the other social worker. She was surprised and made compliments when I did a small thing. So I realised now that I could change myself and do something on my own.'
>
> Client 3: 'Previous social welfare workers often berated me by focusing on what I did wrong, but my present case manager always supported me by complimenting me and having a positive attitude. I am sure they learn something new.'

Other clients mentioned significant changes in their lives such as interacting more with family members or friends, compared with being very reserved prior to the sessions. Many had a rather cynical and pessimistic view of life, and they were often sceptical of other people's words.

They had low self-esteem and low self-confidence. But after the sessions with their practitioners, the clients were more active and happier, were more confident in themselves and had brighter hopes for the future.

These interviews suggest that the practitioners understood and applied the principles of SF well, and in part this is likely due to the vigilance of the supervisors.

Conclusion

My colleagues and I learned through our experience of supervising this project and other, similar projects, that when practitioners are under SF supervision consistently for at least three years, they understand that the SF approach is not just a skill but a completely different paradigm. When practitioners first learn the SF approach, they generally think the approach is very simple. But most practitioners who had received training in the SF approach and participated in these projects told us that consistent supervision was needed in order to adapt to the SF approach.

We knew the SF paradigm was very important in helping both clients and practitioners feel respected and gain self-confidence. The SF approach is more than just a set of skills; it is an attitude as well. Through my own journey as an SF supervisor, I have learned even more that it is not easy to supervise with an open and curious mind-set. However, the effort paid off as I have gained a deeper understanding of the SF approach by using this mind-set.

References

Kim, Y., & Hwang, H. (2006) *Manual of strengths perspective solution focused case management*. Seoul, South Korea: Ministry of Health and Welfare & Solution Center.

Noh, H., & Kim, Y. (2014). *Strength-based solution focused case management*. Seoul, South Korea: Hakjisa.

Noh, H., You, S., & Park, H. (2006). *Strength based case management for female heads of low income families: Evaluation and management measures*. Seoul, South Korea: Ministry of Health and Welfare & Soongsil University.

Solution Center. (2008). *Reporting 'Follow up research: The project of strength based case management for female heads of low income families.'* Retrieved from www.solution-center.org.

21

BE THE SUPERVISOR YOU WISH TO SEE IN THE WORLD

Lilian Ing

Introduction

The application of a solution-focused (SF) approach in agency settings (McAllister, 2007; Pichot & Dolan, 2003; Turnell & Edwards, 1999) and in supervision in a number of different settings has been well documented (Wheeler, 2007). What is different about this chapter is not only the focus on the supervision of supervisors, but also why this approach has proven so helpful within an Asian context. In this chapter I share my experience of what has worked in practice in supervising supervisory managers in the social and educational sector, whose roles run the gamut from managing task performance, to providing specialist input on complex matters to emotional support.

Why solution focused?

Solution focused (SF) supervision holds certain assumptions about the supervisory relationship that supports collaboration, notices and encourages particular ways of thinking and behaving, and inspires excellence in the supervision of others and oneself (Thomas, 2013). Thomas describes the role of supervisor as one that helps supervisees to learn to learn. Cantwell and Holmes (1994, p. 37) call this 'leading from behind' and in my work I attempted to model this through my supervision with supervisory managers. I believe that they are doing their best, that they want what's best and that whatever challenge they bring is just a blip on the radar screen of their journey, a challenge that will enable them to learn new skills or reinforce those they already have.

In Asia, in both the educational and social sectors, many supervisory managers have indicated that they themselves, and their own managers, tend to take a critical view of failure, which does not always result in a balanced view of themselves or their work. Asking 'What went wrong?' and 'Who did that?' are frequently the first steps into problem solving, leading to blame and shame. They have openly expressed that their fear of loss of face and of being perceived as 'weak' by their managers and peers, thus inadvertently bringing shame on their organisation, families, even their community, weighs heavily. I have also been told by many that they were not raised and schooled in self-reflection or that cultivating self-awareness does not come easily. Instead, they are more comfortable with the pragmatics of doing something to remedy a problem.

Taking an SF approach does not require one to know the details of the problem in order to help the client formulate what they want instead. Further, applying an SF approach to arrive at a better outcome than what is currently happening requires that one 'stay on the surface', rather than use a theoretical framework to understand the 'cause' of the problem.

In addition, I have frequently felt the need to be a 'super' supervisor . . . and quailed at the thought. The SF approach lets me off the hook from being the expert, providing some relief at times when I was tempted to disseminate my own experience and pontificate on my own opinions. By taking a non-expert, 'not-knowing' stance, I could instead draw on the deep and broad competence of my clients quite naturally. To do this, I ask questions. However, I have not withheld information when it lies within my domain of expertise. I offer this as an approach that they might find useful, in order to adequately address a risk-related, legal or ethical issue.

Lastly, these supervisory managers have a range of different theoretical orientations. O'Connell and Jones (2001) in their successful application of the SF framework in the supervision of counsellors, regardless of their theoretical orientation, provided footprints for me to follow.

For these reasons, taking an SF approach to supervision has proven helpful and achieved the desired outcomes for those whom I have supervised and me, as a supervisor.

Playing hopscotch in the field of dreams

The solution circle model by Daniel Meier (2005), a Swiss coach and trainer, has been my framework of choice in supervising supervisors, particularly where my assignment has included reporting on organisational themes, since the model has been successfully applied to teams and organisations. It is based on the solution-focused framework, developed by Insoo Kim Berg and Steve de Shazer. Figure 21.1 depicts the process.

The key elements of this model are the following:

1   Preparing the ground

In order to ensure that supervisory managers are supported, I always obtain their manager's sponsorship. This is important in Asia, where the manager's authority and power is both recognised and required. In the initial meeting, I strive to deepen my understanding of the expectations of and outcomes desired by their manager and we agree on the process and goals. (Where I am contracted to work with a cohort of managers, we also explore the organisation's desired outcomes.) Managers' best hopes for supervisory managers tend to largely focus on professional and organisational improvement.

2   Setting goals

With the supervisory manager, our initial meeting deals with the following: the supervisory framework; expectations and desired outcomes (which in contrast to their managers', inevitably tend to be more personal in focus); performance highlights; personal strengths and resources; previous helpful supervisory experiences; 'hot topics' (what they must get right in order to be acknowledged by the organisation for their contribution, rather than what they are doing wrong) and their commitment to, rather than compliance with, supervision. This is important here in Asia, where irrespective of personal beliefs and feelings, compliance is often the norm in the workplace.

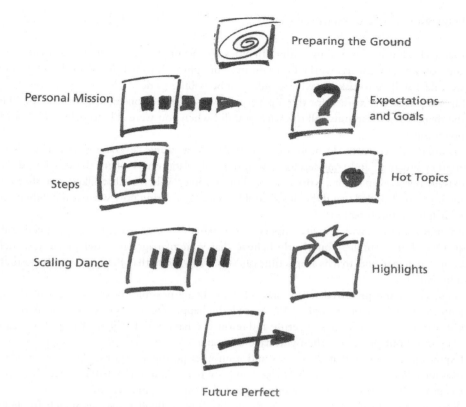

FIGURE 21.1 Overview of the steps in the solution circle.

(Credit: Taken from p. 149, *Team Coaching* [2005] by Daniel Meier. Published by Solutions Books. Reproduced with kind permission of Solutions Books.)

Using scaling, we measure the gap between where they are currently and their personal preferred future. This has allowed those who may be thinking of leaving the organisation to clarify their decision and to manage their departure effectively. It also provides a platform for those ambivalent about their role to resolve their position either way, and to facilitate connection and new meaning.

We explore the next helpful steps on their journey, and the resources (for example, people, practices, processes, decisions) they might need to support them.

Seemingly paradoxical, in meeting personal needs, organisational needs are met.

3   Steps in the direction of the personal mission

Supervision plays out as a structured, purposeful yet appreciative conversation, ensuring a balance between identifying hot topics and valuing behaviours and practices that are working, and examining helpful actions and possible resources (both within and external to the organisation) that might support them in reaching their personal mission or preferred future.

My questions are designed to encourage:

- Practical solutions for dealing with difficulties. For example, 'You know your manager well and you know what has worked for you in your approach to her. You also know what you would be willing to risk. So what would you be willing to do?'
- Eliciting what has worked for the supervisee, given systemic constraints. For example, 'Given the manpower constraints, tell me what you did when you were able to deliver to a deadline previously?'
- Encouraging people to do more of what is already working; leveraging what is working in another situation; and considering areas, times and relationships where the problem does not exist or is less, even if not a work context. For example, 'When we last talked, you shared with me how you handled that difficult stakeholder. I am wondering how what you did there might be helpful in this situation?'
- Providing context, which invites supervisees to reframe and gain a different perspective about an issue. For example, 'You clearly believe that your manager is under pressure to deliver to his manager and that is impacting on you. How does that help you to do something different?'
- Focusing on the preferred future and what might be possible 'next time' versus the usual pattern of events. For example, 'What would be happening in your best case scenario?'
- Unearthing the supervisee's expertise and resources that might facilitate change. For example, 'Tell me about the times when you have been at a 7 (on the scale).'
- Exploring behaviour that showcases and reinforces personal responsibility and choice. For example, 'When you were on that project and you put your mind to making it work, you chose to engage. What do you suppose others noticed about your behaviour?'
- Noticing and affirming the supervisee's approach to difficult situations which has led to a positive outcome. For example, 'You told me that was impossible! How were you able to do that?' Without offering direct or effusive affirmations or compliments, which have tended to be brushed away modestly with my Asian clients and even refuted, my approach has been to ask questions that indicate both interest and curiosity, inviting them to tell all. My supervisory managers have blossomed when they were affirmed and validated in this way, since they revealed that compliments, encouragement and positive strokes are largely in short supply in a predominantly Asian workplace culture.

The transcript below provides an illustration of this kind of conversation between the supervisor (S) and supervisory manager (SM):

SM: I am struggling to deal with a supervisee who is leaving. We both agreed that her skill set and values were not a good match for her role, but I just don't have any peace about this.

S: What might having peace look like for you?

SM: (wistfully) If I can only truly believe that I can have that . . . We both come to agree on differences we have had and accept it, but . . . I don't want to feel there is bad blood, at fault, criticised, incompetent.

S: What will you be feeling and thinking instead?

SM: We have contributed to each other's life. This is a phase. I have learned.

S: Tell me about the times when this has happened before?

SM: In the past, when people have gone over my head, like she did, and told my boss about their unhappiness, rather than come to me, I told myself, I can't give them what they want. They are looking for something I cannot give.

S: How were you able to do that?

SM: I trusted my judgement. I firmly believed that my evaluation was right. My manager also endorsed my decision. I let myself off the hook. I behaved in a professional and polite way toward her, acting rationally with her, not on the basis of my disappointed feelings.

S: On our scale, where are you currently and where will enough be for you to feel you have resolution?

SM: 4.5 . . . 6.5

S: What is happening that tells you that you are at a 4.5?

SM: Because I believe it is not possible to end on a good note.

S: Suppose you were able to believe.

SM: (leans forward in chair, alert, engaged) 4.5 – I am not alone in my assessment, since all parties are in agreement. I continue to see evidence of low standards in her work every day, which confirms my assessment.

S: What would be happening at a 5.5?

SM: (looking sad) I would allow myself to grieve the loss of this relationship . . . I realise how important relationships are to me, and how angry and sad I feel when I do not get what I want from my relationships.

So, what's worked?

Feedback from supervisees on their experience has been positive, with a senior supervisory manager reporting that her supervision with me had been her best experience of professional supervision in her career. Why?

- 'You appreciated and accepted me!'
- 'You gave me time and space to think for myself.'
- 'You were there when I needed you. You listened to my story.'
- 'I see the world and me the right way up, in a good way, after supervision. It is never a waste of time!.'
- 'I learn so much . . . there is so much to think about.'
- Me? I am working on what works and intend doing more of it!

The value of this approach to supervision in Asia has been to provide a balanced view to supervisory managers of both their strengths and challenges. This has enabled them to explore, surface and then leverage their considerable resources, which are forgotten, downplayed or modestly taken for granted when facing challenges. It is also a good culture-fit, since SF takes a respectful approach, while assuming competence to deal with 'stuck' situations where not only the supervisory manager, but also their team, can be part of an effective solution.

Where a number of supervisory managers are in the same organisation or agency, organisational themes of what is working as well as hot topics can be identified for addressing, without criticism. Further, recommendations can build on what is already working and leverage existing know-how and resources, so as to facilitate improved performance. This has given both managers and their organisations a sense of hope – of already having started on the journey, as well as being able to learn from what is working, so that learning can be leveraged.

Given this positive experience as a supervisor, I end with a quote that has become my mantra:

Do something. If it works, do more of it. If it doesn't, do something else.

(Franklin D. Roosevelt)

References

Cantwell, P., & Holmes, S. (1994). Social construction: A systemic shift for systemic therapy and training. *Australia and New Zealand Journal for Family Therapy, 15*(1), 17–26.

McAllister, M. (2007). *Solution focused nursing: Rethinking practice.* Basingstoke, UK: Palgrave.

Meier, D. (2005). *Team coaching with the solution circle. A practical guide to solutions focused team development.* Cheltenham, UK: SolutionsBooks.

O'Connell, B., & Jones, C. (2001). Solution-focused supervision. In S. Palmer & J. Milner (Eds.), *Counselling: The BACP counselling reader*, 2 (pp. 402–408). London, UK: Sage.

Pichot, T., & Dolan, Y. (2003). *Solution focused brief therapy: Its effective use in agency settings.* New York, NY: Haworth.

Thomas, F.N. (2013). *Solution-focused supervision: A resource-oriented approach to developing clinical expertise.* New York, NY: Springer.

Turnell, A., & Edwards, S. (1999). *Signs of safety: A solution- and safety-oriented approach to child protection casework.* New York, NY: Norton.

Wheeler, J. (2007). Solution focused supervision. In T.S. Nelson & F.N. Thomas (Eds.), *Handbook of solution-focused brief therapy: Clinical application.* New York, NY: Haworth Press.

22

'PULLING UP THE SHOOTS TO HELP THEM GROW' AND OTHER ORIENTAL PEARLS OF SOLUTION-FOCUSED WISDOM

Alan K. L. Yeo

Introduction

'The skills of a solution-focused supervisor resemble those required for a solution-focused therapist' (Pichot & Dolan, 2003, p. 160). I attribute the joy of learning the solution-focused (SF) approach for me and my supervisees to the same climate of trust I create during therapy, where mistakes can be shared safely, and where a spirit of co-learning and co-teaching helps build rapport and confidence.

When Chinese speakers converse, they routinely pepper their narratives with idioms to help convey their messages more eloquently. In this chapter extracts from my supervisees' cases illustrate the use of these idioms to enhance learning during supervision and/or application during therapy.

Each idiom (or other figurative phrase) has some or all of the following functions:

- Addresses an aspect of Asian culture and values, demonstrating that the SF approach is applicable to case scenarios commonly associated with Asians
- Enhances a teaching moment in supervision, helping supervisees remember SF principles
- Parallels an SF tenet, suggesting influence by Asian philosophies
- Is familiar among today's Chinese speakers; idioms are useful and current
- Is easy to understand; non-Chinese-speaking SF practitioners may share similar ideas with their supervisees, regardless of language
- Can be useful when shared appropriately with clients, as well as in supervision

The key Chinese characters and *pinyin* (Romanised pronunciation) are shown in the opening part of each section.

My first precious lesson in SF supervision

> *'If you want to lead them (people), you must place yourself behind them'*
> 欲先民、必以身後之 *Yù xiān mín, bì yǐ shēn hòu zhī*
> (Laozi as translated by Muller, 2011, Chap. 66)

'Leading from one step behind'

(De Jong & Berg, 2008, pp. 50–51)

I first honour my own SF supervisor, who showed me the light at the end of my long and lonely SF tunnel when I was a budding SF therapist. Due to my insecurity, I would share with my clients my psychology and counselling knowledge to help them realise there is only this way to end their problems. I was not only leading from the front, but dragging my clients along. Of course that didn't work. Yet I would try harder, seeing my advice-giving as responsible prudence. My supervisor neither encouraged nor discouraged this. One day she asked, in a hypnotic, Eriksonian manner, 'Was it Maslow who said, "If all you have is a hammer . . .?"' I waited for her to complete the quote. She said, 'Sorry, time's up. Ask *Gǔ gē* (Big Brother *Gǔ*)'. 'Ask *Gǔgē*' is a Chinese pun on 'Go Google'.

I realised much later that my supervisor was probably 'leading from one step behind' (De Jong & Berg, 2008, pp. 50–51). This episode contained several SF principles: 1. Asking is more impactful than telling. 2. Trust that your supervisee can reach his destination by himself. 3. Try not to rob your supervisee of his own discovery; nurture independence, and 4. Subtlety goes a long way; indirect expression (e.g., planting an idea) takes longer to piece together, but keeps the mind actively self-discovering. While some of these principles are specific to counselling, 'SFBT therapists . . . make questions the *primary* communication tool . . . an overarching intervention' (de Shazer & Dolan, 2007, p. 4).

I felt that in Googling, I discovered Maslow's quote myself. With that sense of ownership, I shared it passionately with many of my supervisees. A common application of Maslow's idea is, if all we have is advice-giving, we will 'see' that advice is what our clients need.

For most beginner therapists, taking some credit for the success of our clients can be healthy self-affirmation. So, perhaps this quote from Tolle provides a more realistic and encouraging balance in recognising our work with clients than Laozi's: 'The teacher and the taught together create the teaching' (Tolle, 1999).

The power of reframing

'A journey of a thousand miles starts with one step'
'千里之行 始于足下' *Qiān lǐ zhī xíng, shǐ yú zú xià*

(Laozi as translated by Muller, 2011, Chap. 64)

'Small steps can lead to big changes'

(de Shazer and Dolan, 2007, p. 2)

Leng's client was a retired Chinese language teacher. When her husband passed away she was devastated. Both were still healthy and had plans to travel. The client attempted suicide but luckily her eldest son, a doctor whom she lived with, managed to revive her. During therapy, the client exhibited ambivalence, wanting to move on yet not finding the strength or reason to do so. Leng held her client's hands with empathy, and said respectfully, 'It must be really tough. I'm not sure if this saying is meaningful to you: A journey of a thousand miles . . .', and paused. Her client contemplated this, sighed with relief, nodded and completed the quote. She added, 'I procrastinated seeking help for a long while, but today I let my son bring me here'.

I use this proverb to encourage my supervisees when they lament about their mandated or 'resistant' clients. The SF approach reframes 'resistant' clients as 'not yet ready'. The proverb helped my supervisees to view their clients as having already made the first step to be in the therapy room. Even if therapy was not their choice, they were polite to the therapist (i.e., another baby step). Or, if their responses were monosyllabic, at least they were not silent. With these reframes, the ball is in our court, so we can empower ourselves to be creative with our interventions, rather than bemoan the client's lack of motivation.

An SF take on self-disclosure

> *White-haired person sends off black-haired person* (Chinese idiom)
> (Child dying before his parent is unbearable grief)
> 白头人送黑头人 *bái tóu rén sòng hēi tóu rén*

Ivey and Ivey (2007, p. 356) describe self-disclosure as 'shar(ing) your own story, thoughts, or experiences briefly' with clients. The pros and cons of self-disclosure are discussed in most counselling courses. De Jong and Berg (2008), however, discourage self-disclosure as the process could be more of the therapist's frame of reference than the client's.

Lian learnt the limitation of self-disclosure in therapy, with her experience with an 89-year-old grandfather. He was grieving the loss of his favourite son. In her attempt to provide solace, Lian disclosed, 'I too lost my father many years ago. We were also very close. I know what you are going through'. Lian was taken aback when the grandfather retorted with some indignation, 'No, you don't know. White-haired sends off black-haired'. The grandfather lamented that he was not allowed to attend his son's funeral (bad luck), a practice common among more traditional families. Lian apologised for not being sensitive enough, and continued to use the SF approach to bring some closure for the grandfather.

Lian's experience reminds us to use self-disclosure sparingly, if at all.

Clients prefer to be told what to do

> *Pulling up the shoots to help them grow* (Chinese idiom)
> (To spoil things through excessive enthusiasm)
> 拔苗助长 *bá miáo zhù zhǎng*

> *Slow is faster, fast is slower; 'Go slow'*
>
> (Pichot & Dolan, 2003, p. 172)

There is a perception that Asian clients see their therapists as experts, and seem to prefer advice over self-discovery. Some of the authors' colleagues found the SF approach to be slow moving and preferred the quicker way of telling clients what to do, or asking questions leading clients to acknowledge their unhelpful strategy. It is tempting to believe that clients also prefer this approach. De Shazer and Dolan advocate patience and 'giving clients new opportunities to envision their future and begin to make plans to move toward that future'(2007, p. 162). It takes longer to come up with customised questions (e.g., miracle question, exceptions, relationship questions, scaling, etc.) that have these aims, and often even longer for a client to answer them.

However, the quality and commitment that comes from the client's response is more likely to lead to small but realistic and significant changes in the client's life.

Hock shared that he tried to convince his client that counselling does not quite work by telling parents what to do. 'You know your child better than I do . . .' he began. The mother interrupted, in a somewhat upbeat tone, perhaps to disguise her anxiety, 'If I do, how come my son blames me for pressuring him to the point where he blacked out on the first day of his exam? I'm doing something wrong'. She continued, 'Please *lah*! Tell me what I should do instead. You are the expert'. Hock paused, and used the idiom 'Pulling up the shoots to help them grow' to kill two birds with one stone. Firstly, the idiom struck a chord with the over-eager mother as she realised her high expectation of her son's academic results contributed to his breakdown. She had always seen her effort as what all 'Tiger Mums' need to do to motivate their children 'for their own good'. Secondly it also dawned on her that if the counselling was not used to explore solutions from the mother's and her son's frame of reference, then being told what to do by the therapist would be ineffective in the long-run. The idiom had a calming effect, which allowed Hock to elaborate: 'My expertise is in asking you important questions. And from your answers, *we* (emphasis intended) will have a much better idea of what suggestions work best for you and your son. I am tapping on your expertise as a mother to your son for 12 years. I've only had 12 minutes with him'. During the end-of-session feedback, the mother said, 'When I came in, I thought, "When my son fails, I fail". Now I am hopeful. I can begin to see my strengths and my son's strengths as we move forward, in a more measured way.'

A variation of SF scaling questions

> *Broken mirror difficult to put back* (Chinese idiom)
> (A broken relationship is hard to mend)
> 破镜难圆 *Pò jìng nán yuán*

> *Broken mirror can be put together* (Chinese idiom)
> (A broken relationship can still be mended)
> 破镜重圆 *Pò jìng zhóng yuán*

'Scaling questions have great versatility' and 'can help clients to express complex, intuitive observations about their past experiences and estimates of future possibilities' (De Jong & Berg, 2008, pp. 106–107).

Kee's client, Seng, 63, disowned his transgender son for bringing shame to the family. That was 20 years ago. Since then, his wife passed on, and his health has deteriorated in the past 2 years. He came for therapy to 'make peace with his son' before Seng dies. He kept repeating, 'broken mirror difficult to put together', followed by a list of regrets and negative ruminations.

Kee empathised with and affirmed Seng, and attempted to scale his confidence towards his goal.

Kee: Suppose at 10, you believe 'broken mirror can be put together', and at 1 you believe 'broken mirror is impossible to put together', where would you say you are now?
Seng: 2.
Kee: How come not lower?

Seng: I don't know . . . if my father disowned me, whether I would ever forgive him.
Kee: So does 'making peace' mean he has to forgive you?
Seng: I never thought of that. Please elaborate?
Kee: Well, some clients seek forgiveness. Recently I had a father who disowned his drug addict son. He just wanted his son to attend his funeral. No need to forgive, no need to call him 'Pa'.
Seng: It would be good if he forgives me. Actually, I just wish he doesn't hate me. I am so tired carrying this guilt. When he needed me most, I turned him away. He was just a child then. Maybe he has also moved on. I think he has. How else can he be a successful lawyer, and now an actress?
Kee: What else tells you he has moved on?
Seng: Well, she is younger; more energy. I'm the old fool, stuck in my ways. It should be easier for her.
Kee: I noticed you sometimes use 'he' and sometimes 'she'. Any particular reasons?
Seng: Oh, habit I guess. No *lah*, I know what you psychologists are thinking; that subconsciously, I still wish he is my son. She is successful, and happy. I also feel proud when I read about her in a new serial. She is no drug addict or criminal. Before my wife died, she told me, 'Don't take this guilt into your next life'.
Kee: What else?
Seng: After talking to you, I believe a broken mirror can be put together. It won't be perfect, but it can still reflect what is important. I'm at an 8 now.

During two subsequent sessions, Seng role-played and rehearsed how he was going to contact his daughter, what to say, etc. When they met, Seng could only manage an implied apology, as a prideful man would. That was good enough for his daughter. A few months later, he died, peacefully. His daughter called him 'Pa', arranged for his funeral and forgave him.

Conclusion

Words of wisdom often reflect the universality of humanity. We learn them in schools. We hear them in conversations, in movies, in literature. They connect us intra- and inter-generationally through a history of shared knowledge and experiences. Some supervisees, including non-Chinese speakers, observed that even if they used the English translation of these Chinese idioms, they could still make a good connection with their clients. Their clients took delight in explaining the idioms, if needed. As I come to embrace the SF model of supervision, I appreciate how it has helped me create a climate of respectful support, laced with appropriate puns, fun, and humour, and filled with 'Wahs' (Wows) and 'Aha' moments. It is my supervisees' and my wish that these examples be ideas worth spreading.

References

De Jong, P., & Berg, I.K. (2008). *Interviewing for solutions* (3rd ed.). Belmont, CA: Brooks/Cole.
de Shazer, S., & Dolan, Y. (2007). *More than miracles: The state of the art of solution-focused brief therapy*. New York, NY: Routledge/Taylor & Francis.

Ivey, A.E., & Ivey, M.B. (2007). *Intentional interviewing and counselling: Facilitating client development in a multicultural society* (6th ed.). Belmont, CA: Brooks/Cole.

Muller, C. (2011). *Daode jing*. Retrieved from: http://www.acmuller.net/con-dao/daodejing.html.

Pichot, T., & Dolan, Y. (2003). *Solution-focused brief therapy: Its effective use in agency settings.* New York, NY: The Haworth Press.

Tolle, E. (1999). *The power of now: A guide to spiritual enlightenment.* Novato, CA: New World Library.

SECTION 3

Solution focused practice in education in Asia

23

INTRODUCTION TO SOLUTION FOCUSED PRACTICE IN EDUCATION IN ASIA

Debbie Hogan

The interest in quality education is a world-wide concern and recently the spotlight seems to have been on Asia. Not only do Asian schools excel academically, they also cultivate a culture of achievers. The pressure to succeed and excel academically is unrelenting, and this pressure is felt across the board – by the school, the parents and the students. In this chapter I will put the spotlight on the educational environment in Asia, and share some personal observations on the importance of education in Asia and its impact on teachers, parents and students. I will shift to how SF practice can make a positive difference with these challenges and examine some research on the effectiveness of the SF approach in education. I will conclude with introducing the nine compelling chapters in this section that relate how the SF approach was used successfully in the educational setting by SF practitioners in Asia.

Brief look at educational environments in Asia

Schools in Asia are amongst the top schools in global rankings in test scores (Coughlan, 2015) and in maths and science (McSpadden, 2015), and international schools in Asia are also amongst the top-ranked globally (PryceWarner, 2011). No longer are international schools in Asia simply the domain of expatriate children. Many of them are filled with Asian students, and, for some, the majority of their students are Asians.

The prediction is that international schools catering to Asian students who want to attend English-language schools will increase in Asia (ICEF Monitor, 2014). Needless to say, Asian schools are like a pressure-cooker. There is unrelenting pressure to achieve academically, and these high expectations are placed on every child. What impresses me is how resourceful and hard-working Asians are. There is an undeniable tenacity and drive for excellence.

Observations on the importance of education in Asia

Several years I ago I saw a cartoon of an Asian pregnant mother, standing in line to register her unborn child for school, holding a Walkman with earphones over her pregnant belly, playing educational tunes. While many of my Asian friends found this amusing, they agreed that it really does depict the concerns of Asian parents. One of the first words of the local vernacular that I learned when moving to Singapore 28 years ago was 'kiasu'. Originating from the Hokkien dialect, it literally means 'scared to lose' (Oxford English Dictionary Online, n.d.). The 'kiasu' parent will do anything within their power to make sure their child gets into the right school, studies hard to make the top grade and eventually is accepted into a top school to have a solid head start in life. Getting their child into a top university gives them a better chance to have a good future with a good job, social status and the family pride associated with this success. The 'kiasu' mentality, however, is not limited to Singapore as it is prevalent in many countries across Asia and globally.

My daughter was born in Singapore, and when she was ready to attend pre-school, I wanted to find the best school for her. I discovered that the best rated nursery school was in our neighbourhood and enrolled her. Yes, I was a 'kiasu' parent! My daughter brought home graded artwork and was given homework, which she did diligently, still excited about going to school. That was until she started to learn the Chinese language. Verbally she excelled, but written Chinese was very difficult. The Chinese language teacher used scolding to 'motivate' her, which did not work. When it was time to enrol her in primary school, My husband and I visited several schools and interviewed the principals. Or should I say, they interviewed us. They quickly told us that we should not expect special treatment just because we were expatriates, and that my daughter would be expected to perform well in the school. I realise now that this is part of the process of inculcating Asian educational values, and the training starts at a young age. It helped me appreciate the seriousness and focus of Asian schools in preparing their young people for the global marketplace.

Impact of academic pressure on teachers, parents and students in Asia

Schools in Asia are busy environments with pressures from many directions: academic performance, initiatives from management, and expectations from parents and teachers. Asian schools cultivate a culture of achievers, and schools are rewarded and rated for good academic performance.

Teachers. Teachers expect every student to succeed. There's a lot of rigour and focus in the classroom, and teachers often feel squeezed in the middle – between the expectations of the school system and the parents on one side and the students on the other side. They're eager to find ways to effectively manage these challenges.

Parents. Many parents feel they have no choice but to place high expectations on their child. Parents try their best to support and motivate their children to perform well academically and do all they can to 'guarantee' a positive future for their child. When their child does not do well academically, they often blame themselves and place even more excessive demands on their child. Many seek parent-coaching to learn effective ways to manage the situation.

Students. Asian students feel enormous pressure to achieve academically, rooted in the cultural values placed on education and the fierce competition for admission into higher education. After-school tuition is a way of life in order to excel in national exams. This can put a financial strain on the family to provide these services, and in return, parents expect their children to perform well. Lin and Chen (1995) report some of the negative consequences experienced by students who have to cope with this unrelenting pressure. 'Double pressure from family and schools has turned many a child's life into one of depression, nervous breakdown, and dissatisfaction' (p. 154).

While these realities in the educational system are not new, what is changing is the realisation that perhaps old methodologies to manage these challenges are not effective, and there is a growing recognition that a more strengths-based approach does have its merits.

How the SF approach can make a difference

A central focus in SF practice in education is building a strong alliance with the student that facilitates trust, respect and co-constructing meaningful goals with the student. Many studies show that when there is a positive relationship with the teacher, students do better academically (Birch & Ladd, 1998; Hamre & Pianti, 2001). Lee's (2007) study with Korean middle school students identified trust between teacher and student as an important factor for successful academic performance. Noddings' (1992) findings showed that students work harder to achieve academic success when the teacher shows interest in them.

SF practice is embedded in a philosophy about the nature of change and motivation and places a premium on respect. Motivation is already inherent in every student, and SF counsellors use elegant questions and curiosity to explore the competencies of the student. The SF approach is very pragmatic and facilitates cooperation that leads to ownership and responsibility for desired changes and improvements. It requires a mind-set change from problem solving to solution building based on the co-construction of what is wanted, while looking for existing competencies that already demonstrate capabilities and resourcefulness.

The SF approach to classroom management – WOWW Coaching (Berg & Shilts, 2005) – trains teachers to use the key SF ideas in the classroom and with individual students, like a coach. Some schools in Asia have adopted this approach, and the results have been amazing. Teachers like the simplicity of the tools and the way it enhances cooperation with students. Students like being acknowledged for their accomplishments and efforts, which leads to confidence. The collaboration that is built by using this approach leads to students taking initiative and responsibility and even 'policing' each other for agreed classroom goals. The results shared by teachers and students after I conducted WOWW training in schools indicate both qualitative and quantitative improvements, such as a reduction in truancy and absenteeism, an improvement in academic grades and increase in student engagement and cooperation.

Research into the effectiveness of SF in education

There is growing research that supports the effectiveness of SF practice in Asia – e.g., from Hong Kong, Korea, Taiwan and India. By 2014, 180 studies had been published in Mandarin alone (Macdonald, 2015). The effectiveness of the SF approach in education is one of the most researched areas. As described in the section on schools, SF practice is very suitable with Asians because of the focus on outcomes and the way it is structured. Its focus on strengths instead of pathology, and clarity on the desired changes, is believed to help Asian clients address their problems. The SF approach also enables the practitioner to co-create simple and concrete solutions that honour the Asian values of group cohesion and filial piety.

Contributions by authors

School counsellors face many challenges when working in the Asian education system, and the following examples demonstrate the elegant way in which the SF approach can be a meaningful impetus for change in students, parents and teachers. Nine authors share their unique approach to using SF practice in various educational settings in Singapore, Cambodia, Hong Kong, India and Indonesia and the positive impact from using a solution focused approach in a variety of situations.

The first two chapters involve school counsellors in local schools in Singapore. Joan Low works at a Junior College and suggests ways in which to effectively respond to students who repeatedly say 'I don't know'. Yana Ricart talks about the importance of taking a 'not-knowing' stance and how to maintain curiosity when working with students.

The next four chapters focus on school counsellors in international schools, serving a huge population of Asian students. Bradley Barrett shares examples of adapting and integrating the SF approach in a Cambodian international school. Emily Meadows gives us insight into the competitive environment of an elite Hong Kong international school that serves a high percentage of Asian students of wealthy families and how a scaling tool was used to work with young children. Patricia Joudrey highlights the use of the SF approach to help a student deal with conflict in managing the family cultural values and school expectations in India. Colleen Steigerwald shares examples of primary-aged Asian students and how they found hope in troubling situations at a top international school in Singapore.

The next two chapters focus on the use of SF practice when multiple stakeholders are involved – the school, parents and students. Vania Djohan, an SF practitioner and owner of a private school in Indonesia, shares her experience of dealing with school bullying and how she facilitated a peaceful resolution with the school, parents and the students involved. I share a case in which a school referred a student for anger management and how I worked with the school, parents and student to build cooperation and collaboration among the key stakeholders which facilitated the desired outcome.

The last chapter offers a unique and creative alternative for students who have dropped out of school. Joe Chan works with youth in a community setting who have been referred by the juvenile court system for gangsterism and truancy. His approach involves creative programmes to engage at-risk youth.

We hope the reader will be inspired and encouraged by these real client stories.

References

Berg, I.K., & Shilts, L. (2005) *Classroom solutions: WOWW coaching*. Milwaukee, WI: BFTC Press.
Birch, S.H., & Ladd, G.W. (1998). Children's interpersonal behaviors and the teacher-child relationship. *Developmental Psychology, 34*, 934–946.
Coughlan, S. (2015, May 13). Asia tops biggest global school rankings. *BBC News*. Retrieved 10 December 2015 from: http://www.bbc.com/news/business-32608772
Hamre, B. K., & Pianta, R. C. (2001). Early teacher–child relationships and the trajectory of children's school outcomes through eighth grade. *Child Development, 72*, 625–638.
ICEF Monitor (2014, 18 March). *New data on international schools suggests continued growth*. Retrieved from: http://monitor.icef.com/2014/03/new-data-on-international-schools-suggests-continued-strong-growth-2/

Kim, J.S., Franklin, C., Zhang, Y., Liu, W., Qu, Y., & Chen, H. (2015) Solution-focused brief therapy in China: A meta-analysis. *Journal of Ethnic and Cultural Diversity in Social Work, 24*(3), 187–201.

Lee, S.J. (2007). The relationship between the student-teacher trust relationship and school success in the case of Korean middle schools. *Educational Studies, 33*(2), 209–216.

Lin, J., & Chen, Q. (1995). Academic pressure and impact on students' development in China. *McGill Journal of Education, 30*(2), 149–168.

Macdonald, A. (2015, November 18). *Solution-focused brief therapy evaluation list.* Retrieved from: http://www.solutionsdoc.co.uk/sft.html.

McSpadden, K. (2015, May 13). Here's where you're going to find the best schools in the world. *Time Magazine.* Retrieved 12 December 2015 from: http://time.com/3856834/worlds-best-top-schools-survey-asia/.

Noddings, N. (1992). *The challenge to care in schools: An alternative approach to education.* New York, NY: Teachers College Press.

Oxford English Dictionary Online. (n.d.). Kiasu. Retrieved 12 December 2015 from: http://www.oxforddictionaries.com/definition/english/kiasu.

PryceWarner expatsvillage. (2011, July 6). *Top ten international schools around the world.* Retrieved from: http://www.prycewarner.com/blog/2011/07/top-ten-international-schools/

24

WORKING WITH YOUNG PEOPLE WHEN THEY SAY 'I DON'T KNOW'

Joan Low

Introduction

'If I could get a dime each time I hear the reply "I don't know" from our students, I would be a millionaire by now!' This was something a frustrated colleague shared with me not so long ago. Indeed, in my practice as a school counsellor, it's not uncommon for me to hear 'I don't know' from students in response to any of my most well-crafted or best-intentioned questions, especially if it wasn't their idea to come see me in the first place. In this chapter, I will explore how a solution focused (SF) school counsellor deals with this common response from students, and how persistence pays off when you hold to your firm belief that perhaps they do know, or eventually they will know.

'I don't know'

With young people, replying 'I don't know' to any question asked of them seems almost like an automatic reflex. Either they think it's an enormous inconvenience on their part to process the question or they are just genuinely helpless and confused, and hopeful that I would both ask the question and answer it for them. For this reason, it can often be an incredibly frustrating or nerve-wracking experience working with young people. To illustrate this, the following is an excerpt of the first session with a student, Gabriel, who was referred to me for persistent late attendance issues.

Joan:	So what needs to happen in our session today in order for you to say it was worthwhile coming here today?
Gabriel:	I don't know.
Joan:	Right . . . so whose idea was it for you to come today?
Gabriel:	My teacher.
Joan:	So what do you think your teacher wants to see different so she'd think it was a good idea she asked you to come today?
Gabriel:	I don't know . . . you'd have to ask her.

Joan: Sure. Maybe I'd do that some time but I'm interested in what you think is important for you . . . what you want to see different so coming to see me today wasn't a waste of your time?

Gabriel: I don't know.

This goes back and forth for another five minutes before I asked some other questions in a bid to gain some form of rapport and break the ice.

Joan: So Gabriel, I'm curious . . . what made you decide to come to Junior College (JC) after O levels?

Gabriel: My parents.

Joan: Right . . . so it wasn't your idea to come to JC?

Gabriel: I don't know . . .

Joan: So what makes your parents think it's a good idea for you to be here?

Gabriel: I don't know . . . they want me to become a lawyer or a doctor.

Joan: I see . . . and what do you make of that?

Gabriel: Huh?

Joan: I mean . . . what do you think about what they want?

Gabriel: *shrugs* I don't know.

Joan: You don't seem to think much of it, huh? What your parents want? What *is* important to you then? What would you like to see happen in your life?

Gabriel: I don't know . . . I don't know . . . I don't know!

Perhaps Gabriel didn't really say 'I don't know' in the last sentence three times but it most certainly felt like it. This dialogue is fairly typical, especially when it comes to students who are mandated and sometimes even with students who are self-referred. It can be very exasperating and bewildering to be on the receiving end of multiple 'I don't knows', all the time wondering how in the world I can work as a solution focused counsellor with these students, believing they are the experts in their own lives (De Jong & Berg, 2013), when in that moment they often seem anything but.

Literature has shown that when clients repeatedly say 'I don't know' in the session, it could often mean a number of things, including being resistant to the helping process (Cowan & Presbury, 2000). I suppose that could well be the case in some situations. However, I've come to notice that in the majority of the cases where the students repeatedly say 'I don't know', they don't seem to be saying that as a way to frustrate the proces; rather, they genuinely do not seem to know what they would like to see different in their lives. This seemed to be the case, especially with the Asian youths whom I work with.

Cultural imprinting

As I thought about the way I was brought up in an Asian family, I began to understand a little better why these students often seem confused and lost. It has helped me to understand that they are not deliberately saying 'I don't know' as a way to frustrate me or be disinterested in the counselling process. Growing up, I was seldom, if ever, asked for my opinion about things. The assumption then, which I think is still very much the common assumption now, is that things have to be a certain way because our parents and teachers said 'it was so'. No questions asked; no room for critical inquiry. On the rare occasion when I challenged my teachers about certain ideas I found unreasonable and illogical, I was thumbed down as being rude and rebellious. Affirmations were also a rare commodity at both home and school, and I grew up learning to see myself from a place of deficit and being 'not-good-enough', as well as believing that my opinions didn't really matter.

A recent meeting with a parent of a student somewhat confirmed this view. Even though decades have passed from when I was a child, this cultural dynamic in Asian families, for the most part, seems largely unchanged. In that conversation, the parent repeated to me several times that the ultimate solution to the issues the student was facing was to simply listen to her advice and obey the 'rules of the household' and everything would be okay. The parent took the time to belabour the point that she had been trying her best to 'listen' to her child by telling her exactly what she should do, which just didn't seem to make sense to me. In that moment, I understood a bit better the sense of helplessness my student felt, being in an environment where there was no space for her opinion or to explore what was important to her and what she valued in life.

It made me wonder: In an environment such as this, can the egalitarian and collaborative nature of solution focused therapy (de Shazer & Dolan, 2012) work? Can we really formulate therapy goals with our Asian students, believing they are the experts of their own lives, when they have had limited opportunities to express their own opinions or make their own choices, especially with regards to complex and difficult situations?

Forming goals with the lost and confused

One of the most influential articles that has helped shape the way I think about forming goals with lost and confused students is '*The Common Project*' (Korman, 2004). Korman talks about the importance of asking the 'common-project' question as the first thing we say to clients when we start the session. Instead of 'How are you' or 'What brings you here', he asks solution focused counsellors to explore the 'common-project' question first: 'What would you like to see different, perhaps something small, as a result of talking to me today so you'd feel that it was worth your while coming here?' Korman then discusses various ways in which we can go about formulating concrete therapy goals with clients depending on the way they answer the 'common-project' question. I've personally found this question to be one of the most difficult SF questions to ask because even before we can build any rapport with the client, we are already asking them to think about what they want to see differently. With Asian students, I worry that the question is ultimately unproductive and I just come off as being rather weird. Korman also states that 'asking the common-project question is far from simple . . . the foundation for the common-project-question is a firm belief – or knowledge – that clients know what they want, even if they don't yet know that they know' (p. 14). In a sense, this highlights the fact that while SF techniques are deceptively simple enough to learn and almost everyone can learn to ask SF-like questions, at the heart of it, to work in an SF way, one must have that 'firm belief' that clients indeed know best. I have struggled with keeping this firm belief, especially when the students I work with often seem genuinely lost and confused as to the difference that they want to see in their lives. However, I have also learned that by holding on to my firm belief and asking the 'common-project' question persistently in different ways, this can often lead to surprising responses.

Case example

Lisa asked to see me and said that she had something very serious to talk to me about. I started by asking the 'common-project' question.

Joan: Lisa, thanks for coming today. What would you like to see different, maybe something small, as a result of having talked to me today so that the time we spend here would have been worthwhile for you?

Lisa: (surprised look) Hah? I don't know . . .

Joan: (waits 6 seconds, pretending that the student had just said 'I don't know . . . yet').

Lisa: I don't know . . . I guess I was hoping that we could talk about my relationship with my parents.

Lisa then went on to say that she had been sexually abused by her father when she was 12 years old. The case had been brought to the police, and her father was still serving time for what he did. Lisa talked about having regrets reporting the matter to the authorities as it permanently damaged her relationship with her mum. I listened to her story for a while, explored how she coped with the situation and then decided to approach the 'common-project' question with her again.

Joan: Lisa, I'm sorry that things were so tough for you and I'm just amazed at how you've tried to cope with it all. By coming to talk to me today about this, what were you hoping could be different?

Lisa: I don't know . . .

Joan: (waits another 6 seconds without nodding, moving or blinking)

Lisa: I don't know . . . I suppose I want to be living life without regrets.

Joan: I see . . . what will you see yourself doing when you are living life without regrets?

Lisa: Well, for starters, I won't be talking to a counsellor about this issue anymore. I will be out there living life, having fun, hanging out with friends . . .

Joan: Wow . . . living life . . . having fun . . . that sounds awesome! Hmm . . . suppose we could spend the rest of this 30 minutes working out ways in which you can be 'living life', will that be helpful?

Lisa: Ha-ha . . . if we could, then, yes.

We went on to discuss what 'living life' would look like for her, explored some scaling and exceptions and arranged to meet again the next week to see what was better. Mid-way through the week, Lisa texted me to say that she thinks she's fine and doesn't need to see me anymore. In her text, Lisa said that she has seen many counsellors before but none of them had ever asked her what she wants to see different in her life. Most had spent considerable time exploring what had happened with her father. When I kept asking her what she wanted to see different, that was the spark she needed to realise that she didn't want to be stuck in the past anymore, and she wanted to move forward 'living life'. It was a very humbling moment for me, to realise the power of a question that I was once so afraid to ask for fear of looking ridiculous, and it was yet another stunning example of how even when clients say they don't know, they in actual fact do know.

Reflections

Since that experience with Lisa, I remind myself to always be persistent, even if the response is often 'I don't know'. I've learned to not freak out when students don't seem to 'get' the process of figuring out what they want to see different in their lives, and I've learned to not feel like I need to jump in and clear their confusion for them. Most importantly, I've learned to always trust in the fact that the students I see are indeed the most resourceful and creative experts in solving their own problems, even when they don't see themselves as capable . . . yet. This, I've realised, is especially important when it comes to working with Asian youths because it's so easy to fall into the culturally expected role of the school counsellor as an adult advisor. And, as I've come to experience for myself over and over again, when we are able to trust in students' ability to trust in themselves, that's when they learn to see themselves from a place of immeasurable strength.

Acknowledgements

My heartfelt gratitude to all my SF teachers who have either taught me directly or whose writings I have been influenced by. Thank you for being an inspiration in the profound respect you give to all of your clients and the creativity and wit you show in the process: Steve de Shazer, Insoo Kim Berg, Debbie Hogan, David Blakely, Therese Steiner, John Henden, Yvonne Dolan and Harry Korman (to name just a few).

A big thank-you to all my students, who ultimately became my best teachers. Thank you for bearing with my weird questions and for showing me what you are truly capable of.

References

Cowan, E. W., & Presbury, J. H. (2000). Meeting client resistance and reactance with reverence. *Journal of Counseling and Development*, 78(4), 411–419.

De Jong, P., & Berg, I. K. (2013). *Interviewing for solutions* (4th ed.). Belmont CA: Brooks/Cole, Cengage Learning.

de Shazer, S., & Dolan, Y. (2012). *More than miracles: The state of the art of solution-focused brief therapy* (2nd ed.). New York, NY: Taylor & Francis.

Korman, H. (2004). *The common project*. Retrieved from: http://www.sikt.nu/wp-content/uploads/2015/06/Creating-a-common-project.pdf.

25

'NOT KNOWING'

Curiosity as a tool for working with students from different cultures

Yana Ricart

I have no special talent, I am only passionately curious.

(Albert Einstein)

De Jong and Berg (2013, p. 20) suggest that if we want 'to put clients into the position of being the experts about their own lives', we need 'to learn how to adopt a posture of *not knowing*'.

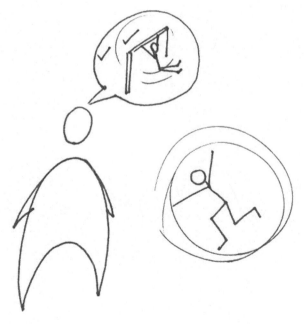

FIGURE 25.1 Imagining possibilities.
(Credit: Xochitl Ricart)

From the moment I arrived in Asia from Latin America, I wanted to learn how to approach different cultures respectfully, in order to engage in positive relationships with people. 'Not knowing' was a reality for me. Later, through training in solution-focused brief therapy (SFBT) and my early experiences working in the Singaporean educational system, this attitude became a tool ingrained in my practice.

This chapter describes examples of how curiosity and this posture of 'not knowing' helped me to counsel students in both local and international schools in Singapore.

Understanding my curiosity

When I began working at a counselling centre associated with the Singapore public school system, I went with a team of counsellors to conduct workshops at a secondary school. We were going to work with classes from different educational 'streams'. In Singapore, secondary students are placed in three different streams based on their exam grades at the end of primary school.

After the workshops, when we were reviewing the students' behaviour and attitudes in the different classes, I realised that since I was new to the system, I had confused the higher- and lower-ranked classes. I could see more strengths in the students from the lower-ranked classes precisely because I did not know the labels. This engaged my curiosity immediately.

The discussion with my other colleagues had an impact on their curiosity as well. Initially they did not understand how I could confuse the streams, and they thought it was very amusing. As we discussed what I saw and felt, they began to look at the students from a different angle, and I gained understanding about their views as well.

It was surprising: Looking at things differently produced a domino effect that opened possibilities to all of us involved.

FIGURE 25.2 Understanding my curiosity.
(Credit: Xochitl Ricart)

This incident took place while I was training in SFBT, so I could observe the concepts in action. I learned a very valuable lesson about 'learning to think differently' (Metcalf, 1995) and being genuinely open to the students' potential. I realised how to use my 'not knowing' and curiosity as a tool for approaching students in this culture.

Understanding the students' curiosity

The government program that sent us to conduct workshops in different primary schools also required regular individual sessions with students. As I started conducting these sessions, I noticed that when they told me which class they came from, some students made a special effort to tell me which 'letter' followed the grade they were in, for example 4H or 5J. I observed from their body language that these 'letters' seemed very important to them.

I did not know what it was about, so I started to pay more attention. The students seemed to expect a specific reaction from me when they mentioned these letters, and the fact that I was not reacting the way they expected seemed to make them curious. I found out later that these letters were an indication of their grades; the lower the grades, the further down the alphabet the letter was. Just by mentioning the letter, they expected to be seen in a different way.

My 'not knowing' served to clear the slate: No mental images or attitudes were attached to these letters. The effect on the students was interesting. In the counselling room they seemed to feel free from the letter labels; they were more curious and open to explore new behaviours.

Afterwards, I had conversations with parents and teachers that contributed to the students' progress as well. Through conveying respect for their culture and sharing the attitudes observed

FIGURE 25.3 Understanding the students' curiosity.
(Credit: Xochitl Ricart)

in the counselling room, they were able to look at the students in a different way. They could see hints of possibilities and hope for their children.

Understanding curiosity on both sides

The students I saw within the local system were always referred to as 'a program'. Since they did not come voluntarily, at the beginning, many did not even want to see me. In the case of a particularly angry Malay teenager, he conveyed his lack of desire to be there by being silent and looking annoyed the whole time.

I tried to engage him in different ways, and none had any effect. During one of the first few sessions he started to look angrier within his silence, and after a while he had an outburst of anger and shouted: 'You don't know anything.' I waited to see what would happen next. I was wondering if he would continue expressing his anger.

After it was clear that he was not going to say anything else, I answered by saying: 'You are absolutely right.' At that moment he looked at me for the first time; it seemed that he was not expecting that response. I continued by explaining that I did not know anything about his culture and that I would like to know more about it, if he was willing to explain it to me. We didn't exchange many words more in that session, but a significant change took place at that moment.

Berg and Szabo (2005, p. 208) said that 'it is a buyer's market and the customer is always right'. During that outburst, by accepting that he was right and admitting my 'not knowing', he felt validated. In the next session he was willing to start a conversation. Both our curiosities were engaged: He realised that I was truly curious about him, and that made him curious about what could happen during these discussions.

FIGURE 25.4 Expressing anger.
(Credit: Xochitl Ricart)

FIGURE 25.5 Allowing openness.
(Credit: Xochitl Ricart)

From 'not knowing' to complimenting

Everybody is a genius. But if you judge a fish by its ability to climb a tree it will live its whole life believing that it is stupid.

(Albert Einstein)

FIGURE 25.6
(Credit: Xochitl Ricart)

FIGURE 25.7
(Credit: Xochitl Ricart)

In my experience, students in Singapore public schools as well as students in international schools start cooperating more when discussions focus on their strengths. Students realise that we genuinely see a more capable side of them, and they begin to reflect that view in their behaviour.

I noticed that this posture of 'not knowing' was a very helpful tool for finding students' strengths, which I could later use in complimenting them. The following are examples of using some aspects of this 'not knowing' posture for finding strengths.

Openness. One of the Korean students referred to me would not look at me at all in the beginning. By being open to a different interpretation of the behaviour and accepting it as a natural part of the culture, I was able to find strengths in the few words uttered by the student. The fact that I maintained an open, comfortable attitude about this behaviour, and at the same time continued complimenting the student's strengths in each session, allowed the student to slowly open up in ways consistent with the Korean culture. Eventually, a strong counselling relationship developed between us, and the student started to meet the behaviour required by the school.

Curiosity. By maintaining a curious attitude about the students' words and their world, some Singaporean and other Western and Asian students were able to look at difficult emotions (e.g., anxiety, feeling overwhelmed) in a different way (e.g., exploring when they had felt similar body sensations in other moments of their lives). Because they were thinking differently, they were able to identify present or past successes in seemingly unrelated areas (e.g., sports or school activities). From the strengths and successes found, I could give them 'reality-based compliments'

(De Jong & Berg, 2013) that allowed them to discover culturally appropriate ways of behaving within the situation they needed to deal with.

Compliments. Since sessions created an open, curious environment, and there was a focus on strengths and compliments (both individual and cultural), some students started naturally to include strength-based comments in their language. Sometimes, while they were relating their experiences, as they shared their difficult moments, they also shared their proud ones. They were instinctively sharing what was better, which created a virtuous cycle of complimenting.

'Not knowing' as a lifelong process

De Jong and Berg (2013) mention that learning how to adopt and maintain this 'not knowing' posture is a lifelong process. The following is an example of an incident that happened years after I started using this 'not knowing' posture more consciously in the schools.

On one occasion a student wanted to make an appointment with me due to a 'writing problem'. I immediately thought this was not a counselling problem and I was about to refer the student to the school's learning support team, when luckily I allowed my 'not knowing', curious attitude to take the lead, and arranged an appointment for the next day. It ended up being an anxiety-related writing problem. We explored other situations and possibilities during the session, and I complimented the student about his strengths.

The student approached me again voluntarily a few weeks later. Upon arrival, I asked what was better about the 'writing issue'. The student looked at me puzzled and mentioned that the writing problem did not bother him anymore; he was coming for a different issue this time. I was happy that the 'not knowing' posture had helped me to be present for a student, so he could find his own solutions.

Examples like the previous one keep reminding me that this need to remain constantly alert is certainly a lifelong process, especially when working with students from cultures different than our own. It reinforces the fact that 'to re-invent life . . . to ask students and really hear about their worlds is not easy . . . it requires courage, risk and commitment' (Valenti Batlle, 1994, p. 49). But it is such a rewarding commitment that we keep on finding our own strength to remain in our 'not knowing' attitude.

References

Berg, I. K., & Szabo, P. (2005). *Brief coaching for lasting solutions*. New York, NY: W.W. Norton & Company.

De Jong, P., & Berg, I.K. (2013). *Interviewing for solutions* (4th ed.). Belmont CA: Brooks/Cole, Cengage Learning.

Metcalf, L. (1995). *Counseling towards solutions*. San Francisco CA: Jossey-Bass.

Valenti Batlle, M.T. (1994). *¿Quién educa a los educadores?* [Who educates the educators?]. Santo Domingo, Dominican Republic: Susaeta.

26

SOLUTIONS FOR CHALLENGING DILEMMAS IN CAMBODIAN EDUCATION

Bradley Barrett

A quick drive through the city of Phnom Penh and one is immediately reminded of the problems of living in this city. There is the dust, the traffic, the ankle-deep sewage when it rains, and the flies collecting over unrefrigerated meat being sold on the street corners. Considering the fact that only 40 years ago Cambodia endured a horrific season of genocide led by Pol Pot's Khmer Rouge (Ly, 2003), one begins to appreciate the magnitude of the problems in Cambodia. Despair is not an uncommon reaction to the grim picture depicted above, and no one feels it more than the Khmer people themselves. With the twentieth-century horrors faced by this country, it is not surprising that pathology tests have labelled whole communities of Cambodians with Post Traumatic Stress Disorder, which includes many children who were not yet alive to face the genocidal travesty (Mellen, 2012). Here, problems run deep and wide, and local education has not been spared. For the majority of Cambodian youth, a public education is all that is economically feasible, and this substandard primary education leaves them unprepared to face the academic rigors of university and acquire gainful employment (Jeong, 2014). Yet, as one who has lived and worked in Cambodia for six years, I am struck by their resilience and resourcefulness. For many young students, a drive to succeed permeates all they do. As a school counsellor, it is important to engage these students in a dialogue that empowers them to recognise their own talents, draw from existing resources and envision a future where their lives are conduits of change for Cambodia.

Given the problem-saturated environment in Cambodia, it seems all the more important to consider how a solution-focused approach could make a significant impact in schools and in the individual lives of students. I'm curious how we can help these young people build a hopeful future instead of merely getting over their horrific past (de Shazer, 1988). It will likely prove to be an important journey of individual and personal resilience. This journey to envision a hopeful future, one small step at a time, may prove to be the catalyst for significant change.

One such attempted solution to the poor public education is the development of private educational institutions, such as Logos International School, where I work. Logos School exists, along with its umbrella organisation, Asian Hope, to bring quality holistic education to Cambodian youth. It not only prepares them for university and significant employment, but offers them the tools and character to be the very embodiment of solutions that this country needs. Solution-focused brief therapy (SFBT) is a very natural fit to the context in which I have the privilege to counsel many Asian youth as they seek solutions to problems and experience positive change. This chapter will comprise brief examples of common problems Cambodian students face and illustrations of how SFBT has been effective in this setting.

Integration of SFBT in a Cambodian school

Being excluded. With a deep yearning to be included, youth of all ages find it stressful to be excluded from peer groups. Many young Khmer youth may find it particularly daunting to be excluded from peer support if it proves to be their primary support structure. With many Cambodian parents struggling to repair their past while navigating the challenges of rearing children, a significant number of Cambodian children find themselves experiencing an emotional chasm between themselves and their parents (Field, 2013). This chasm exacerbates the exclusion experienced at school and increases their distress. In addressing this challenge, I have found SFBT extremely effective.

CF makes a difference. The first few complaints about Duong being excluded came from a concerned friend (CF): 'I thought my class was including everyone, but now I realise I was wrong.' When CF asked how he could help Duong, I facilitated a solution-focused conversation.

Therapist:	What you want is for Duong to be more included with your peer group?
CF:	Ya, I mean, I like him but I know some others don't.
Therapist:	What difference would that make if he were included?
CF:	It would mean he could be happy and not so down all the time.
Therapist:	Okay, that would be a good difference for him. What about for you?
CF:	I would be able to hang out with him and my other friends and not have to choose. Like this Friday, my friends want to go to the mall but they told me not to bring Duong.
Therapist:	You don't want to choose between hanging out with Duong and your other friends?
CF:	Ya.
Therapist:	What else would be better if he were more included?
CF:	I wouldn't have to stick up for him. I will say things like, 'He's just trying to help us be closer to God.' They don't like to feel judged.
Therapist:	So, you wouldn't have to stick up for him?
CF:	Not all the time, anyway.
Therapist:	What would you be doing instead?
CF:	I don't know, I'd be just talking normal stuff with my friends.
Therapist:	Who would be the first to notice when you were just talking normal stuff?
CF:	Probably Navy. He's the one who's the meanest to Duong.
Therapist:	What would Navy do that would let you know he noticed?
CF:	He would talk more with me.
Therapist:	It's encouraging that you want to help Duong connect better with his peers. Tell me about the times when Duong was more included? What was different about those times?

Exceptions surfaced, and there were at least a dozen times where Duong was not excluded. When I asked what was different about these times where Duong was included, a very obvious pattern emerged. With the clarity of this pattern of behaviour, I worked with the concerned friend and prepared him to engage Duong in a series of solution-focused questions that helped

Duong explore acceptable alternative behaviour. CF reported back about a week later that Duong was getting along much better with a particular student and his peer group was more accepting.

Pressure to succeed. In an Asian context it is not unusual to have extremely motivated students who are eager to excel in all subjects with the hopes of securing a spot in a top university, with its promise of a lucrative career. Cambodia is no exception. For many of these students the only ones more motivated and determined to see them excel are their parents. In an environment where so many have sacrificed so much to create a better future for themselves and their family, parents can be found crossing the line from child advocate to academic dictator. This extreme pressure to succeed sometimes creates conflict and intense emotions for Cambodian adolescents.

Malai wants balance. It was not unusual for me to see Malai looking stressed. In light of her academic aspirations and the pressure she received at home to succeed, Malai lived with a certain level of stress day in and day out. However, on the day she came into my office to 'just talk', I sensed that the academic stress and pressures from home had reached a boiling point.

Malai:	SATs are stressing me out.
Therapist:	How can I help you with that?
Malai:	Well, I need more help with my English and the essay section.
Therapist:	Do you have someone you can ask for help?
Malai:	Ya, I need to ask them before the weekend.
Therapist:	What is it that you hope to improve in your current situation?
Malai:	(Tears begin to well in her eyes) It is so stressful at home right now. My mum paid for me to take the SAT and she expects me to study every waking moment.
Therapist:	Wow, that's a lot of studying!
Malai:	I just wish she would see that I am trying so hard. I don't always study as hard as I could, or as hard as she wants, but I need some break times too.
Therapist:	It sounds like you are working really, really hard to prepare for the SAT.
Malai:	I am but it's not good enough for my mum. She wants me to study morning, noon, and night and still do my regular chores and regular studies.
Therapist:	It sounds like you want your mum to see that you're trying really hard.
Malai:	Ya, and to realise that I do care about my future and getting into a good college but I need a little balance between study and friends.
Therapist:	You want her to know you care about your future and allow some balance between studying and being with friends.
Malai:	That would be good but it won't happen, she just keeps pushing and pushing. When I get home I just want to take a five minute break and she sees me sitting there and starts complaining that I need to get going on my studies.
Therapist:	What difference would it make if she recognises how hard you're working?
Malai:	It would let me know that she is proud of me and knows I'm doing my best. But I know that my best just isn't good enough.
Therapist:	What would be the first sign that she recognises your hard work and wants to help you find this balance?
Malai:	She would help with my chores if she expects me to study so much extra for the SAT. She helped my sister when she was studying for the SAT but for some reason she expects more from me.

I asked the miracle question to help paint a clearer picture of Malai's preferred future. Her vivid portrait of a future without the problem included a contented peace, a smiling, helpful mother, a study schedule that both Malai and her mum agreed upon, and a weekend with a few hours to spend with friends. Particularly interesting was her description of a conversation she would be having with her mother at the breakfast table. This conversation included a time of encouraging one another and compromising on the daily chores to be done. After complimenting Malai on creating such a vivid preferred future, the following conversation ensued using scaling questions.

Therapist: Malai, on a scale of 1–10 where '10' is this wonderful picture you described happening on a consistent basis and '1' being about the worst you can imagine, where are you on the scale?

Malai: 4, I guess.

Therapist: How come 4 and not 3?

Malai: I know that my mum does care. She's just so concerned that I get above the average SAT score so I can get scholarships for university.

Therapist: What else?

Malai: I know that this major pressure will be gone once I take the SAT in October.

Therapist: So you recognise that your mum cares and you see a light at the end of the tunnel?

Malai: I do get to have some time with friends, just very little without my mum calling to ask when I am getting home to study.

I continued to explore her existing resources and exceptions using scaling and relationship questions. When asked where she would like to be on the scale within the next 10 or so days, she smiled and positively announced that she believed she could reach a 7. Malai felt that one important sign that she was at a 7 would be a compromise between her and her mum on a study schedule, one in which they could both agree. As a small step within 24 hours that would increase her chances of reaching that 7 on her scale, Malai made a commitment to talk to her mum about making this schedule. After the weekend I asked a more refreshed-looking Malai, 'What was better?' and she reported having made the schedule and enjoying some uninterrupted social time over the weekend. Taking a few moments to amplify and reinforce her progress allowed her to see the value of continuing to do what's working.

Conclusion

Like many problem-saturated contexts, it is tempting to look at the problems we face in detail, hoping that by taking a microscopic look at the challenge, small details will be seen, analysed and found to offer insight that will address the concern. In Cambodia, the problems many face on a daily basis are so great that most do not know where to begin. With challenges mounting, it is encouraging to know that there is an alternative to focusing on the problem – a focus on solutions. When we focus on solutions we see that there is a possible future to be embraced, differences that make a difference, goals to be set and small steps to help us get there. As an educator and school counsellor in Cambodia it has become increasingly clear to me that a student body that is expected to support each another, work extremely hard and take the reins of this country and lead it to greener pastures needs to be a student body that knows how to find solutions to the problems of today and the challenges of tomorrow. A positive, hopeful future is possible, one student at a time, one step at a time.

References

de Shazer, S. (1988). *Clues: Investigating solutions in brief therapy*. New York, NY: W.W. Norton.

Field, N.P. (2013). Parental styles in the intergenerational transmission of trauma stemming from the Khmer Rouge regime in Cambodia. *American Journal of Orthopsychiatry, 83*(4), 483–494.

Jeong, H. (2014). Legacy of Khmer Rouge on skill formation in Cambodia. *Journal of International and Area Studies, 21*(1), 1–19.

Ly, B. (2003). Devastated vision(s): The Khmer Rouge scopic regime in Cambodia. *Art Journal, 62*(1), 66–81.

Mellen, G. (2012, Apr 22). *PTSD from Cambodia's killing fields affects kids who were never there*. Long Beach Press Telegram. Retrieved from http://www.presstelegram.com/technology/20120422/ptsd-from-cambodias-killing-fields-affects-kids-who-were-never-there.

27

RESETTING THE BAR

Solution-focused scaling with children in Hong Kong

Emily Meadows

You come to Hong Kong because you're very good at what you do.

This maxim clarifies the wealth of high-achieving professionals who move their families to the cosmopolitan 'Pearl of the Orient' in order to advance their careers. Hong Kong attracts the ambitious, the well connected and the brilliant. Families come from around the world and across Asia to the fast-paced city of Hong Kong. And they all require schools for their children.

As a primary school counsellor at a prominent international school in Hong Kong, I have the privilege of supporting the very youngest of these children. Culturally, Hong Kong breeds high expectations and extraordinary standards; we are accustomed to success. However, all children encounter challenge as part of the learning process, and this can unsettle even the most confident. In my practice, I redirect the focus from flaws, weaknesses and worries toward assets, potential and growth.

This chapter illustrates how solution-focused (SF) counselling marries with a competitive college preparatory school setting, and why the developmental traits of early childhood lend themselves to SF work. Anchored in practical examples, the chapter outlines various applications of a scaling tool designed for use with children as young as four years old, revealing how solution-focused counselling can benefit one of the most perfectionistic populations in the world.

The what

SF scaling tools are basic instruments that offer a sort of litmus test on how a person perceives their personal situation. The tool I created for use with young children (see Figure 27.1) is simple and covers the main elements of their life in early childhood.

An initial session with a student might produce something similar to the scale pictured in Figure 27.2. The counsellor also has the option to write notes in the margin from the session. For example, one young student struggled with his parents' expectation that he would sit for 90 minutes each evening to complete homework assigned by a private tutor. I asked the student to mark on the scale how he was feeling about home and school, which reflected this frustration. The smiling face indicates positive feelings, and the frowning face indicates negative feelings. Through use of scaling, the student was able to suppose what it would look like to bump up his current mark. Rather than eliminating the cultural expectation that young children should be doing homework each night, the child was able to identify a coping strategy (keeping a soft toy in his lap while working), and moved up the scale by using his own resources to find a solution.

Should a follow-up session be applicable, the child may be invited to mark their updated responses on the same sheet as was used in the initial meeting (see Figure 27.3). This allows both child and counsellor to identify areas of growth, or notice where more support may be required.

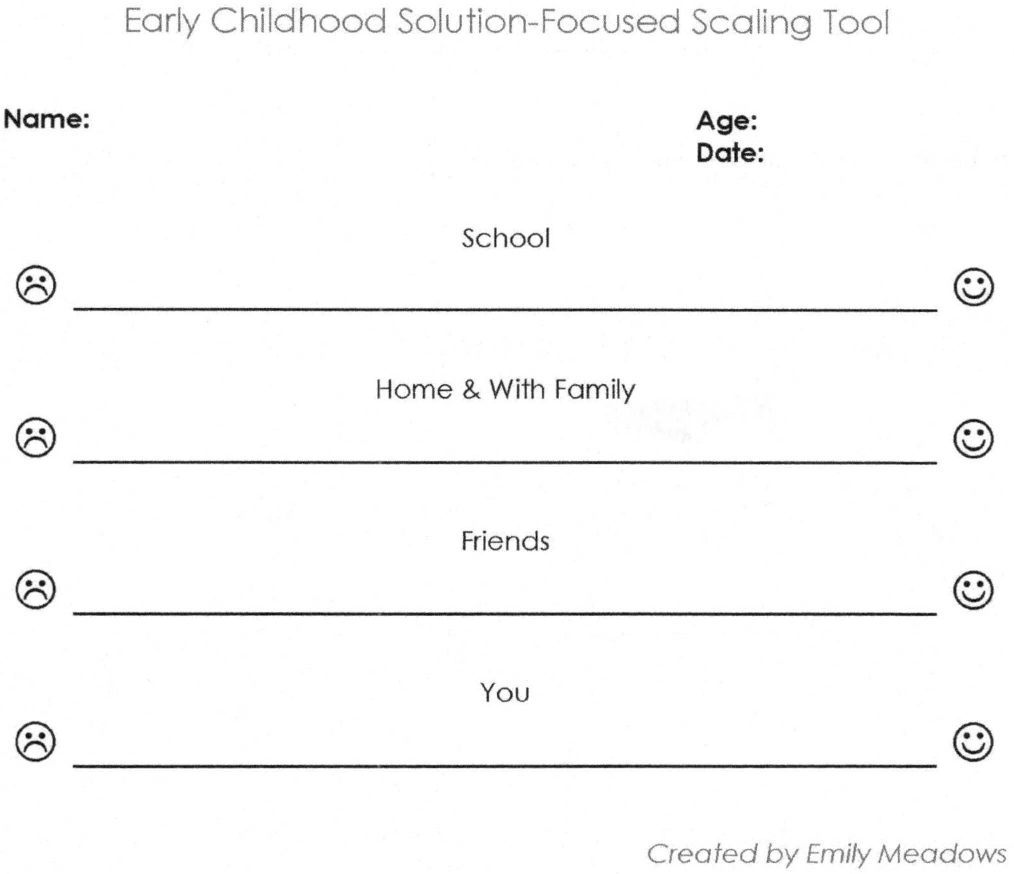

Early Childhood Solution-Focused Scaling Tool

Name: **Age:**
                                                     Date:

School

☹ _____ ☺

Home & With Family

☹ _____ ☺

Friends

☹ _____ ☺

You

☹ _____ ☺

Created by Emily Meadows

FIGURE 27.1 Early childhood solution-focused scaling tool.
(Credit: Emily Meadows)

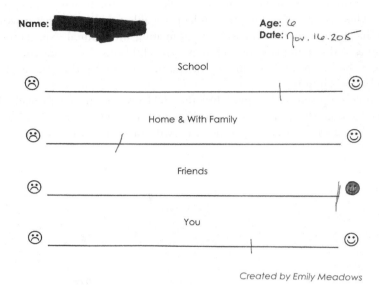

FIGURE 27.2 Solution-focused scaling tool at initial session.
(Credit: Emily Meadows)

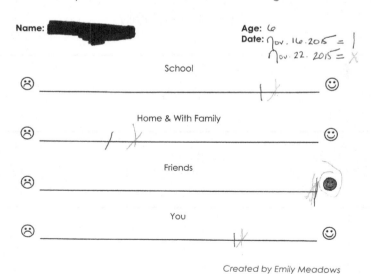

FIGURE 27.3 Solution-focused scaling tool at follow-up session.
(Credit: Emily Meadows)

The when, how and why

The scaling tool can be used in various situations with a student who is not yet reading or writing. Minimal verbal skills are required, a relief for younger children who may require time to warm up in a conversation. For counsellors stretched thin with heavy case loads, scaling allows for brief and effective interactions with students, and provides direction for the next steps, without the student missing valuable instructional time. The following examples show how an SF scaling tool was used in a variety of situations with Asian students.

Anxiety and perfectionism. In our school, where admissions are competitive, there is a prolific sub-industry of private businesses touting interview skills and test preparation for 3-year-olds. Imperfections must be concealed and limitations quickly targeted and remedied. Children are tempted with rewards such as an outing to Hong Kong Disneyland or Ocean Park if they perform as they have been trained to during intake screenings. The pressure is intense, and, once admitted, these children join the ranks of privileged students from around Asia who will start their education amongst the elite.

As unpalatable as the admissions process sounds, it is the reality of pre-school in Hong Kong. The determination to achieve near-perfect standards loads children with an unrealistic expectation of how to please others. They may become hyperaware of small mistakes, and self-esteem is compromised. With students who have been referred to their counsellor for anxiety, low confidence or perfectionism, they are initially hesitant to take risks. While often very bright, these children may still prefer the stock answer, 'I don't know', or even silence, rather than put themselves in a vulnerable position where they might make a mistake. They tend to stick within the boundaries of the familiar, which can be deleterious when the aim is to stretch and grow.

One young Asian student, referred for anxiety, was apprehensive about meeting with me, and direct eye contact was culturally too aggressive for her. We sat side-by-side, and I kept my focus on the tool instead of directly looking at the student. As this child had also been through multiple transitions before arriving in Hong Kong, I helped ease her apprehension by explaining what the session would be composed of, and what to anticipate. 'First, I will ask you to pick out a colour of pen that you like, then I will ask you to mark your thoughts on a paper. At the end, we can play something from my collection of games.'

The scaling tool offered relief from the black/white, right/wrong thinking common among perfectionistic students, and provided an unlimited spectrum of acceptable choices. The student responded positively to a non-judgmental stance, which increased her comfort.

Limited language skills. Young children are still developing the diverse vocabulary necessary to fully express themselves. They may have strong feelings, but often lack the specific words to describe them. They may be aware that something is amiss, but are uncertain how to talk about it, especially to an adult they may not know well.

In addition to the considerations of early language development, it is common for international schools in Asia to offer modified programs for English Language Learners. Many local families seek an Anglophone education for their child so as to increase their prospects of eventually attending a prestigious university abroad. This has led to a proliferation of schools where students are learning English as a second – or even third – language. Professional counsellors are responsible for cultivating these students' social and emotional growth, irrespective of whether they are trained in working with speakers of other languages.

In using the scaling tool, it is important to use the child's vocabulary and elicit familiar words to describe both ends of the scale: 'What does it mean when you smile?' If the child gives an answer in a language you do not understand, this provides an opportunity for her to become an 'expert' within your office, which can strengthen the connection between you and will encourage early language learners.

The SF scaling tool eliminates the need for complex language, and can bridge the gap between a child's inner thoughts and their outward expression. Simple words such as 'family', 'school', 'you' and 'friends' make the tool accessible to almost any child. This accessibility facilitates professionals' understanding and support of children from a variety of linguistic backgrounds.

Relationship-building/alliance-forming. Parents who have elected to send their children to our school are typically supportive and collaborative with the educational professionals who care for their child. This facilitates a smoother connection between the child and the school counsellor.

However, young children's bonds are strongest with their primary caretakers. Once a child becomes comfortable with regular attendance at school, usually by age 3 in Hong Kong, connections also begin to form with their educational caretakers. The classroom teacher, the specialist teachers and other trustworthy adults usually become a part of the child's support circle.

With many early childhood programs in Asia falling short of the 250-to-1 student-to-counsellor ratio recommended by the American School Counselor Association (2005, p. 70), students are often not familiar with their school counsellor. They may have met them, but will likely be unaware of their role, and possibly be uncomfortable with meeting them directly. An SF scaling tool allows the counsellor to demonstrate sincere interest in the child and to begin to develop an alliance, while moving into the work of assessment. While some children will benefit from an even softer approach, perhaps beginning with a game or a story, most are drawn into the relationship-building nature of the scaling activity and quickly catch on that the counsellor's intent is safe and supportive in nature.

Depending on the cultural background of the counsellor, Asian families may seem relatively private. To bridge the gap with a reserved child, I take note of various hobbies, interests or personal experiences the child makes reference to, as these can serve as means in getting to know her. Parents may be wary of receiving a phone call from their child's counsellor, as they may interpret this as a sign that something is wrong. When contacting parents regarding their child, a scaling tool allows me to focus on the positives that their child inherently possesses and highlight the resources they have already identified to me in the SF process.

Cultivating a growth mind-set. Stakeholders in a child's future are apt to look for concrete indicators of success. We often use report cards, test scores and other hard measures to communicate whether or not standards and expectations are being met. With competitive international Pre-K through Grade 12 institutions being perceived as so-called 'feeder schools' for the Ivy League and other brand-name universities, there is a tendency to expect consistently exceptional results. Teachers and parents alike are highly invested in the child's education, and want to ensure that they meet the mark. In a community where parents commonly hold impressive titles, accolades and diplomas, it is implied that their children will aspire to the same.

Children, however, do not operate on a pass/fail dichotomy. They are perpetually in transit along the growth spectrum, and their success is far more nuanced than can be denoted by a series of met/unmet benchmarks. While formal assessments and their resulting scores may be valuable tools in providing information about a child's skill and knowledge base, they can also be misleading and trigger the deceptive interpretation that some children have reached the summit already and, of course, that some have not. This can be falsely satisfying or devastating to those who care deeply about a child and their future. The truth is that there isn't a precise summit. Instead, each child is on a personalised path, and our job is to meet them where they are and walk the next step with them. With this perspective, we can assist the child in their learning, regardless of their starting point. This lowers the stakes from 'passing' an arbitrary mark to the more manageable 'moving forward'.

Children in competitive Asian schools may experience some cognitive dissonance if their mark on the scaling tool does not lie at the top, as strong messages are pushing them to aim higher. Regardless of where the child's response point lies along the scale, I reinforce the validity of the answer. Clearly establish that there is no wrong answer; the child is the one who knows the most about their response, and the counsellor is learning from her. If a child senses a judgment is being made, it could impact the way they respond to future questions and skew your reading.

One child I worked with, who was very eager to please, often resisted doing school work, as she worried that she would give the wrong answers. Though she was competent in many ways, she preferred leaving a blank response over taking the risk by giving an answer she was not entirely certain about. During our first session, she was reluctant to even try the scaling tool, wary about displeasing me or putting the 'wrong' mark down. However, as she slowly warmed up to the idea, and observed that I was accepting of her responses as the 'expert', she became more confident in asserting her own voice. With time, this translated over to classroom work as well.

An SF scaling tool illustrates and reinforces the growth mind-set concept; that is, we all possess the agency to move forward, accumulating competence and confidence as we progress, rather than completing any singular achievement. Parents, teachers, and children discover gratification in the understanding that a child is not 100 per cent happy/unhappy or successful/unsuccessful in any given situation, but is working to develop tools and strategies to keep them on a positive course.

Conclusion

Using the scaling tool is a powerful way to connect with young children, especially international students where language barriers may pose a challenge. It is a simple instrument that can be used in multiple ways to promote growth and development. This chapter demonstrated the use of a scaling tool with young students in various situations and with those with minimal words. By using this tool, children were able to respond in a way that led to increased confidence, feelings of safety, and anxiety management. The scaling tool helped them to 'reset the bar'.

Reference

American School Counselor Association. (2005). *The ASCA national model: A framework for school counseling programs* (2nd ed.). Alexandria, VA: Author.

28

THE MELDING OF TWO DIFFERENT CULTURES

Finding balance between school and home

Patricia Joudrey

I am a school counsellor at an International School in Chennai, India, and work with Asian students attending the school. Asian students in international schools grapple with melding two very different cultures, the one that they go home to at night and the one that they face during the day. In the following chapter, the effectiveness of using solution-focused brief therapy will be demonstrated using a case example of an Asian student to demonstrate how to address culturally sensitive issues and find the balance between the home and school cultures.

Creating the preferred future with students

Imagine yourself in a time and space when your problem is solved . . . your difficulty no longer exists! What are you doing? Who is the first to notice? What would they say?

This new and imagined reality enables students to contemplate change in a unique and unthreatening way. The creation of their best hope in the student's mind allows the scenario to become real and the future to be realised in the present.

Student: I would wake up with a smile and say good morning to my mother!'
Counsellor: What would your mother say in response to that?
Student: She'd say good morning and we'd have breakfast together.'
Counsellor: What difference would this make?
Student: I'd feel good. It would make me happy. I like having breakfast with my mother.

By constructing the hopeful future, a student was able to see the small beginnings of her imagined reality. Focusing on what to do when the problem is solved makes it possible for a student to be aware, to act and to change in a positive way in the present. Asian students are not used to being asked what they want and often have difficulty expressing their own opinions. They are used to having their parents tell them what to do and how to solve their problems. Helping them to see a glimpse of their possible desired changes allows them to think of possibilities, which leads to forward movement and small signs of progress. Including the parents' perspective acknowledges the parents' position as one of a supporter and respects their authority, both important aspects of Asian families.

Various cultures under one roof

As a school counsellor at an international school in Chennai, with over 30 nationalities attending, two of the most common issues are student adjustment and transition. Only when a new student is feeling comfortable, safe and at 'home' is that student able to be motivated and focus on the actual learning at hand. Manoeuvring through this transition while going through the personal and physical changes that accompany adolescence, and maintaining a high academic standing, are simultaneous challenges these Asian students face. SFBT works well with adolescents as it allows students to determine solutions for themselves while maintaining their cultural values and, consequently, to know what changes they need to make to get there. Adolescents appreciate this process, and the autonomy they attain.

The school system in which I work has various inherent expectations for students, such as having self-advocacy, asking questions in class, having homework done on time, seeking help when one is experiencing difficulties and taking responsibility for one's own learning. However, these are not the same expectations that one finds in an Indian or Asian school system. In an Asian school context, the behavioural expectation in the classroom is such that the teacher is considered the 'guru', one who imparts knowledge, and the student accepts and regurgitates the information for assessments and does not question the teacher. The class size is often very large in Asian schools, and hence it is difficult for the teacher to be on top of each student's progress and homework submissions. An Asian student, therefore, is grappling with melding two very different cultures, the one that they go home to at night and the one that they face during the day. When homework is regularly not completed, or a student is reluctant to participate in class, or when a student does not seek out extra help when they need it, teachers will sometimes refer a student for counselling to see if there is another issue underlying the behaviour. On the surface, this appears to be lack of motivation, and resistance to learning, even to the point of defiance of a teacher's direction. However, from an Asian child's world, discussions with the teacher in class and coming in at lunch or after school and 'asking' for help is very foreign to them. Admitting this to their parents or teachers could lead to scolding or shame.

Mary's development and self-discovery

Mary, a middle school student from Korea, had difficulties in getting work turned in on time. She also turned in homework that was clearly copied from the web. Mary's teachers met with her and explained the importance of responsibility, digital citizenship and being honest in her work. However, Mary did not make the appropriate changes and was again caught cheating and plagiarising a few weeks later. She was referred to me, the counsellor. The teachers wanted to learn more about why she continued to make the same choices for herself when she knew it was wrong and to help her make better choices for herself.

The following is a brief summary of how a solution-focused process enabled Mary to find her own solutions to her problem.

Mary explained that the reason she cheated was that she didn't have enough time to do her homework at home. Each morning her mum woke her up at 4:30 a.m. when she left for church and again at 6:30 a.m. when she returned, to get her up for school. As a part of their Korean values, it was important for Mary's mum to maintain her daily attendance at the Korean church services while living in India. Typical of many Korean fathers who are sent by their companies to work in India, Mary's father was often travelling and worked extremely long hours, and consequently was unavailable to support Mary at home. So it was important for Mary's mother to make sure Mary knew where she was at all times. However, Mary was perpetually tired. All she wanted to do was to fall asleep when she got home and she did not do her homework. Every day after school, she would fight with her mum and did not want to answer her barrage of questions, and she would end up going to her room to sleep.

Counsellor:	Suppose this session was really helpful for you, what do you want better as a result of talking to me?
Mary:	I would get my homework done and not get in trouble with the teachers. I wouldn't cheat any more.
Counsellor:	What difference would that make?
Student:	I would be happier, my teachers would be happy, and my mum would be happy.
Counsellor:	If you were one small step closer to being happier, what would we be talking about?
Student:	We would be talking about getting my homework done and being honest to teachers.
Counsellor:	What would you be doing differently when you are happier?
Mary:	I would be talking to my mum, I would say hello to my teacher when I came into class. . . .
Counsellor:	What would your mum notice about you when you are happier?
Mary:	I would talk to her, answer her questions . . .
Counsellor:	What difference would this make?
Mary:	I would tell her about not having time to do my homework and I could be honest with her. If she knew that the reason I couldn't get my homework done was because she wakes me up so early every day, then maybe she wouldn't do that anymore. Then I would not be tired and I could get my homework done.
Counsellor:	So if you were able to tell your mom about your problems, this would help you with homework and not get into trouble with your teacher? Is that something you would like to change? Is that something you would like to work on today?
Mary:	Yes.
Counsellor:	I'm going to ask you a very strange question, and you will need to use your best imagination. Suppose after you get home from school and this evening go to bed at your normal time, and while you were sleeping a miracle happens. This miracle is that all the problems that we have talked about today have been solved. But because this has happened when you are asleep you don't know it has happened. When you wake up in the morning, who will be the first to notice that things have improved?
Mary:	My mum
Counsellor:	What would she notice?
Mary:	I would say 'good morning'.

Counsellor: What difference would that make?

Mary: When I talk to my Mum, she likes it. She likes to ask me a lot of questions about school. She would think I'm doing better.

We explored the positive differences this would make and how it would improve things at home. She realised that it was important to explain things to her mum. We explored the differences it would make at school.

Counsellor: Who will be the first to notice things were better at school?

Mary: My teachers and my friends would notice because I would smile and say hello to them.

Counsellor: What else?

Student: I would be friendlier to my teacher. I would be able to say the truth about why I handed in my work like that.

We explored the courage it took for Mary to talk to her teachers about her situation and how that would improve things for her at school and at home.

Counsellor: On a scale of 1–10, with 10 being you are very comfortable talking to your teachers and you know what to say, and 1 is you are not comfortable and you don't know what to say, where are you now?

Mary: At 3.

Counsellor: How did you get to 3?

Mary: It's not that I don't want to talk. I want to tell my mum that I'm afraid to tell my teachers the truth about why I cheated and that I'm sorry.

Counsellor: What else?

Mary's transformation

Mary successfully negotiated with her mum to answer only one question each evening at home. She was able to tell her mom that it was too difficult for her to wake up at 4:30 a.m. each morning and that this was affecting her ability to get her homework done. She was able to tell her teacher what happened about her plagiarising and cheating and she was able to apologise. She also told her teacher that she wanted to have a better relationship and rebuild the trust. Mary felt good that her strength of character could now be used to resolve her difficulty and pull her through the consequences that she had to accept as a result of her plagiarism.

Mary and her mom were able to continue with the agreement, and Mary was able to complete her homework each night. Mary was able to feel happier and confident both at home and school. Her relationship with her mum and teachers improved over time.

These changes that Mary made resulted in her being happier, and she came into my office with smiles on her face after this. There were still occasions that she didn't complete her homework but Mary was able to tell the teacher the reason for it and accept the consequences. She wasn't sent to the office after this. Mary was now smiling in the corridors and answering more than the minimum one question to her mum. As a result of these sessions, Mary was able to integrate her own unique cultural home routines and interactions with the school's expectations of homework and communication with teachers. A once timid, trapped and non-assertive girl developed into a more open, more honest and happier student and daughter.

Conclusion

One of SFBT's basic assumptions is that the solution is not always directly related to the problem. When Mary first stepped into my office, the solution seemed clear to the teacher – that if Mary understood the consequences of her plagiarism, then she would not repeat the action. However, the real solution came with Mary being able to communicate with her mother.

The Asian sense of respect and duty of a child to their parents is a wonderful and strong cultural bond among family members. However, this Asian expectation sometimes seems to conflict with the expectations that students put on themselves. It is therefore, even more important that communication between child and parents, and teacher with child and parents, be strong. On the other hand, empathy and understanding of where an Asian student is coming from is equally important. Mary's work with the counsellor facilitated her development to openly communicate with her mother and with her teacher, something that was culturally difficult for her, but which solved her problems that she was facing at school. Mary was able to successfully manoeuvre through both her cultural family obligations and school challenges and make her own goals based on her own cultural context of what was right for her.

29

PRIMARY-AGED STUDENTS FIND SOLUTIONS IN ASIA

Colleen Steigerwald

Our lives are sustained by what we hope for. I have witnessed Asian students finding solutions to their problems within the school setting after discovering their capabilities, strengths and resources. As a school counsellor, I see the student as the expert and I work collaboratively with them. I take a not-knowing stance, which allows the student to find their own solutions. For many Asian children this is a paradigm shift, as culturally the idea that Asian children are 'seen and not heard' still prevails. With the right tools, Asian children can identify what works, when things are better, what they want and how they might get there. In this chapter I will highlight my work with primary-school-aged Asian students and how they found hope in their troubling situations.

Culturally adaptive students

Some common issues that arise in working in a multi-cultural school setting revolve around being a third-culture kid (TCK) (Pollock & Van Reken, 2009), transitions, varied cultural differences and academic expectations. Many of our Asian students are TCKs, in that they have lived in different countries with multiple experiences of having to adjust to new schools and making new friends. One of the unique features of TCKs is their ability to adapt and be flexible. To best support these culturally diverse students from Asia, solution focused (SF) practice is ideal, in that we focus on how they are able to adapt and how their experiences can be utilised in the present. This sense of control and view of competence through uncertain times reinforces self-efficacy and builds confidence.

Supporting culturally diverse students

As a school counsellor, I support Asian students within a broad range of academic, behavioural and social-emotional issues. These include learning difficulties, executive functioning difficulties, anxiety, autism spectrum disorders and emotional regulation. With Asian students who have lived abroad in many different countries, I find that the SF approach allows me to stay focused on their abilities and capabilities to help them successfully manage their difficulties, and my curiosity enables me to explore this, rather than focusing on the complexities of their life.

Building confidence with Jane

Jane, aged 9, was an adopted child from Indonesia. She did not develop secure attachments living in an orphanage and wore down her adoptive parents with endless tantrums at home. Her mother described frequent hour-long tantrums, which included screaming and sobbing. At school Jane did not have tantrums but would frequently tell lies and occasionally steal.

The teacher found handwritten notes in Jane's desk that read, 'I hate myself'. The problems were many and layered. Trying to understand the root of the problems could take years and lead nowhere. My time with Jane focused on building a predictable and caring relationship, highlighting the things that were going well, and clarifying what Jane wanted. Adhering to the SF approach, every time we met I began with, 'What's better?' I was never disappointed as she eagerly shared her stories.

Despite the struggles, I discovered there were many positive things in Jane's life. She could sing beautifully, loved to perform and loved to read. When I consulted her mother, we quickly got lost in the problems. I complimented the mother for maintaining such strong hope for her child, in spite of the difficulties. This hope strengthened the parent and also reassured the child.

With young children, the miracle question is a very powerful tool when asked in a very simple way. With Jane, it allowed her to imagine what she would do or feel when things improved for her. I asked Jane this question when we discussed the 'lying problem'.

C: What will be different tomorrow morning after the miracle happens?
Jane: I would feel proud, Mum would be amazed, people at school would be happy to know exactly what happened, and it would be less stressful for me and my mum.
C: When things are less stressful for you and your mum, what would happen instead?
Jane: I would feel calm . . .
C: Tell me more . . .

The tantrums at home did not totally stop; however, they occurred with less intensity because Jane explored what calmed her. Finding what worked and doing more of it led to hope and lasting change. Jane's mother supported the changes Jane identified that helped her to stay calm instead of telling her what she should do.

Building courage with Tanvi

Tanvi, aged 8, came to my office almost daily during recess. Tanvi avoided the playground because she believed she had no friends and that nobody liked her. She felt hopeless. We built a picture of what she wanted with lots of details.

C: How will you know when things are better and you don't have to come here?
Tanvi: I'll have friends that I can play with.

I took out a list of students in Tanvi's class and asked her to circle the names of students whom she had played with, or who had been kind to her. She circled one name.

C: What difference will it make if you play with this girl?
Tanvi: Then I will know that someone likes me.

Tanvi began to see possibilities, and one week later, she was back in my office during recess, proudly declaring she had asked the girl to play and she seemed really pleased. I was genuinely impressed and complimented Tanvi on her courage.

Compliments are an important part of every interaction I have with my students. Compliments acknowledge that there are things going right, despite the difficulties. Validating what students are doing right gives them hope and confidence to change. In my experience Asian parents do not typically compliment their children as they believe it may create laziness and the children may stop trying. As a result, Asian students may struggle with accepting a compliment. A genuine and trusting relationship between the student and counsellor is necessary for this to be an effective tool.

Building self-management with Hwan

Unlike Jane and Tanvi, Hwan (aged 10) did not meet with me willingly. His teacher referred him because of a bald patch on the crown of his head. It was not necessary for me to discover why Hwan was twirling and pulling out his hair because in SF work, there is not necessarily a connection between the reason for the behaviour and the solution. Hwan already knew that when he wore a cap, there was a physical barrier that stopped the hair pulling. The challenge was, Hwan did not want to wear a cap to school because he felt singled out and did not want to lose face. For his Asian parents, it was difficult to let Hwan be in charge of the situation. There was one month until a long holiday, and Hwan was confident he could tackle the problem then. Having confidence and respecting the student's decision to manage the solution was a key element. When school resumed, I was not at all surprised to see that Hwan's hair had grown back as he had worn a cap over the break. I used his success as an opportunity to compliment Hwan on his ability to follow through with a goal. It was an important reminder for me that it's best to lead from behind and let the student be in charge of how fast or slow they want to go.

Shinzo takes the lead

Shinzo, aged 9, was a boy who learned to take the lead. He had significant anxiety, often triggered by thunderstorms, dark clouds and rainy weather. Living in Singapore, this is a daily occurrence, and Shinzo would end up in tears during instruction as the weather shifted from sunny to cloudy. Shinzo told me he wanted to be home, as he feared for his family's safety. As we began to discuss this 'thunderstorm problem', I asked Shinzo to tell me about the times he didn't cry. Obviously, Shinzo wasn't crying the majority of the day! He told me that when he didn't look out the window and didn't notice the dark clouds, he felt less anxious. SF therapists know that no problem happens all of the time and in looking for the exceptions to the problem Shinzo discovered a skill he already had within his reach – one he could use immediately.

C: What will your teacher notice when you keep your back to the window?
Shinzo: That I won't be crying.
C: What will you do instead?

During the next thunderstorm, Shinzo used his idea and was able to hold back the tears. Once he could identify an exception and feel a sense of control, he was able to manage the situation. This brought a sense of hope and competence.

Asian students are masterful

I find that SF tools are easily adaptable with the rich diversity of students from many parts of Asia. My students love to scale. I use scaling to check progress, to see how well things are progressing in the right direction and to better understand how a child feels about a particular situation. It does not matter where on the scale they fall. They just need to identify where they are in the moment, and together we determine what would help them move up, even a tiny bit. I have yet to work with a student that can't identify something. I am mindful that often young children want to please and will offer a number they think you want to hear. I help them describe what is happening at that point on the scale and what else could happen that would contribute to their successes. The number is insignificant; however, their awareness of how they got to where they are is important, as is their sense of accomplishment in moving up the scale. Scaling to me is like a compass. It lets me know where we are so we can determine in which direction we need to head.

Advait finds motivation

Advait, aged 10, was a student who struggled with motivation. On standardised assessments, Advait's score indicated that he was a capable student, yet his teacher complained that the quality of his work was poor. His Indian parents were frustrated with his lack of motivation towards homework and often nagged him. When Advait and I met, we scaled his motivation.

C: Advait. On a scale of 1–10, where 10 means you have all the motivation you need and 1 means none; where are you now?
Advait: With schoolwork I'm at a 3
C: How did you come up with 3?
Advait: I don't want to disappoint my parents and teachers.
C: So, you care about pleasing them?
Advait: Yes. They think I don't care at all, but I do.

We explored other indicators that he was at 3, and his energy went up. Then we explored what a 4 might look like.

C: Suppose you move to a 4. What would your teacher notice?
Advait: I would check my work in class and take time to fix mistakes.
C: What would your parents notice?

Advait: I'd do my homework without my parents nagging me.
C: On a scale of 1–10, how willing are you to experiment with this?

After a pause, he smiled.

Advait: I'm at an 8, because it would be really great if my parents stopped nagging me.

Advait found hope in a very difficult situation because he was willing to do something different and challenge himself.

Conclusion

The SF approach is simple but not easy. One of the elements that make it simple is time, as it does not require large time commitments. Students work with me as it fits within the schedule of the school day, and it's even possible to make a significant impact during a brief interaction. I have seen success using SF tools and questions with students from various corners of the Asian continent. There is no prescriptive formula; rather, the effectiveness of the various SF tools and the respectful relationship between the counsellor and the student can lead to change. Respect begins by allowing the student to be the expert on their own life, remaining curious, and empowering the student to find their strength, capabilities and resources.

Reference

Pollock, D., & Van Reken, R.E. (2009). *Third culture kids: The experience of growing up among worlds.* Boston, MA: Nicholas Brealey Publishing.

30

TURNING BULLIES INTO ALLIES

Vania M. N. Djohan

Dealing with students' problematic behaviour in school can be tricky, especially with multiple stakeholders involved, such as the parents and the school leaders. The author, a solution focused practitioner (SFP), is one of the owners of a private school in Indonesia, and uses the solution focused approach in the day-to-day running of the school. She shares two examples in which she facilitated a solution focused process to address bullying. Both examples highlight how a solution focused approach facilitated collaboration and ownership in resolving the issues among the key people involved, thus allaying the fears of concerned parents and ensuring that no parties ever lost 'face', both important factors in the Asian context. The process also demonstrates the importance of including the students involved in the incidents, to become part of the solution instead of part of the problem.

Example 1: It takes a village

This is a case about a group of boys who were bullying their classmates and how the school principal leveraged on all the parties involved to arrive at mutually agreeable solutions.

During the school year, the Grade 3 cohort contained several boys who dominated the class by being loud and rude and bullying some of the 'weaker' students. Their classmates were frustrated; the teachers were exhausted and resorted to frequently sending them to the principal's office.

Eventually, a father of one of the boys involved in the bullying initiated a meeting with the teacher and the principal. They met with the concerned parent and discussed how they might deal with the situation. They decided to enlarge their workforce to include all the parents of the boys who had been bullying their classmates, their teachers, key members of staff, and the school counsellor.

A week later they met with the larger group, and the principal shared her concerns regarding recurring conflicts, bullying and behavioural issues involving this group of boys. The principal wanted to ensure that the meeting was conducted in a respectful way to avoid 'losing face' and made it clear that the meeting was not to assign blame but, instead, to facilitate an open discussion to deal with the situation. She suggested that they all work together to resolve these issues in a way that all parties would feel satisfied and address their concerns. In order for this to happen, they agreed they would need to explore resources and strategies that would help everyone work towards solutions.

The principal facilitated a discussion on the topic of a preferred future – what they all hoped to see at the end of the school year, and what success would look like for the children. They began to look at steps they could take to achieve these goals, and broke up into smaller groups for further dialogue, which the principal and the school counsellor facilitated.

In the parents' group, the father who had initiated the first meeting shared his ideas with the parents in a discussion of life at home. He was concerned about the amount of time the parents were spending with their children, the children's unsupervised access to social media and video games and how the parents tackled conflicts. They explored what was working and what was not. They bounced ideas off each other about how to best support the boys, and came up with a list of ideas including spending more time with their sons, and making sure they all 'spoke the same language'.

At the other table, facilitated by the school counsellor, the school personnel deliberated about what they could do. As educators, they thought it would be helpful to initiate a new series of C.A.R.E. (character and religion enrichment) lessons about building skills to help with conflict resolution, anger management and relationships in general, for the whole grade, not just the boys involved. They agreed that it would be helpful to build lessons promoting community responsibility, respect for others and integrity, instead of focusing on 'no bullying'. They agreed it would be important to include the boys in this process to rebuild the relationships and include them in the solutions instead of focusing on them being the problem. The school counsellor suggested she could have several sessions with all the boys to discuss their ideas for managing the situation and conflict resolution strategies, and would offer individual support if required.

The principal went back and forth between the two groups, and eventually brought everyone back together to share their findings. They were all energised by what they heard. They each agreed to what they were willing to do to improve the situation. Everyone left determined, but at peace, and agreed to meet in four weeks.

Follow-up meeting. One month later, the teachers reported a decrease in incidents among the boys and said they were all trying to learn how to build better relationships. The parents appreciated the school's intervention and praised the personnel for being effective in teaching skills and strategies. The school personnel complimented the parents on their hard work and showed appreciation for parental support. The principal reported that the new C.A.R.E. curriculum had been useful for the whole school, and a new review date for parents and school personnel was set to ensure the progress could be maintained after the initial intervention. The school counsellor had met with all the boys in several group sessions and individually. She reported that the boys had decided to apologise to the ones they had bullied in school and some had become friends as a result.

A number of smaller follow-up meetings ensued as school personnel monitored behaviour, reviewed progress and addressed issues. Most of the parents shared that individual sessions with the school counsellor had been helpful. Over time, the boys were asked scaling questions regarding personal growth and group dynamics, and the results were very encouraging. The school developed another C.A.R.E. lesson, this time on the issue of cyber safety, and the school counsellor presented a talk for parents regarding the effects of media on children and planned future parenting forums.

Final review. At the final review, everyone involved in the joint intervention celebrated a victory. The boys had learned what their triggers were, how to prevent situations from developing further, and when to ask for help. The whole of Grade 3 experienced a noticeable reduction in conflicts. The school benefitted from the new C.A.R.E. curriculum. The parents welcomed more parenting talks. And finally, the school personnel grew in effectiveness by partnering with parents. They learned that proactively tackling the issues together was more effective than 'fighting fires' as the conflicts arose. The typical way this might be handled in Indonesia is to have conflict between the parents and school as to how to manage the situation, and, typically, the bullying will not be dealt with effectively. Usually, parents feel shame when their child is in trouble at school, and this results in punitive measures by the family. Using the solution focused approach ensured that all stakeholders involved were treated with respect and solicited their ideas toward effective solutions, which were achieved effectively, with the full support of all involved.

Example 2: Will the real victim please stand up?

This case is about how one male student caused the public humiliation of a female classmate through social media and how it led to his life being threatened by her boyfriend. The school principal was able to facilitate reconciliation and a successful resolution of the issue.

A student named Ned from Grade 11 snapped an unflattering photo of Nancy, then showed the photo to some classmates, and they all had a good laugh. Humiliated, Nancy told her boyfriend, who attended a different school. The boyfriend made threatening calls to Ned for the next few days, and brought a gang to school to beat him up. Ned asked his older brother to help him fight, but before anything violent happened, a watchful teacher warned the principal of the impending battle.

Principal Sim called for a meeting with Ned and his family and asked me to facilitate. I met with the parents and brother first, and thanked them for coming to help settle things. I remembered Ned from elementary school – how he was kind-hearted, curious and playful— and I looked forward to helping the family. Ned's parents expressed concern that their son had received threatening calls, that Principal Sim had falsely accused him and that he wasn't safe at school anymore.

I assured them that school safety was a shared goal, and invited the principal to tell us what he had gathered from speaking with various students, including Ned, which might 'fill in the gaps' in case we were missing crucial information.

Principal Sim shared how Ned had confided in him not only regarding the severity of the threats but also about *why* the threats had started. He explained the picture-taking incident, and that Ned had told the principal he had deleted the photo immediately. However, several of Ned's classmates had told the principal that Ned had shown them the photo, and that they all had a good laugh about it.

Ned's parents apologised to the principal for their earlier accusation and said they wanted to help sort everything out. Then we invited Ned to join us.

SFP: Ned, I haven't seen you for a few years – you've really shot up to become a tall and hand-some young man.

Ned: Thank you Ma'am.

SFP:	I had a nice chat with your parents and your brother and I am glad we can all meet together. Ned, what needs to happen in this meeting to make it worthwhile for you?
Ned:	I haven't been sleeping well and I'm scared – some boys sent me threatening messages.
SFP:	Well, I hope we can use this meeting to help you feel safe. I may need you to help out with a few details. Is that ok?
Ned:	Yes, Ma'am.
SFP:	I trust that all of us will remain calm and be honest and do our best.
All (In unison):	Yes.
SFP:	Ned, what would you like to see happen so that you can walk out from this meeting feeling relieved?
Ned:	I want the threatening messages to stop. I know I made a mistake but I didn't mean to insult Nancy. It was only a joke, and I already deleted the picture.
SFP:	What do you think you might do to help the threatening messages stop?
Ned:	I will apologise to Nancy and I will never do it again.
SFP:	Thank you, Ned. Is there anything you would like to tell your parents while we are here?

The principal was aware that Ned had not told his parents the whole truth, which led to the parents' misunderstanding and initiating the meeting in the first place.

Ned:	Mum, Dad, I didn't tell you the whole story. Actually, I took an unflattering picture of Nancy and showed my friends. I was only joking.
Parents:	We will talk more at home, son.
SFP:	Thanks for telling the truth, Ned. Now, suppose Nancy were your sister and her friend in school took the same picture, and showed it to some other boys – would you think it was just a funny joke?
Ned:	No, I would be upset. I wouldn't think it's funny. I would be angry
SFP:	Thanks, Ned. What are you willing to do that might help the situation?
Ned:	It was disrespectful of me to do that. I will email her parents tonight and apologise and I will talk to Nancy tomorrow.
SFP (to the principal):	Thank you, Ned. I'm impressed you see this clearly. You have been a model student here and we are glad to have you. We want to make sure that every student feels safe in school. Now I will do my best to help you feel safe.
SFP	I'm so impressed that Ned is honest and a gentleman. He realises his mistakes and is quick to apologise. He understands that he needs to respect his fellow students, and is being brave and honest. Great qualities I hope many students his age will have.
Principal:	Yes indeed. I appreciate that in him as well.
SFP:	Ned, the principal and I will meet with Nancy and her family now and see what can be done to stop the threats against you so you can get some sleep, OK?
Ned and his parents:	Thank you!

Conclusion

A more typical way of handling this kind of situation in Indonesia would be problem focused, with blame finding and punishment. Alternatively, rather than completely avoiding the issues due to shame, or being overly direct and insensitive to anyone's feelings by using power, significant changes were facilitated as a result of some key solution focused conversations. It was important that Nancy's family felt their concerns were heard and that they felt respected and did not 'lose face.' Because of this collaborative approach, all parties appreciated how the matter was handled. The family dropped the case against Ned, and called off the boyfriend and his gang. Instead of a punitive approach, Ned was given the opportunity to reflect and decide what he needed to do to resolve the situation. He felt heard and respected, and learned about empathy and respect. The parents' appreciation for the school increased, and the school personnel experienced the collaborative power and impact of using solution focused conversations.

Final reflections

Bullying is a hot topic in most schools, if not all. The impact and consequences can be devastating. We have heard some horrifying outcomes when the cases of bullying, in any form, did not get resolved quickly. The community at this school learned that we can always turn a negative situation into a positive learning opportunity as long as we set clear mutual objectives and open solution-focused dialogues among all the stakeholders. These examples have served as great models for many parents. It is indeed possible to turn bullies into allies.

31

'AMY THE AMAZING' IMPLEMENTS 'PROJECT CONTROL'

Building collaboration between student, parents and the school

Debbie Hogan

As a psychotherapist in private practice specialising in solution focused practice, I work extensively with students, parents and schools regarding school-based issues in Singapore. When students are referred by the school, it is very important to understand and manage the expectations of the school and the parents to support the desired changes in the student. I will share an example of a 6-year-old girl who was referred for 'anger management' by the school, and how a solution focused approach was utilised to work within the social system of the child to help support the necessary changes in a way that was respectful and realistic for all stakeholders. The example further illustrates the important steps for maximising cooperation and collaboration between all the parties involved.

Setting the stage for collaboration

Six-year-old Amy was brought by her parents to see me regarding concerns from the school and their recommendation that Amy work on 'anger management'.

I welcomed the family and thanked them for coming. In Singapore it is rare to have both parents come for counselling, and I could see the high level of care and concern they had for Amy. Asian parents often feel shame and embarrassment when their child gets into trouble at school and often blame themselves or become punitive with their child. I was immediately impressed with the way these parents viewed the situation. They wanted to talk with me before I contacted the school. They were interested in how I could work with them to improve the situation.

Amy actively explored things in my office, and I offered her several things she could do while I talked with her parents. I could see Amy was listening while her parents shared their concerns as she glanced at me several times. I occasionally turned to Amy to compliment her on what she was doing. I thanked both parents for taking the time to come to the session. I turned to Amy and said I would like to get to know her a little bit. I asked what she enjoyed doing when she was not in school. Amy was eager to say that she loved to read and draw and go swimming, especially with her friends. We played a little game. I tossed a soft ball to Mum and asked, 'What is Amy good at?' Then Mum threw the ball to Amy and asked 'What is Dad good at?' The three of them took turns. Amy was quick to add what Mum was not good at, and we had some good laughs.

Understanding the landscape

The challenge for me was to make sure I understood the desired outcome for the parents as well as understanding what the school principal and the teachers expected in terms of behavioural changes from Amy, and approached it in such a way that Amy was able to meet these expectations. Before talking with the school, I needed to find out what the parents wanted from our sessions and how I could work with Amy about addressing these concerns. Amy was busy doing her artwork while I listened to her parents. She created some colourful cards with stickers and coloured markers.

The school principal had contacted the parents several times about Amy's 'unacceptable' behaviour and wanted it addressed. The school reported that Amy was resorting to biting, kicking and hitting when she didn't get her way, especially with her classmates at school. She was disruptive in class, talking and disturbing those around her. Her teachers and the school counsellor had tried all they knew to change her behaviour, but nothing seemed to work. The principal suggested they seek outside therapy for 'anger management'.

Clarifying what is wanted

At this point in the session, I felt Amy was responsive and open to me. I inquired as to how I might help in order to make a positive difference for them.

Deb: What needs to happen in this session for you to be able to say that it has been worthwhile for you?

Parents: Amy needs to learn how to manage her anger. We don't want her to get into trouble at school anymore. And the school principal wants Amy to learn 'anger management'.

Deb: I see. What are the expectations of the school?

Parents: That Amy no longer gets into trouble and can get along with her classmates. No more biting, hitting, kicking when she doesn't get her way.

Deb: I see. So it's important that some things need to change.

I asked the parents to mention things about Amy when she was getting along in school. The parents described Amy as a child who was very social and enjoyed playing with other children. At times she was a little 'bossy' and insisted on her own way. They said she wanted to be accepted and wanted to please the teachers. I saw this as a possible way to collaborate with Amy.

Building mastery and competence

I turned to Amy, who continued doing her artwork, to explore her understanding of the situation.

Deb: Amy, I hear that you really like playing with other children. And you want to get along with them, is that right?

Amy: I don't want to get into trouble in school. I don't like that the teachers always blame me when it's not my fault.

Deb: I see. So, sometimes you get into trouble when it's not your fault and you don't like that? What do you think needs to change so this doesn't happen anymore?

Amy: I need to stop biting and hitting when they don't want to play with me.

Amy explained further that her best friend had started to befriend another student, which upset Amy. It made her 'angry' and she wanted them to like her. She also understood that she needed to handle her upset in a different way. For a 6-year-old, I was impressed with her ability to express herself and have a good understanding of what she needed to change.

I decided to explore what Amy already knew about controlling her anger.

Deb: So, what do you do instead?

Amy: I can count to 10 when I'm angry. I can breathe. I can take turns.

Amy knew quite a lot about managing her anger, and I decided to explore the idea of developing good habits, instead of the bad habits.

Deb: It sounds like you have some good ideas. Suppose we can give a name to this little project we're going to work on. What name do you want to call it?

After some thought, Amy decided she would call our project 'Control'. I described our work together as 'developing a new habit' of 'control'. We talked about other habits she had developed, like brushing her teeth and taking a bath. She liked that very much, and the parents were pleased that Amy was on board. It was more desirable for Amy to work on something she was interested in doing instead of focusin on 'anger management'.

Deb: Let's talk about how your parents can help you with 'Project Control'. How do you want them to help you?

Amy described some things her parents did and the school did when she got angry that did not help. It made her feel bad and even more angry. It was important to Amy that she be treated fairly and not be targeted or singled out for being the class 'trouble-maker'.

Deb: What do you want them to do instead?

Amy: My mum can whisper 'control'. (She demonstrated it to me in my ear.)

Deb: And what about the teachers? How can they help you?

Amy: They can whisper 'control' to remind me, too.

Deb: And how will this help?

Amy: If they remind me, then I can do it myself.

Deb: Aha. You really want to practice how to do it yourself! That's great. I can see how much you want to do this.

We discussed ways in which the teachers and parents could help support Amy. What emerged was an agreement between the mother and Amy to buy a special stone that Amy could keep in her school bag. She liked the idea of having a little reminder she could touch and hold when she needed to remind herself to do other things when she got angry.

Building collaboration with the school

I contacted the school principal and teachers to better understand their concerns and how we could all work together to support Amy in the changes she needed to make. Amy's teachers explained the things they had witnessed and how they had tried to tackle the situation, but it had not made any difference. After getting a good idea of the school's expectations, they agreed to try some 'experiments'. The school principal was supportive of our ideas. They also made it clear that they had other students to care for and this behaviour would not be tolerated, as other parents were also complaining. I validated their concerns, and that we all wanted Amy to succeed in her 'Project Control'. Schools in Singapore are a beehive of activity, and most teachers have a student ratio of 40:1. Given the time constraints and the reality of what they could manage, I made a few suggestions to the teachers, to help them support Amy:

- Notice and observe Amy doing things that support the changes you want to see and not comment on the problematic behaviour, during 'Project Control'. (This latter part was emphasised, as Amy was used to getting criticised for her 'bad habits' and she needed time to develop her new habits.)
- Catch these moments and reinforce them as soon as possible. For example, noticing when Amy listens in class, takes turns or shows interest in what others are doing. A simple compliment can be given, e.g.: 'Thank you for listening and paying attention in class today.'
- Send a little note home with Amy to give to her parents. Explain that the note will be positive things the teacher observed during the day.
- Take note of times that Amy needs support, by whispering 'control' to her.
- Notice when she touches her special stone, and compliment her on practising her skill.
- Make note of improvements, and send the counsellor a short email at the end of the week.

At the end of first week, it was reported by some of the teachers that they had noticed Amy touching her special stone a few times. Some teachers reported that Amy was no longer disturbing her classmates. And some reported that Amy had shown anger in school, but was making improvements. The parents reported that Amy was practising 'control' at home and things had improved.

By the second week, the teachers and parents reported that Amy had completely stopped her 'bad habits' and was no longer doing the things she had been asked to change.

Amy returned to our next session with her mother and I explored 'What is better?'

Mum: Well, it's quite amazing because Amy has really improved things at school.
Deb: Tell me more! That sounds wonderful.

The mum started to brag about all the good reports from teachers and read some of the notes to me. Amy had even been given a little certificate during school assembly for showing 'acts of kindness'. Amy was beaming.

Deb: I think I will call you 'Amy, the Amazing'. What is better for you?
Amy: I've been practising 'control' and touching my stone. My teachers say I'm doing good. And I made a new friend who likes to play with me.
Deb: Wow! How did you do all that?

Amy: Well . . . I just did it! My mum helped me. My teachers helped me.

Deb: So, just like that? You decided and then you practised?

Amy: Uhuh.

Deb: And you like it that your teachers helped and your mum helped?

Amy: Yes! Because last time I always got in trouble before and got blamed for everything. Now, I'm not in trouble anymore.

I reviewed all the good things that Amy had accomplished. By the end of the session, Amy was beaming and determined to keep it up. She really enjoyed the positive attention. Highlighting her successes made Amy even more confident.

Deb: I wonder . . . how many more times do you think you need to come here to say: 'I don't need to see Ms. Debbie.'

Amy: Two more!

Scaling for progress

I asked Amy where she was on a scale to help her have a visual representation of her progress. I asked her to help me draw the numbers, 1–10 on pieces of paper and place them on the floor.

Deb: On this line, '10' stands for all the things you know – your good habits – you know, 'Project Control' and you are the best! And '1' is when you first came. Where are you now? Can you stand on the number?

Amy: '8'

Deb: Wow! For everything you have done to make it '8', please tell me and hop up one number.

Amy proceeded to mention many things that she had done to make things better, and with each hop to the next number, she beamed with pride. I also asked the mum for her ideas, which added up to quite a list of items.

Celebrating the accomplishment

I suggested that at the last session, we would have a celebration party for 'Amy the Amazing'. We explored what it would be like. She mentioned grapes, balloons, ice cream and strawberries, which Mum agreed to. At the last session, which was exactly the number that Amy had predicted, we had a celebration party. I blew up balloons and put them around the office. We had ice cream and strawberries while reviewing Amy's accomplishments since the previous session and how she would continue to practise her good habits. I presented Amy with a certificate: 'To Amy, The Amazing: For Outstanding Success with "Project Control"'.

Final check-in with school

I continued to check with the school to make sure things were improving in the right direction. The principal and teachers were satisfied that the initial problems had been resolved and that Amy was no longer biting, kicking or hitting her classmates. There were no other incidents at school. The next school year, the mum sent me a note saying that Amy was doing well in her new school and had really developed lasting 'good habits' in dealing with her anger.

A small difference goes a long way

As a result of this collaboration and the significant changes with Amy, some of the teachers started experimenting in small ways. One teacher changed her approach with another student who was failing a subject and disruptive in class. By noticing and commenting on the small improvements, instead of focusing on the problem, the student stopped being disruptive and eventually improved in her class. Another teacher improved cooperation with her students by introducing the scaling tool. Another teacher realised that her traditional approach of scolding to motivate students was not effective and started to recognise that motivation is enhanced when the qualitative atmosphere in the classroom is enhanced. The short-term yet highly effective nature of this approach makes it especially suited for teachers in Singapore, who work within constraints of time and heavy work demands. Making small yet significant changes is like a tiny water drop in a pond. It creates a ripple effect.

32

WHY SHOULD I?

Working with troubled youth in Singapore

Joe Chan

The Singapore government has taken a hard stand against gangsterism, and through their initiative many programmes are offered to help troubled youth. REACH Youth is one of these services, under REACH Community Services Society in Singapore (RCSS). In our various programmes and services, we are mindful of the changing needs and expectations of our youth clientele, the stakeholders that we work with and the national landscape of policies and trends so that we can serve our clientele in the best possible way. One of the common characteristics of our youth is that they don't easily accept help. Many come from broken homes or dual-income families where parents are not able to provide adequate supervision for their children. When they are 'caught' by the system and referred to us, they just play along with the process and don't see that they have anything to work on. Some of these youths are referred to our program through schools and the police because of their risk-taking behaviours.

Using the solution focused (SF) approach, we have come a long way in understanding what works with our young Singaporean clients. We don't view ourselves as the experts of their problems and how they should change. It's the youth's perspective of the issues that's critical, and it's necessary to build collaboration and trust.

In this chapter, I will share the real-life stories of two youths who made dramatic changes in their lives. Through individual coaching, mentoring and various group programmes at REACH, the youth shifted from 'Why should I?' to 'What do I want better for my life?'

Danny and Johnny make significant changes[1]

Danny, at 15 years old, had been arrested numerous times for various petty crimes and sentenced to a court probation order and referred to us. His school leaders were relieved when he completed secondary school and they were finally able to get rid of a highly disruptive and non-compliant student. They didn't seem to care whether he did well for his national examinations and were just satisfied that he didn't create another incident in school. Because of all these issues, Danny's family members were highly concerned about him and felt helpless.

Sixteen-year-old Johnny was referred to us for gang related activities, and was a member of the same gang as Danny. He simply lost interest in studying and stopped going to school. He spent hours on gaming and hanging out with friends. Sometimes, he would play for days on end, only going home to sleep during the day. Coming from a family who earned just enough to meet their basic needs, Johnny had to find ways to earn some extra pocket money. Johnny would also take on ad-hoc part-time jobs during the day time, which made it even more difficult for him to focus on school.

In Singapore, the idea of the 'Many Helping Hands' approach was introduced by Mr Abdullah Tarmugi in 1995 (National Archives of Singapore, 1995). For cases like Danny and Johnny, it's not unusual for them to receive multiple levels of help from various sources. By the time Danny and Johnny were referred to us by the police for their gang-related activities, they had already experienced most of the frontline interventions, such as school counselling, school programmes and court probation orders. It seemed that despite their best efforts, nothing much had changed. It's no surprise that Danny and Johnny saw no benefits from attending our programmes.

Making a difference

Wanting to learn from these experiences, we decided to approach things differently. From the very beginning, we sought to establish a strong alliance with these youths. With the end goal in mind, we explored what the youths wanted to achieve and what would be good reasons to stay in the programme. We invited them to consider some best hopes from attending our programme, even though they were mandated to attend. We viewed ourselves as co-constructors of change with the youths, towards a goal and outcome that would be helpful to them and fulfil the refer-ring agency's expectations.

At the initial stage, I asked the youths:

- How can we work together to help you with what you want for your life?
- What would it take for you to complete this programme successfully?
- Why is it important to you that you complete this programme?

One challenge I faced in working with mandated youths was that I was the delegated authority from the police to ensure that the youth stayed within the requirements of the programme. This was a difficult position to take because it required me to play a dual role as counsellor and enforcer. Because of the collaborative stance of the SF approach, I let the youths choose which role I played. I let them know that I could be counsellor and I could be enforcer based on what they displayed in their behaviours in the programme. When I did that, I was able to manage my roles according to the context.

Shining the spotlight on hidden hopes and dreams

In our Asian context, the emphasis on doing the right thing is often very strong and any form of deviance is highly frowned upon. With Danny and Johnny, the spotlight had already been shone on their deviant behaviours. Instead, I explored the times they did well or were successful. This allowed us to explore their hidden resources and strengths. That was where I discovered that Danny enjoyed cooking for his family. For Johnny, there were times in school when he was not disruptive but engaged. I asked him what was different during the times he was able to keep awake and be engaged in the lesson for 45 minutes. How did he manage to do so? These questions helped to identify the strengths and resources that these youths possessed.

We found powerful information that could be used to generate momentum for change. Thus, in the remaining time of their programme, we no longer focused on the deviant sides of their behaviour. Instead, we shifted the spotlight onto their hidden hopes and dreams and explored details of those dreams being fulfilled, the impact that it had on those around them, and what small steps could be taken towards that hopeful future. So, as we continued to explore in this direction, a lot of space and possibilities were created in our conversations where they were more open to explore.

Reflections by Danny and Johnny

We were curious about the changes that Danny and Johnny had made and what they could tell us about what actually made a difference for them.

Danny

> The desire to change to a better person was when I realised I am at my own disadvantage and upsetting my family if I continue being the way I am. During an Outward Bound school camp it was tough, but it was a great success for all of us. I told myself that I will not give up so easily in whatever I do and strive to do my best for what I want, especially cooking.
>
> For me, punishment didn't help, but heart-to-heart talks did. I felt that to understand teenagers, it is helpful to really listen and know what they want and that is what Joe did. He didn't just tell me what to do or lecture me. He didn't treat me like I was useless. He gave me a chance to learn from my mistakes. Joe was like a big brother, a teacher, a really good friend because he listened and respected me. He asked me what I was interested in. I have this wonderful memory where we played paintball together. I got to shoot him. I felt happy as it brought us down to the same level in the game. This is really different from the way most programmes run. It was like they really cared and helped us find what we wanted in life.

Danny, now 21 years old, is pursuing his interest as a chef and training at a culinary academy in Singapore.

Johnny

> Before I met Joe, I was living a meaningless life. Every day I played around, didn't study, just wasting my life. After we met, he started to counsel with us and understand us. One way that Joe helped me the most was to lead me back to school and study after I had dropped out for 2 years. He helped me understand what I wanted in the future of my life. He guided me along the way and helped me in a difficult time. He helped us open up whenever we talk to him and he found activities to do with us. He asked me what I wanted to do after I finish school. I never gave it much thought because I thought I would never finish. But when he asked me about it, I started to really consider it possible.

Johnny, who is now 19 years old, is pursuing a diploma at an accountancy academy in Singapore.

Customised group activities

In addition to individual work, we customise group activities to develop life skills the youths want to learn. In Singapore, our education system emphasises achieving good results. So, when youths fail to produce good academic results, they begin to feel that they have failed, not only academically but also as a person. Thus, many youths are referred by schools due to problematic behaviours.

Exploration phase. During the exploration stage, we meet with all the key stakeholders at the school to find out their best hopes for the targeted group of students. We seek clarity on the indicators that their best hopes have been fulfilled. This is different from the customary complaints around the problematic behaviour of the youth. At the start, we let the youth know that we are not trying to make them change. Instead, we invite them to create a clear picture of how they will know their best hopes were achieved. This shifts the focus from just doing what the school wants them to do, to what they want for themselves. This approach is very helpful because they are used to being 'put through' talks and workshops where they are expected to change but have no idea what the school clearly wants. In Singapore the common practice is to outsource talks and workshops to external vendors who usually focus on the problematic behaviour. Therefore, what we do in our programme is quite opposite from what they are used to.

Customised programme. After all the input, we meet again to customise a programme, anchoring it to the game of dodgeball. Using a sport as the focus for the sessions enables us to use the rules of the game to teach specific life skills. It's important during rapport building and goal formulation stage that everyone feels engaged in being part of the miracle picture. The miracle picture can even include those who are absent. We use powerful relationship questions to find out the impact the miracle picture will have on others. Throughout the programme, we observe and make note of the times when the youth play an active part and contribute towards the winning of the game.

To monitor progress, we invite the youths and other stakeholders to scale where they think the youth are, relative to the miracle picture they created. We get different perspectives from the group, which helps with self-awareness. The youths often choose to shut down and put up a nonchalant front. But when we have a strong rapport with them, we are able to find out the small baby steps to move forward and bring the scale up bit by bit.

Another key feature of this programme is the conscious connection between their goals and the activities we do. At the end of each session, we focus on drawing connections between how that session has brought them nearer to their goals, as even a small step can become very affirming for the whole class.

During the debrief, we ask three simple questions:

•   What was useful during the session?
•   Where on the scale are you now?
•   What could be better in the subsequent sessions?

This debrief allows each player to reflect on their goals and what they learned that would be useful in their lives. Again, this is a very different format from what they are used to doing in Singapore at school.

S.T.R.I.K.E. dodgeball programme. Besides mandatory programmes, we also have programmes like S.T.R.I.K.E. dodgeball, which stands for Spirit, Teamwork, Respect, Individual Strengths, Knowledge, and Effort. It's designed to reach out to youths who struggle with motivation and may be showing signs of misconduct in school. It's an after-school programme to offer something interesting and challenging for youths. We continue to collaborate with the youths and the school that they attend, to facilitate the best outcomes for all parties involved.

Conclusion

As parents, educators and helping professionals, we often have to learn how to let go of our 'expert' position and work *with* the youths rather than work *on* them. So often we just have to hold on tight to the strings of connection and trust them as they go through the process of growing up. In the case of Danny and Johnny, it would have been so easy to zoom in and focus on the problems and try hard to understand the causes of the problems using our 'expert' lenses. Many of these youths have become so used to being scrutinised by different professionals, to the extent that they have given up hope. Therefore, in our work at REACH Youth, we really have to stay curious and open to the good things that lie waiting for us to discover in our youth and remind ourselves to not push or be too eager to make the client change. We think the SF mind-set aligns perfectly with our philosophy to value each youth, believe in their capabilities and respect their individual uniqueness. We acknowledge that youths need space to make mistakes and learn from them. And they need the opportunity to develop and grow their interests.

Note

1 This case study has also been published in an online article by Chan (2015) and is reproduced with permission from REACH Community Services Society.

References

Chan, J. (2015). *Activating strengths, reaching potential*. Retrieved from: http://www.reach.org.sg/index.php/resources/past-articles/142-activating-strengths-reaching-potential.

National Archives of Singapore. (1995). Statement by Mr Abdullah Tarmugi, acting Minister for Community Development at the World Summit for Social Development, Copenhagen, Denmark [Press release]. Retrieved from http://www.nas.gov.sg/archivesonline/data/pdfdoc/at19950310s.pdf

SECTION 4

Solution focused practice in coaching in Asia

33

INTRODUCTION TO SOLUTION FOCUSED PRACTICE IN COACHING IN ASIA

Peter Szabo and Debbie Hogan

When I (Debbie) first started coaching in the mid-1990s in Singapore, there was very little in terms of coach training or peer support. There were maybe three other coaches I knew, and we were doing career coaching and executive coaching. Twenty years down the road, there are coaching associations all over Asia, a proliferation of coaching programs and a Coaching Circle Support Group. Now, coaching has exploded in Asia. How did we get here? In this chapter, I will provide a brief overview of the history and development of the coaching field, including when solution focused brief coaching came to Asia, and some of my observations on the current coaching landscape in Asia. Peter will share his observations on his coach training in Asia, followed by a summary of eight chapters that highlight the work of solution focused coaches in Asia.

A brief history of the development of the professional coaching field

One of the best resources that I'm aware of that covers the early history and development of the professional coaching field is Brock's (2008) dissertation 'Grounded Theory of the Roots and Emergence of Coaching', including 170 interviews with key influencers and an extensive review of literature. Five points summarise her observations about the emergence of coaching:

1   Coaching sprang from several independent sources at the same time and spread through relationships.
2   Coaching has a broad intellectual framework that draws on the synergy, cross-fertilisation, and practices of many disciplines.
3   Modern patterns and practices of coaching are dynamic and contextual.
4   Coaching came into existence to fill an unmet need in an interactive, fluid world of rapid change and complexity.
5   Coaching came into being in an open integral social network from a perspective of diversity and inclusion.

(Brock, 2008, p. vii)

The coaching field is still developing and forming an identity. During the 1990s, coaching gained momentum and blossomed from 1995 to the present. In the early years, the International Coach Federation defined the field of coaching, and by 1995 they had a professional code of ethics and training standards that included core coaching competencies and professional accreditation (Brock, 2008; ICF, 2015). Other professional coach associations were formed and professional standards were developed. Then, from the mid-1990s, everything changed with the emergence of the external professional coach and the popularisation of coaching.

Coaching in Asia

Brock describes the development of coaching in Asia (2008, pp. 438–440). In 1997, the first coach-training company started in Japan, and in 1999, the Japan Coach Association was formed. Coaching in China evolved independently from other coaching traditions. Wong and Lueng developed their own coach training in Hong Kong in 1996 based on Taoist principles and later took it to China in 1997. In 1998 Phillips conducted the first coach training in Singapore. Wong formed China Coach Association in 2003. Gimm, a pioneer in coaching in South Korea, did the first coach training in 2003.

In 2010, *Coaching in Asia: The First Decade* (Wright, Leong, Webb & Chia, 2010) was published 'to celebrate the impact of the first decade of coaching in Asia' (p. xv) and is a significant milestone in the development of executive coaching within the Asian context, offering multiple views of coaching methodologies. What is also significant, in terms of the purpose of this book on SF practice in Asia, is to highlight that three of the contributors to *Coaching in Asia* are solution focused coaches and that two of them have contributed a chapter to our book.

Where solution focused brief coaching fits into the landscape

The solution focused approach was developed by Steve de Shazer and Insoo Kim Berg and their colleagues during the 1980s. Due to its wide appeal and easy applicability to other fields, the SF approach was easily adapted into the coaching context. Its future-focused, goal-directed orientation was an important alternative to the predominant problem-focused approaches in coaching. The philosophy of SF coaching is based on the core assumptions that clients have competencies and capabilities that can be identified and there is profound respect for the client and what is important to them. The coach and client co-construct the coaching agreement and solicit details of their ideal future without the problem, using a variety of tools to help support the changes the client wants. The SF approach is known for its radical simplicity and attention to language, and great care is given to how the coach listens and formulates questions. Instead of focusing on the problem narrative, the conversation is directed to a future orientation of life without the problem.

The Academy of Solution Focused Training was the first to bring solution focused coaching and accreditation to Asia. Mark McKergow and Jenny Clarke helped launch SF coaching in Singapore in 2004. Mark's book, co-authored with Paul Jackson, based on the solution focused coaching model, *The Solutions Focus: Making Coaching and Change SIMPLE* (2007), has been translated into 11 languages, including Japanese, Korean and Chinese. Peter Szabo joined our coaching program in 2007 and brought brief coaching to Asia. Peter and Insoo Kim Berg's book, *Brief Coaching for Lasting Solutions* (2005), has been translated into five languages, including Japanese and Korean. Solution focused brief coaching is now being taught all over Asia, in China, Japan, Korea, the Philippines, Hong Kong, Indonesia and Malaysia.

This is a very encouraging sign that solution focused brief coaching is relevant and being embraced in Asia. Initially, we didn't know how well SF coaching would be received and applied. In Asia, the coach is held in high esteem and older coaches are preferred and expected to share wisdom with the coachee. Once trust between the coach and coachee is established, the coachee is more likely to open up (Nangalia & Nangalia, 2010). SF coaching places a high premium on honouring the coachee's values and building a strong platform for change based on trust and respect. In my experience, Asian participants are very responsive when their values are respected.

Observations on coaching in Asia from Peter

I remember my first invitation to Singapore in 2007 to offer something on the topic of coaching, and I remember so well wondering if it would work in Asia. It is so amazing how 8 years later a segment of eight chapters in this book is about coaching in Asia. Over this time I have come to experience that the idea of respectfully reinforcing others in who they are and even in who they can become is a most natural thing to do in Asia and probably always has been. It is just that we now have a new name for it: solution focused or brief coaching.

Let me illustrate with three little examples of coaching working in Asia:

1 Yes, workshops can be loudly participative

The evening of my first arrival in Singapore I was invited to work with about 70 employees of an insurance company. I had been warned before that participants in Asia would expect me to lecture to them and that my usual style of involving the audience and inviting them to participate and do exercises in small groups would not work here. I was somewhat worried because my understanding of coaching is very much about involving the clients and letting them reflect on their own experiences and finding answers for themselves. However, about 5 minutes into the workshop, when all the participants were engaged in a small-group conversation, my wife Stephanie came up to me. 'Do you hear the noise and buzz level in the room? Unbelievable! I have never heard an audience engage so naturally and quickly in creating the relevant content for themselves.'

2 Yes, coaching can become very personal

A year later I facilitated coaching workshops in Tokyo and Kyoto. This time I was warned beforehand that it would not be possible for participants to reveal very personal topics in public. I should expect the conversations to stay carefully and respectfully reserved in front of a group or even in one on one conversations. Interestingly, I found quite the opposite to be true. My clients (both men), one in Tokyo and the other in Kyoto, apparently somehow felt safe and comfortable enough to bring up and discuss issues that touched them and brought them to tears. There was such a deep sense of reinforcement and respect in the audience, which made these two coaching moments a fairly comfortable experience to work with and learn from.

3 Yes, in organisations, a chain of natural positive response emerges

The same year at the J-SOL solution focused conference in Japan, I witnessed a group of young employees of a packaging company naturally taking coaching elements and developing them further and creating an even more productive work atmosphere in their team. They had taken the idea of positive reinforcement and invented the tool of OK-Messages. Each evening they would spend five minutes exchanging examples of what had gone well. Surprised by the motivating effect of this on themselves, they even created a booklet where they gathered all these small and significant success stories within their team. At a later stage they even started to send out emails to let other teams know how they had contributed to the OK-Messages. Later, our colleague Aoki created a term for this process: Chain of Natural Positive Response. Aoki discusses this more fully in his chapter on SF in Organisations.

What impressed me most in my numerous contacts in Asia over the last few years is the speed with which change was put into practice. Nowhere else in the world have I seen participants of my workshops work so fast and so thoroughly in doing things differently in everyday life and following through to the entire organisation.

Overview of the current landscape in Asia

We have come a long way since the beginnings of coaching in Asia in the 1990s. Now, when you do an online search under 'coaching', the variety of coaching that is available is incredible: executive, business, leadership, performance, life, relationship, grief, academic, parent, wellness, fitness, spiritual, AD/HD, and the list goes on.

Coaching is moving into a broader marketplace. I'm impressed with how adaptable, flexible and resourceful Asians are in these times of rapid change. The majority of coaches in Asia are executive and business coaches, dealing with performance management, and as more benefits have been experienced, the shift is more directed toward development initiative (Chia, 2010). Seeking coaching is becoming more popular and widely accepted – with much less stigma attached than therapy – a very important consideration in Asia. In Asia, therapy is often associated with weakness and inadequacy, while coaching is identified with successful sports figures or winning teams (Peltier, 2001). As perceptions continue to change and more people see the value in coaching, more therapists are adding coaching to their portfolio.

Organisations are also seeking more leadership coach training to equip their executives to be effective coaches and develop a coaching culture within their organisations. More educational institutions are seeking coach training for their teachers and lecturers to learn important tools to help students successfully manage their academic challenges.

Career coaching is one of the fastest growing sectors in Asia. Organisations are changing very rapidly, and executives and professionals are increasingly turning to career coaches to make important life changing decisions (Skiffington & Zeus, 2003). These are exciting times in Asia for the coaching field.

Professional support – peer-led coaching circle

As the coaching field continues to grow, it will naturally attract more and more people who want to be part of this exciting profession. Developing effective coaching skills is very important as a professional coach. Many solution focused coaches see the value of on-going professional support to continue to develop their coaching competencies. In Singapore, where I am based, we have an on-going peer-led coaching group, called the 'Coaching Circle', of solution focused coaches that meet every month for networking, professional support, lively discussions on some new coaching article or workshop, and peer coaching practice. It's open to anyone that is interested in SF coaching and is a great way to meet other coaches in the region. This group grows bigger each year.

Contributions by authors

After 11 years of teaching solution focused brief coaching in Asia, there have been many impressive stories and examples of how this approach has worked with many different client situations. Eight coaches have contributed to this section and represent six different countries in Asia. I'm very impressed by the variety and unique applications of coaching, ranging from individual and team coaching, to creative use of metaphors, cross-cultural differences in coaching in Asia, and finally a discussion on translation and expectations.

Harliem Salim, an executive coach in Indonesia, shares his experiences in coaching CEOs and business owners to manage work responsibilities while enhancing their personal lives. Marjanne van der Helm explores the use of metaphors in coaching in Singapore and how it created a significant pathway for change for her clients. As a coach in the Philippines, Agnes Hautea Nano shares a moving experience doing group coaching with employees facing redundancy to help them navigate through the difficult transition. Anisha Kaul offers a guide to team facilitation to develop team cohesion in Singapore. As a coach with women leaders in a voluntary organisation in Singapore and Malaysia, Jayne Sim shares the experiences of the challenges women face in Asia and how coaching made a positive difference. Maurice Wan and Raymond Au share a unique application of SF coaching with occupational therapists in Hong Kong, where over 50 per cent are trained in SF coaching and use it in their daily practice. Kirsten Dierolf and Isabelle Hansen, who have done extensive work across Asia, discuss cross-cultural differences between Western and Asian cultures and the universal applicability of SF coaching. Finally, Terese Bareth, a German coach who is a fluent Mandarin speaker, discusses the importance of appropriate translation, assumptions and expectations in coaching in China. Terese created the perfect translation of coaching in Mandarin, which is now recognised and accepted as the appropriate Chinese translation for coaching.

We hope the interest in solution focused coaching will continue. Indications are that coaching will continue to have a strong presence in Asia. We hope that the reader will be inspired to explore solution focused brief coaching and see the value of it, and join the growing network of solution focused practitioners in Asia and internationally.

References

Brock, V.G. (2008). *Grounded theory of the roots and emergence of coaching* (Unpublished doctoral dissertation). International University of Professional Studies, Maui. Retrieved from: https://www.nobco.nl/files/onderzoeken/Brock_Vikki_dissertatie__2_.pdf

Chia, S. (2010). *Coaching in Asia: Trends and development*. Singapore. Candid Creation Publishing.

International Coach Federation. Retrieved 15 December 2015 from: http://www.coachfederation.org/about/landing.cfm?ItemNumber=741&navItemNumber=615

Jackson, P., & McKergow, M. (2007). *The solutions focus: Making coaching and change SIMPLE* (2nd ed.). London, UK. Nicholas Brealey International.

Nangalia, L., & Nangalia, A. (2010). The coach in Asian society: Impact of social hierarchy on the coaching relationship. *International Journal of Evidenced Based Coaching and Mentoring, 8*(1), 51–66.

Peltier, B. (2001). *The psychology of executive coaching: Theory and application.* New York, NY: Brunner-Routledge.

Skiffington, S., & Zeus, P. (2003). *Behavioral coaching.* Sydney: McGraw Hill.

Szabo, P., & Berg, I.K. (2005). *Brief coaching for lasting solutions.* New York, NY: W.W. Norton.

Wright, D., Leong, A., Webb, K.E., & Chia, S. (Eds.). (2010). *Coaching in Asia: The first decade.* Singapore. Candid Creation Publishing.

34

SOLUTION FOCUSED COACHING FOR BUSINESS SOLUTIONS

Harliem Salim

As a solution focused coach from Jakarta, I've worked with business owners, corporate executives, government officials and CEOs in Indonesia and across other parts of Asia. In this chapter I will discuss the coaching process I have used and how solution focused coaching has impacted the executives I have worked with: the positive differences it has made in their work and family life and the ripple effect it has had on the organisations they lead.

Business owners and those in positions of leadership within organisations deal with multiple issues at the same time. They focus on maintaining and increasing productivity, managing employees, satisfying share and stakeholders, handling the media, dealing with legal issues and complying with complicated government regulations, while at the same time hoping to maintain their integrity and stay true to their moral values. No wonder they sometimes find it exhausting to consistently think clearly, maintain a sharp analytical sense, and trust their own judgment when making major decisions! Because most of what they are concerned about is confidential, they often feel that they have nowhere to process their burdens to deal effectively with their responsibilities.

I'm really drawn to the solution focused approach to coaching, as it is very effective and empowering for my clients. This approach enables me to connect with these executives and get to the heart of their concerns and what they want to be different. It provides a wonderful road map through which I can help them navigate these troubled waters and find solid ground. Executives at the top of the ladder are driven and drive their employees. Living in a highly driven, performance-oriented country, like the rest of Asia, executives struggle with finding a good balance between personal well-being and work satisfaction. Through coaching, these executives have made significant changes to manage their work responsibilities well, while enhancing their personal lives.

Building the coaching relationship

When I first meet with my coaching clients, I spend quite a bit of time on establishing the relationship and building trust. I'm interested in who they are and what they do, and I'm listening for their competencies and successes as executives. I ask questions, such as, 'What do you enjoy doing when you're not working?' or 'What do you enjoy most about your work?' or 'What do you feel really good about as a leader in your organisation?' Some of my coachees hold high-profile positions in Jakarta and confidentiality is of upmost importance as some of the coaching issues are sensitive in nature. Sometimes, it takes a few sessions before they feel comfortable enough to move from the rapport phase to focusing on the purpose of the coaching process and sharing mutual expectations. After a while, they feel safe enough to share their problems and frustrations, which eventually leads to ownership in the process. Often, these executives have already experienced the benefits through personal mentoring or coaching. Sometimes, they seek support during a crisis in their business, a personal crisis or a leadership crisis within their organisation. My coachees tell me how much they appreciate the amount of time I give to building trust, as they have not found a safe place to off-load their concerns. In Asia there is a tendency to 'suffer in silence' and not trust others with personal matters. There is a desire to always portray the successful corporate man and never show a weakness or vulnerability as it might be used to get a higher position or get ahead of the corporate game.

Shifting from problem talk to solution talk

The executives I coach are loaded down with multiple responsibilities, and some manage thousands of employees in their organisations. The traditional approach to coaching they are used to in Asia is to talk about the problem and examine and analyse it and then the coach tells them how to solve the problem. It is important to resist the urge to solve the problem for them. From the start I try to set a clear direction for our coaching by asking, 'In order to feel this coaching has been worthwhile for you, how will you know?' It may take a while, so I've learned to be patient. Most of the executives tell me this was a major shift in their thinking and they appreciated the time and space I gave them to think about this. As a result, the coaching is less about problem-solving and more about creating a hopeful and possible future. I often hear that, for the first time as executives, they feel a sense of relief and hope that something can change for the better and they can do something about it.

Coaching topics: Business or personal

In Jakarta, there is tremendous pressure on these executives to perform and deliver, which trickles down to intense pressure on their staff. It is not unusual for these executives to spend more hours at work than with their families. One client began our coaching sessions discussing internal problems at his company but after a few sessions shifted to discussing his marriage. By being able to engage with the client on a personal level, appreciating his responsibilities in his immediate family and understanding the influence of his values, I was able to assist him in matters of importance to him, and to eventually help him with his business problems. Solution focused coaching helps me keep anchored on going where the client wants to go and highlighting what I hear as key values and themes. Sometimes, there is a collision of values within these executives, who realise they are a counter-culture in Jakarta, where often business concerns take centre stage over family and personal satisfaction. For many of the executives I work with, they have come to realise that their personal values need to be more aligned with how they manage their life. This has often led to counter-cultural shifts in their lives. Putting family and personal satisfaction above work and organisational values has been a major challenge for them. However, during our coaching sessions, these executives have been able to identify the steps towards achieving these important goals in their lives, and as a result, have become role models within their own organisations. Ironically, these counter-cultural changes have actually led to higher work performance and higher productivity for these organisations.

Adopting a 'not-knowing' stance

As a solution focused coach, I like to adopt a 'not-knowing' stance, viewing the client as the expert. My clients come seeking help with decision making, seeking clarity, and how to meet their goals and targets and improve employee relations. In helping them identify their coaching goal and how to get where they want, they often realise they already had a clear sense of what they needed to do to make the changes within their organisation. They were able to streamline their resources, increase profits, improve employee welfare and completely redefine their corporate culture as a result of coaching. As solution focused coaches, we have to resist the expectation in Asia to take on the role of 'expert' giving advice or giving solutions. Instead, I prefer to explore the competencies of the client and these executives I work with come fully loaded! They have created multi-billion dollar companies, manage thousands of employees and own multiple companies as well hold significant positions in public office. They often tell me how empowered they feel after our coaching sessions because I focus on their strengths rather than their inadequacies.

Individual impact of solution focused coaching

Most of the executives I have coached reported an increase in their confidence, a better understanding of themselves, improvement in their 'time-management' and 'people skills' and have made a positive difference in how they went about their work in general. One client told me that our coaching helped him to feel encouraged. Another told me that after our sessions, she noticed she could think more creatively. Another said he felt that solution-finding through reflection and discussion with an external person gave him clarity and helped him to feel energised.

After coaching, clients realised that spending time discussing and analysing their roles and actions helped them to develop a better understanding of themselves and their leadership roles at work. The sessions challenged them to think through their lives, their priorities and what contributions they wanted to make to development in general and organisational capacity building in particular.

Organisational impact of solution focused coaching

I have seen many organisational shifts occur as a result of the personal benefits these executives identified through coaching. Changes at the individual level led to improved leadership styles. It led to more inclusive management and more respectful communication. These changes tended to permeate widely through the organisation. For example, one business owner told me, 'Earlier on, no one would oppose me in any decision making, but they would later grumble behind my back. These days, I don't do all the decision-making by myself. It is now shared among all.' This is a very unusual leadership style in Jakarta where hierarchy and position hold high honour and privilege.

Other organisational benefits of coaching reported from top-level management within their organisations include:

- Management was able to differentiate issues from the person, which helped to avoid getting distracted by 'personal attacks'.
- Individual staff worked on issues they felt were important to them, such as communication skills.
- Higher level leadership improved in time management and strategic planning.
- CEOs became more confident in their roles and felt more motivated.
- Management became more aware of potential pitfalls in cross-cultural communication.
- Organisations developed a culture that encouraged learning and values development and embraced positive change.
- Employees felt more valued by their organisation and were therefore more likely to commit long-term; this in turn improved productivity and continuity between programs and delivery, and provided stable leadership within a sector plagued by high staff turnover.

I remain curious about how and when individual change is translated into organisational change. What makes the difference? What kind of individual changes actually impact the organisation in a positive way? In most of these situations, the executives I coached were in key leadership roles and, therefore, became role models for their staff. One executive struggled to keep his marriage together while running his company. Because he was spending most of his time at the plant, he missed important family functions and events. His wife threatened to leave him, which came as a shock. The executive made significant changes in his scheduling and started to attend family functions and spent time with his wife. He wrote in his diary every week to take his wife to dinner, and he left work at 6 p.m. every day, instead of staying until 9 or 10 p.m. He encouraged his staff to do the same, and eventually, many of the men were leaving work earlier to spend time with their families. As a result of higher work and personal satisfaction, the organisational culture started to shift. Overall morale at the plant improved, and productivity increased significantly. Even though they were spending less time at work, they were actually increasing their work performance.

Final reflections

As someone who has been on both the giving and the receiving side of coaching, I have found it to be a very motivating and inspiring experience. When I am feeling stuck, and I engage with a coach who stimulates positive energy in me, and I am able to move forward. I have seen this happen with my clients as well. The solution focused approach to coaching enables business leaders to see the bigger picture and review their life and skills; it is a way to capture a spark of energy and help CEOs take positive action and move towards what they want to achieve or become.

Coaching is a useful leadership development tool for any organisation. It is relevant in commercial sectors, public and voluntary sectors and even religious sectors. As a solution focused practitioner, I have coached clients in South Africa, Sweden, Russia, all over South East Asia,

Asia Pacific and North America, with small business owners and heads of conglomerates. Having coached executives from all over the world and from many diverse cultures, I can say that the basic coaching approach remains fundamentally the same. The differences in culture were insignificant to the work at hand. What seemed to make the most difference was building a collaborative relationship, focused on the client's desired outcome, and highlighting the client's competencies and resources.

35

METAPHORS CREATING MIRACLES

The power and pitfalls of using metaphors in SF coaching

Marjanne van der Helm

As if I was wearing a protective invisible cloth, you know, like in Harry Potter. That's how I'd feel.

(client)

In my coaching practice, I often notice the power of metaphors in clients' conversations. The discovery of an apt metaphor, symbolising a new strategy, a goal or possible solution, can elicit a real epiphanic moment and a strong sense of understanding and direction.

'And how would you notice you had this invisible cloth?' I asked, pretending not to be surprised by this unusual description. 'I would be relaxed, as if I was not in the same room with my ex-husband, or his new girlfriend.' This 5-minute conversation turned out to be a real eye-opener. The almost magical image of an invisible cloth instantly gave her a feeling of protectiveness and an idea of how to act.

This intrigued me. How can metaphors be so powerful? And, more importantly: How can I work effectively with metaphors in solution-focused (SF) coaching? In this chapter I discuss the power, pitfalls and possible ways to use metaphors in SF coaching in an Asian context. To illustrate these, I will use a number of excerpts of coaching sessions with my Singapore clientele. Also, I will share relevant neuro-linguistic research and discuss cultural implications.

Coaching context

With a background in psychology and sociology, I started my career as an organisation development consultant in the Netherlands. I came to Singapore in 2012. A year and a half later, I started my own practice and have been coaching a diversity of clients, Asian and non-Asian, on life as well as career matters.

The bubble

One of my coachees came to see me because she wanted to become 'more in charge at work', as she put it.

Coachee: I get so affected by what my colleagues feel. I seem to carry other people's feelings.
Coach: So what would you like instead?

After trying different questions aiming at describing the desired outcome, I posed the miracle question.

Coach: So what will you notice when you wake up?
Coachee: Oh, I will already notice when I choose my clothes for the day. I will pay more attention to what I *want* to wear. And not think ahead too much about what kind of meetings I will have.
Coach: And what else?
Coachee: I will take my laptop and sit somewhere else on Monday morning. Quiet. To create a sort of *bubble*. Yes, it will be as if there is a bubble around me. I want to feel further away, distance myself. I would still want to sense the others, since it can be handy to know what is going on. But I want to provide a buffer.

At the next session, she told me that the bubble metaphor (see Figure 35.1) had helped her to become more in charge at work already. She visualised the bubble state in the morning, on the

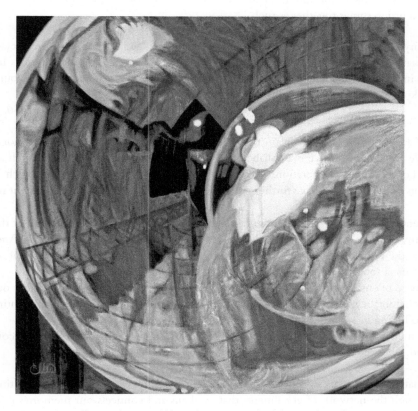

FIGURE 35.1 Rosemary Ellis, *Barbecue Bubble*. Oil on canvas, 30 × 30 inches. ©2012

bus to work. She listed her top three priorities for that day, to help her focus on what she wanted to achieve (and not what her colleagues wanted her to do). When she got to the office, she told people who approached her with questions or orders: 'Send me an email with all the details.' She did not try to answer all of them straight away, as she had done before.

The power of metaphors

So what happened in the example above? How do these metaphors work, and how can they be so powerful in facilitating change in a coaching conversation?

It was long thought that metaphors are just a linguistic phenomenon—figures of speech ingrained in our way of speaking. In 1980, cognitive linguists Lakoff and Johnson proposed that metaphors are not merely a linguistic phenomenon, but more fundamentally, a process that structures our thinking and acting. Recently, this idea has gained more scientific traction (Lacey, Stilla & Sathian, 2012).

Lakoff and Johnson (1980) state that 'the essence of metaphor is understanding and experiencing one kind of thing in terms of another' (p. 125). Examples given by Lakoff and Johnson include: 'Life is a gambling game' (p. 127), and 'Love is a collaborative work of art' (p. 128) or as for one of my clients: 'Acting as in a bubble.'

We seem to think in metaphors all the time. Our brain works largely metaphorically in that we tend to group things together as such.

> Many of our activities (arguing, solving problems, budgeting time, etc.) are metaphorical in nature. The metaphors characterizing those activities (e.g. argumentation is like war, solving problems is like a puzzle, time is money) make sense of and structure our way of looking at the world, our reality.
>
> *(Lakoff & Johnson, 1980, p. 131).*

Lakoff and Johnson (1980) explain that there are schemas underlying our metaphors. Metaphors have entailments. 'Love is a collaborative work of art' can have entailments such as: 'Love is work; Love requires cooperation; Love involves creativity'; and many more. Each of these entailments may themselves have further entailments. The result is 'a large and coherent network' (p. 129).

Different people can have different entailments that underlie their understanding of the metaphor. In my coachee's example, her bubble is *transparent; it enables her to notice others*. And, at the same time, the bubble *distances her*. The bubble is *a buffer*. It is important to realise that someone else may have a totally different set of entailments underlying the same metaphor.

This maze of entailments is held together or represented by the metaphor. It makes our experiences coherent; it makes sense of them. The metaphor provides structure, highlighting some things and hiding or suppressing others.

Some metaphors are more imaginative, creative and new to us than others. According to Lakoff and Johnson (1980):

> What we experience when we think of a *new* metaphor is a kind of reverberation down through the network of entailments that awakens and connects our memories of our past experiences, newly organizes important experiences and serves as a possible guide for future

ones. It can have a feedback effect, guiding future actions which are in accordance with the metaphor.

(pp. 129–130)

This explains the epiphany of discovering an apt metaphor. It creates a real breakthrough, because it gives new understanding. For the client it often captures many things at the same time, combining and organising important thoughts. Also, they remember the insights and the follow-up actions better, because it is all contained in one powerful and meaningful word or image.

Building blocks

A coachee wanted to find a new job. He had an action list, but for some reason this list seemed threatening to him. There were so many actions, often dependent on each other. It paralysed him. So he didn't do them.

One of these actions seemed a little less difficult. I asked him what made that particular one so easy. He answered that it was a *long shot*. It felt like this step was just A possibility and not THE possibility. This helped him to keep his expectations low. Instead of getting stuck with the idea of there being only one way, this train of thought brought him to the idea that there are many pathways.

Then he imagined his action list, or strategy, to be like a tower of blocks. For him, this metaphor combined all of the entailments above. For example, when one block is taken out, the tower is still standing. It doesn't all depend on one action. For him, this took the pressure off. Even the material mattered to him. Wooden blocks, which are not very precious in of themselves, are replaceable.

Metaphors in an Asian context

Metaphors can be very differently understood across cultures. A beautiful example given by Lakoff and Johnson (1980) is of an Iranian student and how he understood and loved the metaphor 'solution of problems':

> He thought of a large volume of liquid, bubbling and smoking, containing all of your problems, either dissolved or in the form of precipitates, with catalysts constantly dissolving some problems (for the time being) and precipitating others. To live by the chemical metaphor would mean that your problems have a different kind of reality for you. A temporary solution would be an accomplishment rather than a failure. Problems would be part of the natural order of things rather than disorders to be 'cured'. The way you would understand your everyday life and the way you would act in it would be different if you lived by the chemical metaphor.

(pp. 130–131)

The metaphors we use in our thinking can largely be explained by the environment we live in, the physical, social and cultural context (Lakoff & Johnson, 1980). How we construct metaphors will be largely 'coherent with the most fundamental values of the culture we live in' (p. 128). For example, a study from Taiwan (Su, 2002) found that metaphors the Chinese use with regard to marriage reflect the current Chinese view of marriage: namely, 'marriage is business' (p. 598).

Even if the same metaphor is used across cultures, the concepts or entailments underlying the metaphor can vary widely from culture to culture. In the example of 'marriage is business', even if the view on marriage is the same, but the person's view on business is different (or vice versa), the metaphor will not fit.

Pitfalls and possible ways to go

Cultural meanings: Be unknowing and unbiased. The above examples show that the same metaphors can be understood differently by different people and different cultures.

As a coach, it is important to be aware of the very personal and cultural understanding of the metaphors your clients might use. It can be difficult to 'stay unknowing' and 'unbiased' when someone from another cultural background uses a certain metaphor that you interpret very differently.

Always remind yourself: 'Don't think you know!' In SF we do not need to understand the metaphor to be able to work with it, as long as it makes sense to our client. Even if the metaphor sounds utterly strange, simply repeat the metaphor and ask relevant follow-up questions, aimed at the practical implications of the metaphor, such as: 'So, how would you notice you are wearing this protective invisible cloth?'; 'How would wearing it make a difference?'; 'What will you be doing differently while wearing this cloth?'

Leave the client in charge. In coaching, the aim is not to find a metaphor. It either comes to our clients or not. We can go along with it if *they say* it is a helpful metaphor.

We follow them in their definition of the preferred outcome. We are in charge of the process, by directing them towards their goal, their resources and actual change. Even if this means that they want to be invisible, so be it. Take them seriously in everything they say. But consequently, ask them how it will make a difference for them, and in their behaviour.

Do not expect the metaphor to be a stable construct throughout multiple coaching sessions. With the bubble example, in the third session the client still used this metaphor, but said that its characteristics had changed. She called it *the Super Bubble*: clearer, thinner, less protective. It gave her the feeling of being in charge, feeling confident and calm. For me, it was a sign that the client was experiencing actual change.

Don't look for deeper meanings – stay on the surface. As Jackson and McKergow (2007) said: 'we can be distracted by theories, complicated language and metaphors, which draw our attention into arid areas' (p. 15). I agree with them that there is no use in exploring every 'common' metaphor or figure of speech a client utters. Generally, I only explore a metaphor when a client clearly claims to have a moment of epiphany or 'aha' moment.

Focus on the positive. Only explore metaphors when they are uttered as *solution- or outcome-oriented talk*. Do not dive into metaphors describing a client's problem situation, since this will only give more insight into the problem, but not into the solution, strategies or strengths of the client.

Make it practical and action-oriented. Finding the metaphor is not the last step. It is only the beginning of finding out what the entailments are that make this metaphor so fitting to the client and their situation.

The key issue is how this new insight makes way for different actions they can take. Make it as practical as possible. Ask clients: 'How does this metaphor help you to deal with the situation better?'; 'How will you be acting differently?'; 'What will others notice you do differently?'

Look for visible, tangible signs or descriptions of changes in their behaviour. For example, with the bubble metaphor, do not leave it at the description of the bubble. Ask how this bubble helps them to behave, talk or walk differently, and what other people would notice with behavioural descriptions.

Also, it is important that the small step a client decides to take is as realistic and doable as possible and focused on changing their own behaviour and not that of others.

Conclusion

'New metaphors have the power to create a new reality' (Lakoff & Johnson, 1980, p. 131). They can help us change the way we look at things and be a beacon to base our actions on. In that respect, they can be tremendously helpful, facilitating change in a coaching conversation, especially when a coach keeps the SF practices in mind and is culturally aware of different entailments underlying the metaphor.

References

Jackson, P.Z., & McKergow, M. (2007). *The solutions focus: Making coaching and change SIMPLE.* London, UK: Nicholas Brealey International.

Lacey, S., Stilla, R., & Sathian, K. (2012). Metaphorically feeling: Comprehending textural metaphors activates somatosensory cortex. *Brain and Language, 120*(3), 416–421.

Lakoff, G., & Johnson, M. (1980). *Metaphors we live by.* Chicago, IL. Chicago University Press.

Su, L.I. (2002). What can metaphors tell us about culture? *Language and Linguistics, 3*(3), 589–613.

36

THE SOLUTION FOCUSED HUDDLE

Assisting employees amidst organisational redundancy

Agnes Hautea Nano

Introduction

Restructuring an organisation can be traumatic, especially for employees selected for redundancy. This chapter describes one company's initiative in facilitating the transition of long-time, dedicated employees who had served the company well. Veering away from an information-heavy program on transition, it shows how solution focused (SF) coaching facilitated valuable exchanges within a group of employees in the Philippines. This group managed to express both their sentiments as well as their best hopes, while discovering their own resources and ways to cope amidst the impending separation.

> *You cannot teach a man anything; you can only help him find it for himself.*
>
> (*Galileo Galilei*)

Personal relationships with colleagues and superiors are among the top job satisfaction factors in the typical Filipino culture. It is commonplace to regard colleagues as family. The quality of this relationship in the workplace is what motivates employees to work extra hours when necessary and exceed job expectations and has been recognised as critical in reaching company targets. Given the role relationships play in productivity in the workplace, being told that one's services are no longer needed can be a tremendous shock for an employee who has dedicated a big part of his life to the company. In some cases, the impact of redundancy programs may also affect the employees who will be left behind as they say goodbye and take on the responsibilities of their long-time colleagues.

Recognising the significance of the relationship with its valued employees, I was asked by a multinational company in the Philippines to facilitate a coaching process for a group of employees who were served notice of their redundancy. During preliminary discussions around the concerns and goals of the company with the coordinator for the program, the articulated goal was to help the employees be more accepting of the redundancy scenario affecting them, and enable them to move on from there. Using an SF coaching format, I tailored the process to fit into an existing programme that was designed and used in the past by their internal Human Resources professional. Inspired by the frequent use of the word 'huddle' in the corporate world, I named the workshop, 'The Solution Focused Huddle'.

Best hopes

I have always been amazed by how simple SF questions can draw out a goldmine of responses on what is important to the client. Setting the directions for the workshop, below are some of the questions I asked the group.

'**What are your best hopes for the workshop?**' Amidst this significant change in their lives, the participants were in different phases of adjustment to the notice of termination. Consistent with the leadership's best hopes, the common goal expressed by the participants was for everyone 'to move on'. While many had been thinking of retiring already and doing something different, some expressed wanting 'to feel better', to be 'confident that there is life after I leave this company', and to have 'advice on how to manage my separation benefits'.

'**What are you good at?**' Taking stock of their strengths and resources was embedded in personal stories of how they arrived at the present moment in their careers. A significant highlight was a shared appreciation of the comfort they felt with one another through the years of working together.

Preferred future. I asked them to close their eyes and do an envisioning exercise to facilitate conversation about their preferred future. After several seconds of silence, with my pen ready on the flip chart, participants began to share that they would be: 'smiling more', 'greeting everyone', 'enjoying a longer lunch', 'laughing', 'playing with children', 'dressing better', 'feeling better', 'having better interaction with colleagues', 'better relationship with spouses', 'a clear financial plan', etc. Others answered that they would be 'more organised at work', so that 'transition of work will be faster and smoothe'.

This exercise seemed particularly helpful in highlighting the connection with their colleagues, as they began to open up and share the impact of this experience and what they wanted to do.

Scaling. On a scale of 1–10, I asked the participants how confident they were that they would be able to get through this phase of their lives. It was interesting that many of them acknowledged that they were already somewhere at the upper end of the 10-point scale (around 8). Identifying factors that aided movement from a 1 to an 8 was useful in helping them see how they had already begun adjusting to the change. Some expressed that the separation package helped them see a brighter future. One member of the team saw the redundancy as an opportunity since she had been planning on retirement as early as 2 years ago. The compensation package was referred to as 'manna from heaven'. Another member saw the redundancy as a way for her to slow down so she could attend to her health problems and work on living a normal life. Others, who focused on coping with the present, mentioned that being able talk about their feelings to their friends also helped them.

The team's high number on the scale really highlighted the Filipinos' ability to be resilient in times of adversity, a valuable reminder of their resourcefulness to cope and manage well. As a Filipino, I understand this all too well, as this has been proven time and again through the various calamities we have been exposed to.

Acknowledging the resources

Through the process of identifying the skills, strengths and resources that helped participants to move on, a number of significant things emerged. As mentioned previously, most had already acknowledged the value and recognition given by the company with the generous retirement package. This had been consistently identified as a resource that would help them plan for life after the redundancy. Additional valuable resources given by the company included support programs. The team-coaching workshop had been helpful in identifying their strengths. Other needs had been addressed, such as how to manage their finances better. Several employees acknowledged the support and understanding they received from their families. As a result, acknowledgement of personal competencies was mentioned. One manager had a light bulb moment when he realised that his skill as a salesperson and the network he managed to build over the last 25 years could help him start his own business. Hearing his plan also inspired the other members to look forward to something positive. Another colleague shared that because she was a good organiser and always wanted to help people, she would be good in doing volunteer work. Several colleagues also shared how their faith and prayers helped them cope better. These colleagues had worked together for quite a long time, which made it more comfortable for them to open up and share their experiences with their extended families.

Small steps

While sharing many positives, some of the group also expressed their fears about the future. Normalising these fears had a calming effect. 'Of course, you will feel that way; it is not easy to do something different after being with the company for 20 years.' It was interesting to see how they broke into a smile, and began to sit in a more relaxed position. Using the three tenets of SF, I challenged them to 'do something different'. I asked them to think of small steps they could take to move forward, into their preferred future. At this point in the process, the colleagues had warmed up, excitedly sharing their ideas, which filled the room with laughter and jest. Ideas flowed, such as going on a vacation, starting a business, spending time with family and grandchildren, taking up a new hobby, bringing their children to school, and applying for a job at a new company.

I concluded the session with the SF feelings tank exercise (Henden, 2008, pp. 146–8). I asked them to name all their fears and imagine putting them in a feelings tank. I asked them to focus on the 'tap', where they could be in control of how much of their feelings they could release to help them feel better. 'And you know what the good news is?' I asked. 'The good news is that you are the one in control of your own life.' The expression on their faces was just priceless. I explored with them how they could use this tap as a pressure-releasing valve and what it would look like. Their small steps included going to a spa, walking the dog, cooking for their family, yoga, breathing and self-care things they could do to feel better, even just a little bit. I also emphasised that small steps can lead to bigger steps and that every little step can count towards feeling better.

I followed up the group four months later, a week before their last day of work, with the help of a series of symbolic activities capturing 'What's better?'. I engaged them in creating a Tree of Hope from post-it notes for leaves and branches of the tree (see Figure 36.1). The leaves and branches were the small steps they have already taken to move up toward their goal. They also created a mandala to show their future perfect world. Making the mandala was stimulated by an appreciative inquiry question, 'What opportunities can arise from your situation now?' After drawing and colouring their mandalas, they shared their steps that reflected even greater openness and readiness to move on.

FIGURE 36.1 Tree of Hope.
(Photo credit: Agnes Hautea Nano)

Reflections

The Filipinos' concept of family has always been a strength and a resource. By blood or by affiliation, it is the tie that binds people together in working toward a common goal. The kindness and sensitivity of the company is an exemplar of the responsibility that comes with this relationship, as it took effort to ensure that each team member was treated fairly and respectfully. Using SF conversations facilitated a process whereby they supported the company's value of relationships, and enabled the participants to own their personal resources, and move forward.

The participants' openness to accept the change contributed significantly to the reported outcome of the workshop. The SF team coaching process helped each of them move up the scale on confidence in their ability to move forward. Before the workshop, some had already been thinking about their personal transition plan, like moving on to a new job, starting up their businesses, taking care of loved ones, etc. The process enabled them to verbalise it and visualise it.

As a coach, it was most helpful to allow colleagues to tell and harvest insights from their own stories. The SF questions were powerful as it enabled them to think of all the possibilities they could explore. The compliments, affirmations and reflections empowered them, and allowing them a venue to share those possibilities also inspired their other colleagues.

Despite the value for personal relationships in the Filipino workplace, this is not always seen in practice. This seems to be particularly true in large, local and multinational companies where productivity is largely defined by profit targets. While it is not an uncommon practice for employees in top-level positions to be served notice of their retrenchment within a very short period, it remains a very difficult process that can put the security and health of the outgoing employees and their families at risk. In such a case, SF coaching can be helpful for both employer and employee dealing with the changes by celebrating how the company has gained from the strengths and growth of each individual with the company, and by mapping out the next steps after termination.

The corporate culture of the company discussed in this chapter is highly commendable for the value it gave to the wellness of its employees amidst their impending termination. It is the value for people that made some of the employees stay as long as they did. It is also this same culture that pushed for a transition session followed by individual personal coaching for the affected employees as well. Thus, the company's all-out support for the needs of its employees was a crucial factor in this process. I, too, was impressed with the 'family like' atmosphere of the company's values, which made some of the employees stay as long as 20 to 35 years. The way this company took care of the members of its family until the end was really amazing!

Reference

Henden, J. (2008). *Preventing suicide: The solution-focused approach.* West Sussex, England: John Wiley & Sons Ltd.

37

SOLUTION FOCUSED TEAM FACILITATION

Co-creating our shared future

Anisha Kaul

Introduction

The solution focused (SF) approach lends itself wonderfully to working with teams in a variety of different contexts including team building; developing vision, mission and values; and strategy and planning. The SF approach is especially powerful in an Asian context as it encourages active participation from all team members. Where other approaches allow passive 'onlooker' behaviour, SF offers tools, processes and an underlying philosophy that setup each individual for success from the start. Who wouldn't want to have the spotlight shone on their greatest achievements – especially when underlying strengths and qualities emerge and can be leveraged even more powerfully in the future? This chapter offers a glimpse into a team intervention grounded on SF principles and supported by SF tools.

Solution focused team facilitation

'But how will we get them to speak up and share what is on their mind? In front of everyone?' Jamie asked. In response to this predictable question from a client in this familiar consulting situation, I smiled reassuringly, 'We will use a solution focused approach'. Jamie sat up straighter. 'Solution focused? Tell me more. . . .'

This is a common scenario when I meet with the leader of a culturally diverse team, listening to them describe a challenge their team is facing and the difficulty in getting team members to work together to decide a way forward. Jamie's team included Westerners and Asians, and while there was harmony, there was low engagement due to the different communication styles of the team members. For Jamie, this situation was proving to be a real test of his leadership. As a Westerner working in Asia for the past three years, Jamie had worked hard to adapt his leadership style to be more responsive to the diverse needs of his team. Jamie explained that while he had built strong and trusting relationships with individual team members, the team as a whole was suffering. Used to working in silos, they needed to come together to align with and implement a way forward.

I had been referred as a consultant and team facilitator to Jamie through an ex-colleague who had explained that the approach I use in team workshops had a way of inviting participation from even the most reticent team members and re-engaging teams.

I answered Jamie's question with my own question 'If they were to speak up and share what is on their minds, what sort of interactions and behaviours would you be observing?' Jamie described what he would be observing, and as I probed for details, it became clear to me that this was a leader who knew what he wanted, but just didn't know how to get there.

External facilitators are often brought in when a team leader knows that something needs to change but is not able to articulate exactly what the issue is. Rather than launching into a lengthy analysis of the root cause of the problem, the SF facilitator reframes this state of not knowing as a platform from which creative solutions can emerge. In an Asian context, where the team leader is often expected to have all the answers, this shift in perspective puts people at ease and offers hope.

Building trust is important. In a setting that invites team members into new ways of thinking and approaching problems, they must be made to feel secure enough to be open, honest, take risks and embrace feedback. In an Asian context, where 'saving face' can often lead to fear of self-disclosure, the SF facilitator uses tools to create and maintain a collaborative environment that is positive, supportive and challenging. This has the benefits of:

- strengthening relationships
- appreciating different communication styles
- increasing trust through self-disclosure
- gathering useful feedback in service of learning
- developing tangible, measurable outcomes

The facilitator's job is to notice and bring to the surface rich opportunities for learning inherent in the team's interactions. In Asia the desire to 'save face' often leads to participants keeping quiet, to avoid being 'wrong'. The SF approach encourages more passive team members to speak up and feel comfortable sharing their views as the focus is on *useful* learning, rather than calling attention to what is not working.

SF facilitators know that positive change in teams begins well before the day of the workshop. My work with Jamie's team began in that very first meeting as I sat across from Jamie. I asked Jamie questions such as 'Help me understand what needs to be different?' or 'What you would like to see happening instead?' versus 'Help me understand what the problem is'. I was very intentional in my choice of words. SF facilitators know that problem talk creates problems and solution talk creates solutions. Before our conversation, Jamie felt stuck in the 'problem' of the lack of cohesion amongst his team members, which he attributed to the different communication styles of the Asians and Westerners on his team.

One of the most powerful realisations I had as a result of my training in the SF approach is that positive change can happen even before the day of the workshop. After that initial meeting with Jamie, I proposed having one-to-one conversations with team members, to begin to build a connection with them. In an Asian context, where it may take longer for individuals to open up to an external facilitator, this pre-workshop contact in which team members are invited to share their point of view in confidence can help earn trust. Just as I had asked Jamie what he would be observing if team members spoke up and shared what was on their minds, I asked team members similar questions.

The questions are designed to uncover the preferred future and what is already in place, and the positive nature of the interview questions focuses attention on what is already working well. Team members are tuned in to report positive 'changes' in the direction of the preferred future. The SF facilitator knows that often these 'changes' already existed within the team but they were not consciously aware of them, especially if they are focused on the problems. I led Jamie's team through an SF team facilitation process that draws from the OSKAR coaching model (McKergow & Jackson, 2007).

The workshop started with an introduction activity in which team members share something about themselves and state their personal objective for the workshop. Giving everyone a chance to speak early on is particularly important as it sets the tone and expectation from the start that everybody is welcome – and expected – to participate. In an Asian context where quieter team members often remain silent, an activity such as this encourages everyone to feel comfortable sharing from the start.

Jamie and his team could already sense that this was not going to be the usual meeting situation in which a few dominant individuals would be doing most of the talking, with the rest being passive observers. By the end of the first hour, everyone had spoken. By sharing something about themselves, it resulted in team members getting to know each other on a more personal and meaningful level. They all had an opportunity to hear everyone's personal objectives for the workshop and by now had a shared understanding of what needed to happen for their time to be deemed successful.

At this point, the expectations that Jamie and his team members had were high. As a facilitator, the pressure was now on me to deliver. However, this is where the SF approach is really powerful, as it hands responsibility back to the team. The output from the question I asked in the next step, which I call 'team alliance', is a powerful source of data for teams to remember in order to work together effectively.

The team alliance question I asked was 'How do we need to be together to ensure that we meet our objectives today?' I probed for a description of behaviours to keep things observable. Several team members said, 'We need to trust each other'. In response to this I asked, 'How would you know trust is present? What would you be observing?' I listed each item on a piece of flipchart paper and asked the team 'Can we all agree to the behaviours listed here to ensure we meet our objectives?' Each and every one of Jamie's team agreed. Taking advantage of this, I took it one step further by inviting each team member to come up and sign their name on the paper.

By now, Jamie's team was feeling good and spirits were high. During the coffee break, Jamie told me that this was the first time he had seen all his team members so engaged and contributing openly to the conversation. He asked me how I did it. I told him that this was the power of the SF approach – we find what's working and do more of it.

You may have noted that we were already half-way through the morning in Jamie's team workshop – and so far there had only been relationship-building activities. We had not yet begun to talk about the problem or the challenge that had led Jamie to bring the team together and to hire an external facilitator to help tackle.

My approach is to put a significant emphasis on relationship building in the first part of the workshop. This helps team members co-create the conditions in which they can each bring their best. Especially in an Asian context, where there can be more formality and it can take longer for people to warm up and feel comfortable contributing, it is important to spend time getting everyone's voices in the room. Spending enough time on this initial relationship-building piece helps build trust and creates a solid foundation for meaningful conversations to take place.

The rest of Jamie's team workshop followed a typical SF framework. I asked the miracle question to uncover the team's preferred future in greater detail.

> *Suppose, you go to sleep tonight, and during the night, while you are asleep, a miracle happens. And the miracle is that the team is performing as a peak performing team. In the morning, when you wake up, how would you go about discovering the miracle had happened? What would you see and hear around you to tell you that you are now a member of a peak performing team?*

Once the miracle picture was built, Jamie's team was able to see how aligned they were on the direction they wanted for their team and organisation. This feeling of all being 'on the same page' helped forge stronger connections between team members. Suddenly, no matter what background the team member was from, it was clear that they all wanted to head in the same direction. This collective witnessing of their shared future emerging was a powerful realisation for Jamie's team members.

After lunch, the team decided which topic to focus on for their planning and next steps. I asked the team to rate, on a scale of 1 to 10, how much was already in place around the chosen topic and we spent time uncovering the team's existing 'know-how'. The team discussed what resources were already in place and what was already working well that they could build on. We looked at this from various different perspectives including the culturally diverse views that existed amongst the team. Exploring Asian and Western values, Jamie's team talked about how to see things from different perspectives and what various stakeholders may need and value. The team was able to acknowledge and celebrate their differences, which led to creative thinking around a shared future that they were all committed to.

This commitment was solidified towards the end of the workshop when we briefly revisited the scale. I asked 'In order to move up one number on the scale, what would we need to do?' Each team member selected one or two actions they could take ownership for. The team had a useful conversation around how to support each other and share resources. Connections emerged that had not been uncovered before.

As the workshop concluded, I reminded the team of a fundamental SF principle: 'Change happens all the time.' In other words, there is a high likelihood that the team's 'preferred future' will have evolved the next time the team gets together. To my delight, one of the team members exclaimed 'We are a solution focused team, and we now have new tools and resources to tackle the challenges and take advantage of the opportunities that lie ahead'.

Conclusions

SF embodies a mind-set that is positive and practical with its focus on what is already working well, which alleviates some of the pressure of needing to 'save face' and thus avoid taking risks. This chapter described the example of Jamie and his team who, supported by the SF facilitation process, were able to feel safe, open up and participate fully, bringing all their diverse perspectives and experiences into play to co-create their shared future.

Reference

McKergow, M., & Jackson, P.Z. (2007). *The solutions focus.* Boston, MA: Nicholas Brealey.

38

LOOK FOR THE SILVER LINING

Jayne Sim

As a mentor and coach in a non-profit organisation that spans eight countries in Asia, I've worked with many women who are constantly plagued with stressful and overworked lifestyles. The typical Asian woman dons a 'hard work is success' mind-set, centred on the constant act of 'doing' in order to feel accomplished, whether in the area of household matters, children's needs or marriage. The women leaders I work with have daily mental 'checklists' to complete to help them feel like a good mother, wife, employee and friend. A working mother today has to hone her balancing act of being a stellar employee at work, and a diligent mother and wife at home. The never-ending demands in both areas — work and home — are usually self-inflicted or imposed by the family or workplace, and are influenced by, and sometimes overwhelm, a woman's belief system. The Asian woman is expected first to be submissive to her husband, taking care of his every need; then a competent, nurturing mother raising up obedient children; while being an excellent homemaker, keeping the home a safe and clean haven for the whole family. In today's affluent society, she has to balance this noble task with the increasing need to also supplement the family income through a full-time job. Consequently, women are bogged down by thoughts of 'never being good enough', leaving them feeling either angry or powerless.

While most women across Asia toil over these same issues, the women I coach and mentor also struggle with additional stressors brought on by their dedication to serve as volunteers in HOPE worldwide, a non-profit organisation. Many of these women are learning leadership and facilitation skills with small groups — gatherings of anywhere from three to six women who meet regularly to talk about all sorts of issues — a kind of peer support group. Taking on these leadership roles is not easy, as they have to help other women work through family issues and insecurities while keeping their own lives in order. They deal with a barrage of burdens that belong not only to them but others as well. Many of these women coaches have often expressed that they feel inadequate about leading effectively, thus my decision to begin training them to use solution focused coaching in their leadership roles. Solution focused conversations have been an effective tool in helping these women leaders overcome their debilitating negative mind-sets. As they trained to become motivators of personal growth, these women have learned how to utilise the strengths of individuals, instead of dwelling on their problems. Their minds are now open to a myriad of ways to deal with a situation as they brainstorm with the women they help. They have also learned that they do not need to be 'experts', but empathetic listeners instead. Their journeys of self-discovery while learning to empower the women they mentor have been the focus during our monthly group coaching sessions and are highlighted in the stories below.

Turning negativity into possibility

The tendency to make problems and weaknesses the focal point when helping others can be crippling to many women leaders as they find themselves sinking unknowingly into a state of negativity. The encumbrance of the problems results in assuming failure too quickly, accompanied by doubts that things could ever turn around. Through training, they have learnt to frame their questions in ways that give hope to those they help and for themselves, seen below in the case of a young woman struggling with loneliness.

Case study: Friendless Frieda

Frieda had been trying to build more friendships while keeping the old ones. Despite her relentless efforts, she found herself feeling lonelier than ever, as if she had no friends at all. During a coaching session with Frieda, I asked her a series of carefully framed questions.

Suppose you found the kind of friend you want . . .

- How would you know?
- Who can you think of in your life that fits what you just described?

Frieda initially found it hard to come up with any names, but by the end of the conversation, she was able to identify a total of 15 names.

The simple questions proved exceptionally powerful in helping Frieda see that the situation was not as bad as she had perceived it to be. Frieda's constant focus on her weakness – her difficulty in building new friendships – was transformed into a focus on the possible friendships she already possessed and could continue building. The numerical evidence made it exceptionally encouraging for Frieda as well. This hopeful shift in mind-set became a catalyst for further changes in her life.

The progress made by Frieda exemplifies one of the many ways these women leaders have discovered how to look beyond weaknesses. They have learned how to bring out the best in an individual or situation by focusing on what is being done well and what could be done for a better future.

Pathways to progress

Using scaling questions has helped these coaches and the people they work with mark their improvement and map out a pathway of progress. Using scaling, the coaches are helping the women they lead discover that the smallest sign of progress (e.g., a 3/10 to a 3.5/10), or the maintenance of a score (staying at a 3/10), can still show growth. Even regression (e.g., a decrease from 3/10 to 2/10), when framed correctly, can lead individuals to consider how they can get back to a 3/10, as they have experienced being at that point before. The coaches have loved learning the scaling tool. They feel it brings hope rather than the gloom and doom that they used to feel when discussing problems. Helping the women they lead to identify where they are, in relation to where they want to go, enables them to make small steps in the right direction. Exploring how they got to where they are on the scale reminds them of the small successes they have already accomplished. By the time a person is at a 6 or higher on the scale, they already know a lot about charting and continuing their pathway to success.

Result-oriented to goal-oriented

When dealing with long-standing issues, many leaders dread going into meetings knowing new problems will be thrown at them while still trying to make their meeting purposeful and forward looking. Wendy, one of the women coaches, asked our group to help her with some relevant questions for her sessions with Susan, which helped Susan think differently about her relationship with her daughter.

Case study: Steamed-up Susan

Susan's 10-year-old daughter, Hazel, had recently been diagnosed with a learning disability. Susan shared that she had become frustrated and abusive when coaching Hazel in her schoolwork, causing a strain in their relationship. Susan was not sure what to work on – her anger management or helping Hazel to become more disciplined. Wendy made use of solution focused questions to help Susan set a clear goal:

- Suppose you woke up and discovered a miracle has happened during the night, that the problems facing you and your daughter are solved; what would be some clues that tell you the miracle has happened?
- What would you be doing differently?
- How would your interaction with your daughter be different?
- How would this make a difference to your daughter?
- Tell me about a time when your interactions with your daughter were close to what you have imagined?
- How did that happen?
- What did you do differently?

While answering the questions, Susan formulated a goal to improve the connection with Hazel and to make Hazel feel more accepted. With the future in mind, some practical steps were agreed upon, and observable progress was made over time. Susan saw how her attempts resulted in a positive response from her daughter, and an improvement in their relationship, which gave Susan hope and encouragement to not give up trying.

Goal formation helps to chart the direction forward as it gives the leader a clear objective for collaboration, hence creating a more effective session that can be felt by the one seeking help. Armed with solution building tools, Wendy then saw herself as a 'visionary' leader, instead of one who felt the pressure of having to 'assess people accurately' or give the 'right solutions'.

Empowering the self through empowering others

Many women coaches see themselves as helpless rescuers in the deep sea – struggling to bring all the drowning women on board at once. Solutions are aplenty, but these women leaders feel they can only help their drowning friends if they jump in themselves, holding the life preserver! By asking questions that lead to personal reflection, they began to see their resources and capabilities. What is remarkable about these women is their ability to shift their perspective and see possibilities that they did not see before.

Leaders who practise solution-focused communication have realised the importance of listening more and talking less. They focus on 'knowing people', 'not-knowing' problems, and channelling their energy to being 'present and involved', rather than being worried about what solutions to provide. As they perceived themselves to be effective listeners, they overcame their insecurities and sought to understand and learn from people instead. As they discovered more about people, they were able to see their strengths, and use these strengths to work towards a desired outcome.

Activity: Strength cards

The utilisation of 'strength cards' has been a useful tool in helping people identify their positive qualities and feeling that their strengths were acknowledged. In one of my training sessions, I placed a set of cards containing positive character traits on a table and the appropriate questions were asked and answered with the cards laid out. Some questions used in the small-group leaders' training meeting included:

- What are your key strengths? Share five and explain briefly.
- What strengths have you had to work hardest to develop?
- What would others say are the strengths of your small group?
- Which strengths do you admire and appreciate in various mentors you've had over the years?
- Which strengths would you like to develop with the help of your present mentor?
- Think of the women in your own small group and list five strengths for each of them.

The women who participated in the above activity felt encouraged that their strengths were acknowledged. Some felt it helped them to be more positive about their groups. One leader expressed that she felt more hopeful about leading, while another realised she could see strengths in the women in her group that she had not seen before. One participant's comment summed up the objective of the exercise: 'It reminded me that everybody has strengths'.

Some of these coaches-in-training turned around and used this tool with their own groups. They reported they were able to bring out hidden strengths in their group members, and they loved being able to help them discover resources they already had. Once again, the focus was shifted from problems. When the leaders focused on existing strengths to empower the people they were helping, they become empowered themselves.

Conclusion

Most of us desire to see 'the light at the end of the tunnel' and hope that a 'silver lining rims every cloud'. Unfortunately, Asian women are often bogged down by the problems at hand, which snatches away the enjoyment of life that they could be experiencing. Being fixated on non-stop worries and inaccessible answers leads to a roadblock of negativity and insecurity. I, too, am a busy Asian woman in a stressed-out society, and I believe that being mindful of the strengths I possess, and helping the women I lead to be mindful of their strengths as well, along with clearly examining situations with the preferred future in mind, helps us journey on with security that we have what it takes to overcome any storm. Storms are inevitable; but we can ride out the storm, and make our own silver lining in the clouds.

39

APPLICATION OF SOLUTION-FOCUSED COACHING IN OCCUPATIONAL THERAPY FOR MENTAL HEALTH RECOVERY IN HONG KONG

Maurice S. H. Wan and Raymond W. C. Au

Mental health services have been evolving from institutionalised care to rehabilitation, and to recovery-oriented practice. Solution-focused (SF) coaching can be a viable option that helps to realise the recovery-oriented practice. This chapter will depict how SF coaching was applied in the Chinese culture of Hong Kong and the various ways in which it led to progress and rehabilitation in occupational therapy (OT), illustrated with a case vignette.

Recovery-oriented practice in mental health

Anthony (1993) describes personal recovery as 'a way of living a satisfying, hopeful, and contributing life even with the limitations caused by illness' (p. 15). In the process, a person develops a new meaning and purpose in life as they grow beyond the catastrophic effects of mental illness.

There has been a swift development in the recovery movement worldwide in recent years (Davidson, Rakfeldt & Strauss, 2010). The psychiatric service in Hong Kong is also changing. The Hospital Authority, being the largest government-funded medical and healthcare provider, set out the future direction in the development of a recovery-oriented psychiatric practice in a five-year mental health services plan (HA, 2010).

The purpose of OT is to empower people with various disabilities to live a meaningful life by returning to their valued life roles at home, work and leisure. In psychiatric rehabilitation, occupational therapists are trained to provide comprehensive assessment and training to deal with clients' functional deficits in work and other daily living skills to overcome these functional limitations. However, it is not always sufficient to support clients' recovery. Occupational therapists need to renew their mind-set and to enhance their knowledge and skills in the new paradigm. They also need to transform their role beyond therapist to the role of a coach to support clients' personal growth in the recovery journey. Therefore, in 2009, SF coaching was introduced to the OT profession in the Hospital Authority of Hong Kong through commissioned training. This was a very timely introduction to support the HA's direction for their mental health services plan mentioned above (HA, 2010).

Mental health recovery and the solution-focused approach

Mental health recovery has shifted the paradigm of psychiatric practice from diagnosis, symptom management and rehabilitation to goal identification, strength finding and development of a meaningful life. Recovery, however, is a set of values that does not provide an approach to operationalise its practice, nor is it supported with specific intervention tools. The SF approach is a way of thinking about how people change and reach their goals, a way of conversation with clients, and a way of constructing solutions interactively (Walter & Peller, 1992). It was adopted as an appropriate intervention tool as it aligns with the values of mental health recovery by occupational therapists in Hong Kong.

The SF approach operates on a number of assumptions that support the realisation of mental health recovery (de Shazer et al., 1986; Peller & Walter, 1989). The guiding principles for a recovery-oriented practice (SAMHSA, 2010) are compatible with many of the core assumptions in SF practice. These are described below, illustrated with some brief case examples.

Positive focus. By focusing on the positive, solutions, and the future, the SF approach facilitates change in the desired direction. Recovery provides the essential and motivating message of a better future that constitutes the important element of hope. For example, by adapting the SF approach with a patient with anorexia during an art jam session, she talked not only about her diet problem but her hope and dream to be Ms. Hong Kong! We then helped her to set small goals of at least improving her present condition if she really wanted to achieve this.

Exceptions to every problem can be created. Clients with mental illnesses often are not aware that there are times when the problem does not happen. By eliciting and constructing 'exceptions' to the problem with clients, it helps the client to develop a sense of control over the problem. This is empowerment in recovery, helping the client to gain control of his or her own destiny. For example, a patient did not think he could have any work-related goal because of his poor mental state. When asked if there were times that he could work even if he felt his mental condition was not that good, the patient gave us several examples! The occupational therapist could then help the patient in identifying his strengths in coping with that situation which could help to enhance the client's confidence.

Small change leads to larger change. Clients with severe mental illnesses often have a sense of hopelessness and helplessness, resulting in a lack of courage to change the problem-saturated situations. By focusing on small changes, clients are empowered to take small steps towards their goals. With the experience of small successes, they are better motivated and encouraged to find solutions to other goals that can move toward larger change. This helps the client to take responsibility for personal change that is important in recovery.

Clients have strengths. People are resourceful. This is the strength-based advocacy in mental health recovery that focuses on valuing and building on the multiple capacities, resiliencies, talents, coping abilities and inherent worth of individuals.

The client is the expert. Instead of relying on professionals as experts, the SF approach advocates clients as experts on what they want to change and to determine what they want to work on. Recovery emphasises clients can lead, control, exercise choice over and determine their own path of recovery to achieve a self-determined life.

Meaning and experience are interactively constructed. Meanings evolve and change in the solution-oriented dialogue between the client and the therapist. A change in meaning leads to a change in experience that could lead to new experience of a positive future. Recovery is a journey where the client rediscovers or develops new meaning and purpose after having a mental illness and ultimately can make his or her choice for a meaningful life.

Solution-focused coaching

Coaching is one of the most popular applications of the solution-focused approach and is defined as 'comfortably bringing important people from where they are to where they want to be' (Berg & Szabo, 2005, p. xi). Enhancing the role of a therapist to the role of a coach in mental health recovery is a more positive and effective way of supporting the client's personal growth toward self-actualisation and transcendence. The elegant model of SF coaching has provided a simple yet concise pathway to coach clients of any type toward their preferred future. The toolbox provides useful and effective questioning skills that can be used where appropriate during the whole coaching process. The model can serve as a map for the therapist to guide clients to explore their goals, to discover their strengths and to take action accordingly. SF coaching's emphasis on strengths and solutions can help to shape the attitude of the practitioners effectively. It also helps to reduce variability and to enhance the consistency of a therapist's practice.

Case vignette

This case vignette is adopted from a local conference presentation (Wan & Au, 2015). Mary was admitted to hospital because of being emotionally unstable after moving house. She felt increased restlessness and poor sleep after a change of medication. She also had a lack of interest in going out and was pacing around at home. She was stabilised in the ward and then referred to a psychiatric day hospital. She attended three half-day sessions a week for training on life skills and received weekly coaching session for about 20 minutes. The following vignette is an extract from a coaching session during her stay in the day hospital.

Coach: What do you want to achieve in this session?
Client: I want to sleep better!
Coach: Suppose you go to bed tonight and magic happens: your insomnia has gone! How will you discover that the magic has happened when you get up in the morning? What small difference will you notice?
Client: Hmm, happier, would like to help more people; I really like to help others!
Coach: What else?
Client: Not to think about death, not to be upset easily.
Coach: What will you do instead?
Client: Do more cooking!
Coach: What else?
Client: Would like to chat with others more, participate in activities more and happier!
Coach: On a scale of 1 to10, with 10 representing this picture you just mentioned and 1 when the situation remains unchanged, where are you on the scale?
Client: 6
Coach: Well, why it is not 5 but a 6?
Client: Oh, I can still sleep for 4 to 5 hours and there is some improvement in my chest discomfort now.
Coach: What helped you to sleep for 4 to 5 hours?

Client: The present day hospital schedule did not allow me to nap during the daytime. My therapist also taught me some tips to sleep better!

Coach: What else helped you to be at a 6?

Client: When I'm not attending the day hospital, I will occupy myself with activities like going out strolling, listening to birds singing and doing household tasks.

Coach: What else?

Client: I learned to shift my focus from worrying about family to taking care of myself. I have also learned and practised relaxation skills. However, I still need a nap after meals.

Coach: Wow! I am really impressed by what you have learnt and done to improve yourself so far! If you would go from 6 to 7, 1 point higher, what will be the step that you have to take?

Client: I will continue my current activities and do more things like strolling, watching the sea, listening to birds, housework during the day time; discuss with the doctor about my medication, practise more relaxation; try not to nap after meals and not to worry much about my children and granddaughter.

Challenges of implementing the SF approach in Hong Kong

What we have experienced is that it is not easy to implement the SF approach within the medically dominant health care environment and the Chinese culture where patients are used to respecting authority! Most of the clients would have difficulties in expressing their preferred future. We needed to have some adaptations to integrating the SF approach with OT practice such as using the Role Inventory and Interest Checklist to assist clients to identify their strengths and goals. Besides, clients need to identify their recovery goals once they are admitted in psychiatric day hospital, and this would also be discussed in the multi-disciplinary case conference. A recovery journal was also developed to help clients to record their goals and progress. This is to make sure the core components of SF coaching are built into the system and that the techniques of SF coaching can be used during the whole process.

As time has gone by, the clients are more confident and vocal in expressing their needs and recovery goals, and they take more responsibility in participating in related treatment activities according to their identified goals. The culture of focusing more attention on strengths and less on problems has gradually developed in the team. Occupational therapists are now more effective in delivering a strength-based, recovery-oriented mental health service.

As mentioned above, the approach is simple, but not easy to use effectively. Continuing professional development and training in this area is therefore important. Quantitative studies on the effectiveness of the approach are, however, still limited. A Chinese SF coaching guideline or manual should be developed with appropriate outcome indicators so that further research could be carried out. In addition, clinical communication through case conferences or ward rounds with more SF language is important in developing and monitoring the care plans of clients. Empowering clients through the SF approach via taking responsibility and identifying goals requires concerted effort of the health care professionals as well.

Conclusion

Recovery for clients with mental health problems used to mean a good clinical outcome of reduced psychiatric symptoms and associated social and occupational problems through proper diagnosis, assessment and treatment. In the new paradigm, recovery is, to many service users and mental health practitioners, a way of living a satisfying, hopeful, and productive life despite having a mental illness. Self-direction, taking responsibility, and maintaining hopeful attitude are the key dimensions of recovery. Instead of focusing on the functional limitation of clients, OT needs to move beyond the role of a therapist to the role of a coach to support clients' recovery journey for a life they want in the future. The SF model of coaching fits the principles of recovery well, and we have found it has been useful to guide OT practice with clients. Further adaptation of SF coaching within the Chinese culture in Hong Kong is, however, needed. We are lucky to have a glimpse of success, but further efforts are necessary for the development of SF practices here.

References

Anthony, W.A. (1993). Recovery from mental illness: The guiding vision of the mental health service system in the 1990s. *Psychosocial Rehabilitation Journal, 16*, 11–23.

Berg, I.K., & Szabo, P. (2005). *Brief coaching for lasting solutions.* New York, NY: Norton.

Davidson, L., Rakfeldt, J., & Strauss, J. (2010). *The roots of the recovery movement in psychiatry: Lessons learned.* Oxford, UK: Wiley-Blackwell.

de Shazer, S., Berg, I. K., Lipchik, E., Molnar, A., Gingerich, W., & Weiner-Davis, M. (1986). Brief therapy: Focused solution-development. *Family Process, 25*(2), 207–222.

Hospital Authority (HA). (2010). *Hospital authority mental health service plan for adults 2010–2015.* Hong Kong SAR, PRC: Hospital Authority.

Peller, J., & Walter, J. (1989). When doesn't the problem happen? In M. Yapko (Ed.), *Brief therapy approaches to treating anxiety and depression* (pp. 314–326). New York, NY: Brunner/ Mazel.

SAMHSA. (2010). *National consensus statement on mental health recovery.* Rockville, MD: Department of Health and Human Services. Substance Abuse and Mental Health Services Administration.

Walter, J.L., & Peller, J.E. (1992). Assumptions of a solution focused approach. In *Becoming solution-focused in brief therapy* (pp. 10–36). New York, NY: Routledge.

Wan, M., & Au, R. (2015, May). *User empowerment in mental health recovery – the application of solution-focused coaching in occupational therapy.* Paper presented at the Hospital Authority Convention, Hong Kong SAR, PRC.

40

SF COACHING IN ASIA THROUGH AN INTERCULTURAL LENS

Kirsten Dierolf and Isabelle Hansen

Intercultural Management is a topic that both Isabelle and Kirsten have been teaching for decades. Both are German and have a lot of experience collaborating with people from all over Asia: China, South Korea, Japan, the Philippines, Singapore, India and Kyrgyzstan. They are also solution focused (SF) coaches and are sometimes surprised at how intercultural difficulties seem to disappear when you consistently work with an SF attitude. SF consulting is sometimes labelled 'very American' both by German and by Asian audiences. The focus on what works well is sometimes misunderstood as Pollyanna positivism and problem phobic. However, none of this seems to matter in actual SF work with clients. It seems that SF provides a third, joint lens for people of two or more differing cultures to use when they are collaborating. Following intercultural models such as Hall (1982); Hampden-Turner and Trompenaars (2004); Hofstede, Hofstede and Minkov (2010) and Lewis (2002), which seek to help explain the differences in general patterns of thought and socialisation, it would seem very unlikely that any approach in coaching would work with similar success in such diverse cultures as European and Asian cultures. We know that European and Asian cultures are both very diverse, so our labels 'European' or 'Asian' are here used for simplification. So why does SF work, chameleon-like, in all cultures that we have experienced?

The intercultural lens

Reporting all intercultural differences between the United States (where SF originated), Asian and European cultures mentioned in the intercultural literature is not possible in this chapter. We only mention those differences that are the most pertinent regarding the assumption that a US-developed coaching approach cannot work in Asia: group and individual orientation, communication styles, and coach status and hierarchy. We then discuss how the SF approach can be adapted to take these differences into account as needed.

Group and individual orientation. Hampden-Turner and Trompenaars (2004) and Hofstede et al. (2010) have identified a different cultural orientation of Asian and Western countries labelled 'Communitarianism' (Hampden-Turner & Trompenaars) and 'Collectivism' (Hofstede et al.)

for Asian countries and 'Individualism' for Western countries. In Asian countries, a 'standard' person would tend to want to be seen as part of a group, as belonging to a bigger entity than himself. He would stress the similarities rather than the differences. In Western countries, a 'standard' (or 'normal', who we are well aware does not exist) person would tend to want to be seen as an independent entity who is identifiably different from their peers. A Western coaching approach would ask about individual contributions and look toward individual agency rather than team agency and would, therefore, probably feel rather uncomfortable for a 'standard' Asian client. A Western coaching approach would focus on developing goals that are attainable for the individual and depend solely on the actions of the client – which might also lead to uncomfortable conversations about differences and 'standing out'. Being embarrassed – losing face – or feeling not treated seriously is, additionally, something that the intercultural experts cited in this paper gauge as having a much worse impact in Asian cultures than in Western cultures.

Communication styles. Several categorisation systems describe the different communication styles of Asian and Western cultures: high versus low context communication (Hall, 1982) and specificity versus diffuseness (Hampden-Turner & Trompenaars, 2004). Lewis distinguishes the listening-oriented (Asian) versus the two (Western) data- and dialogue-oriented communication styles (Lewis, 2002). Oversimplified, one could say that Asian cultures are taken to communicate in more general terms, include more of the contexts in their perceptions of others' communication and are less 'direct', and 'always seem to read between the lines'. Western cultures, on the other hand, are more specific and tend to 'say what they mean and mean what they say' without requiring the communication partner to take into account the context of what was being said.

This factor could pose a difficulty for coaching conversations between Western coaches and Asian clients and vice versa in that the coach misunderstands what is being communicated by the client. The Western coach might not be able to gauge whether the Asian client is actually interested in pursuing a certain line of thought or goal or not, expecting direct answers and direction by the client. In multi-cultural training situations, participants may encounter similar difficulties in dealing with persons from a high-context culture and decoding their ambiguous messages and implicit meanings.

Coach status and hierarchy. The third category of cultural differences is the difference between Asian and Western cultures in how they deal with hierarchies. Hampden-Turner and Trompenaars (2004) call this difference 'achieved and ascribed status' and Hofstede et al. (2010) refer to 'high or low power distance'. The 'standard' person in Asian cultures is deemed to adapt his or her behaviour toward people of different status more noticeably than people from Western cultures. Someone who is ascribed a position of 'high status' will be treated with respect and will be listened to in Asian cultures. In Confucian-influenced Asian cultures, status helps create initial respect and authority; however, trust and respect also need to be built up over time. The most pronounced difficulty resulting from a Confucian influence is the idea of the 'teacher' who imparts his knowledge to the student, who learns by imitation and reproduction. For coaching in Asia, this dimension might pose a significant problem. In SF coaching, the client is held as the expert for their lives and the solutions and developments are elicited or co-created by questions. In China, the general word for the relatively young profession of coaching is 'jiàoliàn' (教练) which also is used for training or imparting a skill. If a Western coach is coaching a mixed Western and European team, the Europeans might dominate the conversation due to this different understanding of the appropriate behaviour in this context and due to the above-mentioned differing communication styles.

SF provides a flexible lens

So why does none of this create a problem in our SF conversations with Asian clients? This cannot be the whole story. There must be something about SF (and about our intercultural adaptation of SF) that makes these perceived difficulties disappear.

First and foremost, SF assumes that you never know what your question was until you hear the answer of the client. It is not necessary for an SF coach 'to understand' the client – the coach uses the language of the client, and both co-construct a process that will help the client move from where he is now to where he wants to be. Unlike other approaches, SF is not based on a 'sender / receiver' model of communication, where the coach or client 'sends a message' and the client 'decodes' it and active listening and feedback is used to ensure communication. SF understands communication as 'doing something together': creating meaning, finding solutions, asking questions, giving answers, etc. The only thing that needs to happen is for the client to be enabled to enter into that joint project of 'doing something together', which is achieved by the coach's use of the client's language. As long as the coach is not blatantly disrespectful (for which knowledge of the cultural differences can help if one is dealing with 'a standard person'), one can assume that the willingness for collaboration is there.

The SF coach will not diagnose, categorise or make any assumptions about the client and works from an attitude of 'not knowing' and resource orientation. In this way, the SF method helps coaches develop the 'tolerance of ambiguity', which many intercultural researchers posit as one of the main factors in intercultural success (e.g. Thomas, Kinast & Schroll-Machl, 2005). Clients will feel taken seriously and accepted no matter what culture or sub-culture they belong to. Being taken seriously and respected, in turn, creates trust and the willingness to think about the questions asked, which is the prerequisite for a successful collaboration between SF coach and client.

As for the specific differences categorised by the aforementioned experts, it is fair to say that SF coaching can be adapted to fit both ends of the spectrum.

Group and individual orientation. Embarrassment of the Asian client resulting from too much stress on the individual contributions, goals and successes can easily be avoided by asking perspective-change questions. Instead of asking a very 'Western' (and even not very SF) coaching question like: 'When have you been able to demonstrate leadership in a C-level meeting?' you might ask: 'When was a meeting in which you acted a little bit more like you want to act? What would your colleagues say about this meeting? What did your behaviour enable your colleagues to do? And when they did . . . what did you then do?' Asking for small observable differences of the change the client would like to see can be done in a very individualistic way (asking about the client), or also in a more group-focused fashion (asking about the environment, the others, and the client). The same is valid for the level of expressed enthusiasm of the coach when hearing about the successes of the client. The Western coach might say: 'Wow!! How did you do that?' and embarrass the Asian client. A more culturally attuned SF coach will use other tools in his or her repertoire like: 'So it seems you are quite happy with this? What do you think contributed to this success? What did others do? What did others see you do?' The aim of 'praise' is not for the client to feel that the coach approves of him or her but for him or her to think about what worked in any given situation and this thinking can revolve around the group or the individual. As stated above, it is the thinking about what helped that matters, not necessarily the expression of (self-) praise.

When working with interculturally mixed teams, SF is very helpful in creating a process that seems 'equally weird' for both sides. In a scaling walk, for example, you can mix Western and Asian participants and ask: 'What have you noticed anybody do that tells you that you are already at an X?' The conversation in pairs and the SF questions allow for a very meaningful exchange which would not happen in other more action oriented coaching approaches (e.g., with the common coaching question: 'What are you going to do about it?')

Communication style. It is indeed difficult to understand when a 'high-context' answer is given and we are not aware of the context embedded in the message and its nonverbal signs, which might not be noticed by someone who is rather used to taking verbal messages at face value. As mentioned above, this is much easier to bear when working with an SF attitude of 'not having to understand'. The one thing, however, that a SF coach or consultant will have to know is where the client would like to go. SF questions ask for concrete signs of things being better and therefore safeguard against running into a direction that the client does not want to go in. Take the following example:

Coach: Suppose this conversation is somehow useful, what will tell you at the end of our session that it was worth your time?
Client: Some more motivation for my team might be useful?
Coach: Suppose there is more motivation in your team, what does this look like?
Client: My team will . . .
Coach: And when your team . . . what would they see you do differently?
Client: They will see me . . .

Coach status and hierarchy. The difficulty of clients wanting an answer from us as coaches is one that might be more pronounced in Asian cultures, but we have also experienced this expectation elsewhere. The mechanisms for clarifying and collaborating are similar and in our experience actually easier when the coach is ascribed a high status. If the coach operates with an SF attitude and is aware of the different expectations, he can easily explain the process of a conversation to his clients: first find out what exactly you want, then see where you are at and what you have done, then figure out what to do. If, in the last step, the SF coach has relevant expertise and the client is hungry for it, there is nothing that keeps the SF coach or consultant from sharing it. As a consequence, a coach in Asia may need a higher flexibility to switch roles and a solid cultural knowledge of the underlying mechanism in the interaction.

Summary

SF offers a flexible lens for coaches. Our understanding of communication as a co-creation enables us to work with a diverse array of people and cultures. Especially in the dynamic Asian context, working on solutions and the overall desired outcome enhances social harmony in relationships, providing a face-giving and appreciative talk at the same time. We do not need 'to understand' but work together to create a better future for the client. SF work fosters tolerance of ambiguity in the coach and grows the ability to talk and work with individuals and not with 'cultural differences'. The SF methodology can be adapted flexibly to many styles of culturally diverse communication and action by the interculturally versatile coach. Clients feel taken seriously and achieve significant results which fit their context irrespective of their cultural background. Mixed teams are enabled to collaborate on solutions in ways that are not possible in any other coaching approach.

References

Hall, E.T. (1982). *The hidden dimension.* New York, NY: Doubleday.

Hampden-Turner, C.M., & Trompenaars, F. (2004). Building cross-cultural competence. Chichester, UK: Wiley.

Hofstede, G., Hofstede, G.J., & Minkov, M. (2010). *Cultures and organizations: Software of the mind.* (3rd ed.). New York, NY: McGraw-Hill.

Lewis, R.D. (2002): *When cultures collide. Managing successfully across cultures* (2nd rev. ed., reprinted with corrections). Boston, MA: Nicholas Brealey Publishing.

Thomas, A., Kinast, E.U., & Schroll-Machl, S. (Hg.). (2005). *Handbuch Interkulturelle Kommunikation und Kooperation.* [Handbook of intercultural communication and cooperation] (2nd rev ed.). Göttingen, Germany: Vandenhoeck & Ruprecht.

41

TRULY MORE THAN A MIRACLE: WHY 'KEQING' AND NOT 'JIAOLIAN' IN CHINESE?

Working with the solution focused approach in China

Terese Bareth

I am a German solution focused (SF) consultant and coach working in Shanghai. I studied Chinese language and business administration and have been living in China on and off since the 1980s. Fascinated with the SF ideas and coaching applications in business, I set up a company in 2007 in organisational development and coaching in Shanghai. Fluent in Chinese, I wanted to introduce SF thinking and transfer the SF language into Chinese. As a result I encountered difficulties with the misunderstanding of coaching embedded in the Chinese language and a realisation that a new and appropriate identity must be created. In this chapter I will discuss my journey through this process and the importance of appropriate translation, assumptions and expectations in coaching and consulting in China. It is my passion and mission to spread the SF ideas in China.

Initial experiences with SF in China

I worked for 14 years for an automotive industry company, the last year in a joint venture in China. I was first acquainted with the SF approach and systemic thinking due to my mentor's influence. Later, as the Head of Controlling and Organisation Development department in a German–Chinese joint venture in China, I had the hands-on opportunity to adapt the ideas and methods in the organisation. Distress was extreme at the time. The company had a lot of needs, so I tried out various things, inspired by Steve de Shazer's motto: 'Find out what works and do more of it, and if it doesn't work, do something different.' The 'findings' worked well. The Chinese employees were passive, were shy and did not dare to take responsibility. I started to discover how to introduce sustainable changes in the company. My 'amateur' coach skills, various books and articles, delight in experimenting and the trust of my former superiors led to the final organisation development intervention, and the change process was started. From this experience, I was inspired to start my own business in 2007, Bareth Management Consultants (Shanghai) Co., Ltd. It was the first company using the SF approach in China.

Fascinated by how the SF approach worked, I looked for more professional knowledge and education, and I pursued training in solution focused brief coaching in Switzerland.

In 2008 as the financial crisis hit China, many told me it would not be possible to survive with a new product in coaching and organisational consulting. Who had heard of that? Who understood what it was? No one here! But I saw that what I was doing was working, so I carried my idea from customer to customer through referrals and the community began to feel the difference of my work. Since 2012 coaching has been a 'hot topic' in China. Currently the market is still in a development phase with all the associated difficulties, opportunities and colourful experiences. For example, people from abroad organise a big coaching event, and most of the participants are foreigners because in the title of the event 'coaching' was translated into Chinese as 'péi xùn' (training) and 'coach' as 'jiào liàn' (trainer, adviser). Or, another example was offering a 'test' session to an HR manager who had already had some coaching experience as a client and who was personally very interested in coaching, to show how SF works. After our session she told me that she felt very well: energetic and full of power. What was surprising for her was that at the end of the session I didn't make any comments about what was good and what wasn't – unlike her other 'coach'.

In China, intercultural differences often come up in the first phase of the coaching process. This is the crucial moment for the coach to adequately react but at the same time to hold on to the process to avoid struggles during the conversation caused by these intercultural misunderstandings.

Coaching in China – An intercultural challenge of misunderstandings

The common translation of 'coaching' into 'péi xùn' (training) and 'coach' into 'jiào liàn' (trainer, adviser) reflects the Chinese understanding, stemming from traditional thinking and education. In this translation – and relationship – one person is an expert and another one a learner who seeks advice. Traditionally, Chinese clients expect the coach to give answers and directions from their wisdom and experience, like masters used to. This has been practised for thousands of years. Knowing this, foreign coaches often feel obliged to follow this course for fear of not meeting expectations and losing authority in the eyes of Chinese clients.

These assumptions and beliefs on both sides led to intercultural misunderstanding that has been counterproductive to the coaching process. The situation calls for a paradigm shift, and it starts with the need for the correct Chinese translation expressing the meaning of coaching as a way to encourage self-development and self-discovery. There is a great need to give coaches in China more confidence by redefining the coaching relationship. Once this is understood, miracles can happen.

Since I am proficient in the Chinese language, it was clear to me that I could not translate 'coaching' as 'péi xùn' and 'coach' as 'jiào liàn' in my company documents and on the website. I wanted to offer 'coaching', not training and consider myself a coach, not a teacher. I had thought a lot about it. What if the Chinese language does not offer a term for the coaching concept? It took me two years to find the solution. The answer presented itself a few years ago after a long discussion with a Chinese friend well-versed in Chinese culture. It was in his living room that the word 'kè qīng' 客卿 for 'coaching' was born! 'Kè qīng' can be translated as 'an interim visit to help to develop' or 'the invitation to assist in development or solution seeking for a specified purpose and in a given time'. It refers to the practice in ancient China, when in the period of The Warring States (475–221 BC) some regents would invite knowledgeable people from abroad to assist them in development of their kingdoms in the areas of need.

'Kè qīng' is the right Chinese translation for 'coaching' for many reasons: 'Kè qīng' reflects the underlying principle of coaching, 'kè qīng' was already a profession in ancient China, and the Chinese pronunciation of 'kè qīng' sounds similar to 'coaching' in English.

For thousands of years Chinese people have shown great respect for those with more knowledge and more experience and traditionally refer to them as 'teachers' (in Chinese 'lǎo shī'). People seek the teacher's wise advice and are ready to follow. It is not hard to imagine what a challenge it is to work in China as a coach! Some foreign colleagues have already discussed the 'impossibility' of coaching applied in China the way it is in the Western countries. The basic attitude of Chinese clients that 'the coach is the expert', and the coach's response 'I should give advice because they expect this', are good examples of an 'expectation of expectation'. Certainly, in addition to the professional attitude and experience, a foreign coach in China needs cultural knowledge and intercultural experience. Currently a variety of coaching approaches appear in China and people are confused by the quantity and various directions. The SF approach is one of them, and according to my observations, we are currently the only SF coaching provider in Shanghai and most probably the only one in China. It is my strong conviction that the SF approach is most suitable to be applied in the countries where systemic thinking has its own tradition.

SF adaptations in China

To keep the SF posture is not easy in an environment that expects a coach to be the expert and advisor with specific knowledge. I see the main difference as being the point of view that the client is an expert. One of the biggest challenges in coaching Chinese clients is maintaining the not-knowing attitude and being only the 'process expert'. It is particularly difficult in the first five to ten minutes of the session. Clients come with the understanding and expectation that the coach is an experienced expert who will help solve their problem and recommend what to do. Very often clients directly express these expectations: 'You're a teacher and you have experience, and I am looking for help, so please tell me what I should do!'

In tricky moments like this it is very hard not to be seduced into giving advice. Once done, it can spoil the whole process. What do I do in such cases? I put clients' expectations aside and ask their permission to ask some other questions before 'we get back to this answer'. Usually, at the end of our coaching conversation, clients are very surprised that the answers and ideas were provided by themselves, the 'real experts', and not by the coach, the 'expected expert'. In such moments I see their eyes shine. It seems the clients enjoy this feeling very much. Some clients at the end of the coaching session still ask me for opinions about their ideas for a solution or about the planned next steps. It is as if they wanted to get the final confirmation that they are really doing the right thing. This is the second tricky moment where the attitude of a professional SF coach is much challenged. It is extremely important to hold on to the professional attitude with confidence and be consciously resistant to slipping into the 'expert role.'

The power of miracles

With the creation and exploration of a dream or a miracle, we generated many success stories, particularly working with company teams. It works 'miracles' – especially in sino-foreign companies, often with very difficult histories and backgrounds. The miracle question made many management teams and their members realise that they all want the same thing. This sometimes came as a great surprise and generated new energy for creating a future together. In my experience and observations in China, the miracle question creates more spectacular effects in the groups rather than in one-to-one coaching sessions.

Current challenges

The current challenges for coaching in China present themselves in a mix of the lack of knowledge and understanding of what coaching is. This is partly due to the use of the word 'coaching' in the sense of 'training' and perception of a coach as a tutor who, like in school, helps one to work on weaknesses to be able to pass exams. Such perception and beliefs create the image of coaching as a service for those who require special care or perform worse than expected. Western companies in China face tremendous difficulties in implementation of coaching as an instrument for staff development because of such perceptions and beliefs. Acceptance and implementation of coaching, whether in a company or in the country, require a paradigm shift.

For the SF approach, the main challenge is the need of paradigm change, so the coaches indeed perceive and treat client as an expert by trusting in the client's abilities, resources and in the process itself. The SF approach is 'simple but not easy', and because of this, it is difficult to learn for the Chinese coach. Once a person feels and experiences how powerful the SF approach is, they appreciate it and wish to learn more. The growing interest in our coaching services and coaching education courses supports this.

The importance of language

Every communication tool shows how important it is to pay attention to language. In the SF approach, language has extraordinary significance.

SF was first developed in the USA among English speakers. SF is very concerned about language. In European non-English speaking countries, e.g., Germany, Switzerland, Norway and France, there were many efforts made to 'transfer' the SF approach into other languages. However, a simple direct translation of SF questions is not enough. It requires good knowledge of the SF approach as well as the proficiency and sensitivity of both, English and the other languages. I was challenged to think deeply about this while working on the Chinese version of our coaching course. At that time my education and previous experience as a Chinese language translator proved extremely useful. In my painstaking work with a Chinese colleague, we made the translation of the main phrases of the SF language. Our intensive and sometimes stormy discussions brought to life, in the Chinese language, the key SF phrases and questions. The effects of the translation have proven successful in my coaching sessions that I provide in Chinese to Chinese clients.

We are still learning about the impact of using solution-focused language, translated and spoken in Chinese in coaching practice, from the exchange with other SF coaches and therapists working in the Chinese language in the Asia Pacific region. We are all looking for further development. The importance and power of language requires that we pay very close attention to translation, particularly in the use of books and teaching materials. 'The language for solution development is different from that needed to describe a problem' (de Shazer & Dolan, 2007, pp. 2–3); this becomes much more meaningful in the SF application in other languages than English. The success of the SF approach in China depends greatly on how it is 'transferred' into and through the Chinese language.

To give just one example: The powerful little question 'What else?' is very often translated into Chinese as: '还有什么?' (Hái yǒu shé me?) or '还有什么事?' (Hái yǒu shé me shì?). Both variants imply that something 'ought to be there'. We translated 'What else?' as '还有呢?' (Hái yǒu ne?). It has a form of an open question, sounds soft and light, yet at the same time it is very concrete and evocative. Depending on how we ask, we get different answers.

I'm interested in an open exchange among SF coaches and therapists working with clients in the Chinese language, making the SF approach as powerful in Chinese as it is in English. The task is daunting, from the language itself to a total paradigm change in communication. But I am confident that the universal SF approach will prove successful in China

Reference

De Shazer, S., & Dolan, Y., with Korman, H., Trepper, T., McCollum, E., & Berg, I.K. (2007). *More than miracles: The state of the art of solution-focused brief therapy*. Binghamton, NY: Haworth Press.

SECTION 5

Solution focused practice in organisations in Asia

42

INTRODUCTION TO SOLUTION FOCUSED PRACTICE IN ORGANISATIONS IN ASIA

Mark McKergow and Dave Hogan

Introduction

Solution focused brief therapy, developed by Steve de Shazer and Insoo Kim Berg, proved successful in quickly helping clients make desired sustainable changes in their lives. By the early 1990s the radically simple but effective approach was being used by solution focused (SF) practitioners in the coaching world and in organisational consulting.

Dave's observations

I first saw the potential for using SF ideas in organisations when I was part of the first SF coach training program in Singapore in 2004 conducted by Mark McKergow and Jenny Clarke. This was the same year they published what they describe as 'the first collection of writings on the applications of Solutions Focus in organisational and management work'. In the book they announced a 'new wave of change', which is not just another model but a 'different *kind* of approach' (McKergow & Clarke, 2004, p. x). It is not interested in spending time analysing past failures, or imposing complex theories and grand designs. The SF consultant is more interested in direct paths to positive change and progress by clarifying what is wanted and by paying careful attention to what is already working in order to amplify solutions already present in organisations. This is what distinguishes the SF approach to consultation from all others. 'What makes organisations – and people – into world class performers does not lie in their (mended) weaknesses but rather in their (developed) strengths' (Jackson & McKergow, 2007, p. 204).

It was not long after that first SF coach training I had with Mark and Jenny that I began to experiment with using the SF approach in the organisations I was a part of and when invited to help other organisations. I noticed that I started listening more carefully, especially when people complained and whined – not to diagnose their problems but to see if I could detect their deep values, hopes and aspirations for themselves and their organisations. I started becoming curious about what was already working for them. I stopped telling them what I thought they should do and started asking about times when things had gone well, even when they felt overwhelmed with problems or discouraged by setbacks. I started asking about what they were most proud of and doing well.

I stopped asking 'why' they were troubled and started asking 'how' they had already achieved so much. And I discovered the power of asking, 'What else?' I learned that when people describe their best hopes in intricate detail, they can more easily notice what the first next step toward that hope might be. And the first small change can lead to even more useful change.

The history of the application of SF in organisations parallels the growth of coaching (as described in the introduction to coaching chapter in this book). Coaching was first born and continues to thrive in the context of business and organisational development in Asia as in the West (Wright, Leong, Webb & Chia, 2010).

The network of solution focused consulting has grown in Asia and continues to develop in the region. The first Asian chapter of the Association for the Quality Development of Solution Focused Consulting and Training (SFCT) was established in Singapore in 2010 and now has 15 members.

The literature on the use of SF in consultancy, leadership management and the world of business has grown enormously in the past decade, as well documented by Mark McKergow in 'Solution-Focused Approaches to Management' (2012). Mark's observation is that 'while controlled studies are possible in the field of therapy, applications in the organizational sphere are much more carried out on an ad-hoc basis; the main concern is to make progress, and whatever helps do this is welcomed' (2012, p. 327). This also holds true for Asia and explains why research on the use of SF in organisations in Asia is still in its infancy.

Mark McKergow reflects on his experiences in SF organisational work in Asia over the past decade, followed by a brief overview of the chapters in this section.

Mark's observations on SF organisational work in Asia

I first came across solution focused brief therapy as a young budding consultant in the early 1990s, and immediately recognised the potential of putting the ideas, techniques and tools in the hands of managers. Over the past quarter century it has been my privilege to be a part of spreading these ideas into the business and organisational field – firstly by learning them for myself, then using them with clients, then writing about them (including the best-selling book *The Solutions Focus* in 2002); I've helped build communities of practitioners such as SOLWorld and SFCT, and travelled around the world to teach people about these fantastically incisive, inclusive and effective methods.

I first came to Asia with Solutions Focus in 2002 when I visited Singapore, and was delighted to discover a small but energetic network of practitioners already working with SF ideas in various settings including family therapy and coaching. Over the years I have seen this group grow and expand to include the authors and editors of this book, as well as many others – based both around Singapore and also in Japan. Yasuteru Aoki, an SF practitioner in Japan, has been a whirlwind of action and encouragement for managers and businesses to try out and build on SF ideas in their work. His J-SOL network is notable for including many more actual practising managers than consultants, and the story he tells in Chapter 43 of this book about the ZACROS Company is one of many shining examples of applying SF ideas from Japan.

When Aoki first came to the UK in 2004 to learn about Solution Focus in coaching and management with us, he made a startling observation. After just one day of training, he took me to one side in the pub afterwards and said, 'You know, SF is so Japanese!' I was surprised and amazed, and wanted to find out more about what he meant. I discovered about the importance of respect and 'face' in Japan and other Asian cultures. It is very bad to lose face – to be seen to be stupid or incorrect. Solutions Focus, of course, focused on what is working and people's strengths – so those involved gain face as an inevitable part of the process. Also, listening hard to the words and language that people are using is a key SF skill – which brings with it a feeling of great respect for those being coached or helped.

I think that Asia has embraced SF for a combination of two reasons: effectiveness and respect. I observe that people across Asia seem to like things to move quickly – which SF work certainly achieves when used skilfully. Combined with the respect shown by listening, complimenting and gaining face, this is a winning partnership. I am not at all surprised that this volume has appeared, bringing with it so many interesting and hope-filled stories of people and organisations moving forward in positive ways with the gentle yet powerful SF approach. I hope that you, the reader, will be inspired to both learn and use these ideas for yourself, and then join in with the various SF networks to share your work with others, learn more and grow this remarkable approach.

Contributions by authors

This section offers examples of 'new waves' of change in organisational work since SF practice came to the shores of Singapore in 1999. Eight practitioners from four different countries in Asia – Singapore, Japan, India and Indonesia—share their experiences and examples of their consulting work with organisations. Readers will be introduced to the basic concepts and processes involved in SF consulting and organisational development and the impact on performance, motivation, success and satisfaction with those involved and why it has been effective in the Asian context.

Yasuteru Aoki describes his disappointment when his initial efforts to 'install SF' as an operating system in an organisation in Nabari, Japan, failed to go the way he expected. His disappointment turned to deeper understanding when he learned how SF ideas had triggered something more pervasive and enduring in the organisation he was working with. He describes his surprising discovery of the impact SF ideas have on an organisation even when only a small number in it are formally introduced to the SF ideas.

Arvind Wable answers the question 'Will the SF approach work in India?' by describing his SF consultation, coaching and team building with a well-established Indian company that needed help managing change and developing new leaders.

Denise Wright describes the SF informed and strategic collaborative process she used to help an organisation achieve its goals to become more effective in team work, more mutually supportive and more productive.

Debbie Hogan tells the story of her work with a successful business owner of a large holding company who wanted to increase his company holdings, improve productivity and strengthen cohesion among his leaders while remaining in alignment with his company's core value, 'Create a better life for all'.

Indry Wardhani shows how the SF approach fits into her consultation work with companies in Indonesia, enabling them to make progress toward their goals and to increase staff motivation.

Karen McDonald highlights the use of the SF approach in a consulting role for two organisations in Asia that had a major conflict and were not able to resolve it satisfactorily. She demonstrates how she and her team were able to facilitate an SF conflict resolution process in a complicated situation in which it seemed unlikely that a resolution could be achieved amicably.

Edwin Choy shows how SF consulting and training with an organisation working with children and youth led to significant positive changes in the caregivers and the children in their care.

Dave Hogan tells the story of how SF coaching and consulting enabled an entrepreneurial manager and director of a successful resort company in Bali to multiply the number of resorts in his company through improving his relationships with his family, his colleagues and his subordinates.

We hope the reader will be inspired by these examples of SF practice in organisations and see the potential for this approach in Asia to impact individuals, teams and entire organisations.

References

Jackson, P., & McKergow, M. (2007). *The solutions focus: Making coaching and change SIMPLE*. London, UK: Nicholas Brealey International.

McKergow, M. (2012). Solution-focused approaches in management. In C. Franklin, T.S. Trepper, W. Gingerich & E. McCollum (Eds.), *Solution-focused brief therapy: A handbook of evidenced-based practice* (pp. 327–341). New York, NY: Oxford University Press.

McKergow, M., & Clarke, J. (Eds.). (2004). *Positive approaches to change: Application of solution focus and appreciative inquiry at work*. Cheltenham, UK: Solutions Books.

Wright, D., Leong, A., Webb, K.E., & Chia, S. (Eds.). (2010). *Coaching in Asia: The first decade*. Singapore: Candid Creation Publishing.

43

'SF INSIDE'

Why the 'SF inside' concept can be useful in organisational development

Yasuteru Aoki

My ambition of changing client companies into 'SF inside' organisations

When I first learned about the solution-focused (SF) approach, I felt it was such a natural and simple wisdom to stimulate positive human interaction. Somehow, I felt like I had always known it. Later, I met many people who shared the same view. I sensed a high possibility of people in organisations utilising SF principles in everyday interactions. As a human communication trainer, I started to dream of enabling organisations to become solution-focused, where all members would share the knowledge and skills of SF communication, and where everything could be managed in solution-focused ways. I named it an 'SF inside' organisation to sound like a computer, in which SF communication is installed as the operating system. My hope was that this kind of organisation would have fewer mental health problems and better productivity as a result of the SF communication installed in everyday interactions.

At first, I innocently believed this was possible because the people I trained in my SF organisational work responded so positively to the approach that they made substantial differences both at work and at home. However, I soon found myself facing a wall. Those results remained personal and did not affect the whole organisation. I dreamed of a CEO finding so much value in the SF approach by hearing about the effects on the trainees that he adopted it as the human resources guideline, 'and the people worked happily ever after'. But it did not happen. I needed to think differently about 'SF inside' if I wanted my organisational clients to be interested in the SF approach as a whole organisational transformational tool. In this chapter I will share how working with one company helped change my perspective on what 'SF inside' means.

Differences between therapy session and organisational situation

On a train from Warsaw to Torun to attend the EBTA conference in 2012, I was lucky to sit next to Dr Alasdair Macdonald. I needed advice for my plenary talk, the theme of which was 'Dissolving SF professional skills into daily conversations'. Dr Macdonald (personal communication) quoted Steve de Shazer to me: 'Therapy is easier than anything else.' I don't think therapy is an easy job at all. But when I think of people in organisations trying to utilise the SF approach, I am aware of lots of differences that require them to adapt. These are listed in Table 43.1.

TABLE 43.1 Different features of SF conversation in therapy and organisational situations

A. Therapy conversations	B. Conversations in organisational situations
One-to-one interactions	Variety of situations
Uninterrupted 1 hour	Interrupted and unpredictable duration
Clear helper and helpee roles	Roles are not always defined
Relationship is limited and terminated	Relationship is long term
Purpose and value are clearly defined by the client	Purpose varies from casual chat to official decision-making

It seems possible to translate SF skills into a coaching model because coaching shares most of the features listed in column A in Table 43.1. However, people in organisations face many diverse situations from within long-term relationships.

From Column B in Table 43.1 it is clear that people in organisations have multiple interactions throughout the day, in predictable and unpredictable ways, and are rarely entitled to secure private, uninterrupted conversations for an hour. You cannot always take the position of inquirer by only asking questions, as sometimes the conversation requires input of your own ideas. It's not only in the other person's interest that you interact, but you also have something you want to gain. You are not free from the hierarchy and priorities that your organisation imposes on you, which often override your wish to behave other ways. So, if I take being 'SF inside' as installing a formal coaching type of conversations in everyday interactions in organisations, it is almost impossible.

As I continued to do SF communication trainings, the people within the organisations became my teachers. They took up SF ideas and applied them successfully in their own unique ways. Their explanation of what happened was interestingly different from that of outsiders like myself, and that led me to think differently about 'SF inside'.

Nobody changed, but the workplace has been transformed!

In 2009 at a manufacturing company called ZACROS, I conducted a group interview about their successful use of the SF approach at Nabari factory in Japan. By email I learned taht their workplace had changed after their managers took SF communication training. I asked permission to do an interview with the managers and workers on site. They accepted, and eight people, including the general manager, a manager, three foremen and three workers, all clad in factory uniforms, welcomed me in their meeting room. Everyone said they had recently been experiencing more positive and lively communication at their workplaces. As a result, the younger staff had developed their job skills much faster, cooperation between the divisions was better, the employee retention rate was higher, the production to wage ratio was better and so on. So they surely must have done something to have made those differences. When I inquired as to 'how' they had done it, they looked puzzled and were very hesitant in answering my question. A strange confused feeling permeated the room.

I re-phrased the question and asked, 'How have you changed?' The first person replied, 'Well, I haven't changed. He changed', pointing to someone else. I asked the same question to that person and again he gave me the same answer, pointing to an entirely different person! That continued for several cycles. Were they kidding me? Or were they just being modest? No. They were saying what they felt was true. I came to realise that when your personal resources are activated through SF communication, it is possible that you don't feel it as a change in yourself. Instead, you are just more of yourself, behaving naturally because you already knew those resources were there within you.

Taking a consulting position, I wanted to describe this great change and maybe identify a hero or two who started all this. But that's not what happened. The workplace was a much better place, but nobody changed! There was no particular hero. It was pleasantly shocking to discover how the insiders' view of what happened in their workplace was different from how outsiders view it. I think it's best to respect it rather than analyse it.

The word 'change' is tricky. Grammatically it is legitimate to say 'SF changed the organisation'. But the people within may not feel they have changed, nor would call it a change because that could mean they were not good before. It's especially true when the changes were small, for example, smiling a little more, helping each other a little more, giving compliments when seeing somebody else doing a good job and so on. You might notice other people doing more of these actions and think they have changed. If it is about yourself, you may just feel you have done only a *little* more of what you had done before and so it's nothing like a 'change'. But when these small things are done by a relatively large portion of the members of an organisation, it should be felt as a positive tangible change in the whole team. So it's only possible to say the workplace changed. From the interviews, it sounded like the more SF their behaviour became, the more they wanted to think they had been that way from the start. That is the insider's view, and I wanted to validate it by accepting the new meaning of 'SF inside' as 'SF was already inside of people'.

Chain of natural positive response (CNPR)

As the group interview continued, I became aware of another significant phenomenon. Out of 300 workers at the Nabari factory, only 20 people had taken a one-and-a-half-day SF training course. Only five people were chosen to take the advanced course. So most of the people in this factory had not taken SF training and heard about SF communication from their boss. Those bosses were not trainers and were not used to talking about something so intangible. They had only had brief sessions at their factory workplaces, to give information about SF communication. The understanding the people had of being SF seemed very simplistic. When I asked for their opinion about the relationship between SF communication and what they had achieved, their voice tone lowered and sounded unsure. So I changed the question to 'What do you think SF is?' Many of them just giggled and said, 'Seeing good in others' or 'Doing good to others'. They basically used three key ideas, namely 'OK message' (compliment), 'future perfect' and 'small step'. Yet, they said they could not really explain how SF ideas related to what they had achieved.

The general manager said smilingly,

> You know, Mr Aoki, recently my subordinates are giving me a hard time. They put all the good meanings on SF, for example, positive, forward looking, resilient, being altruistic, forgiving and so on. When they see me failing to show those qualities, they tell me, 'Hey, Mr GM, you are not SF-tic today!'

I was moved by this useful misunderstanding, or, rather, useful extended understanding, about SF communication. These people seem to hold a certain resourceful meaning of SF communication which is not overtly articulated but shared experientially. They referred to it as 'SF-tic'.

It sounded like this kind of useful extended understanding occurred not accidently but for a reason because SF ideas tend to resonate with the wish for harmony and a good future, which most of us as human beings naturally share.

When these people talked about 'SF', it was not so much about communication theory or methods. It was more about their resources, which impacted their attitudes after they started to do something called 'SF'. They noticed those attitudes promoted better relationships and cooperation. What mattered to them was not what tool they used to activate those resources but what they were experiencing as a result. It's the moon that is important and not the finger pointing to it. Maybe it was good for them to have a minimum input about the SF methodology because they were able to focus on the very things they wanted from using the new method and not the method itself. It could be that 'less is more' was useful when giving SF information, which allowed for more room for useful extended understandings to occur. I realised I only helped the very beginning of the chain of natural positive responses.

During the interview, a foreman shared an interesting example of being successful in developing his young subordinates. His boss took the SF training and came back to his team and told them he wanted to make their workplace the best in their company, utilising something called SF. The foreman did not fully understand what SF was, but he wanted to support his boss because he respected him. So he just took SF simply as 'seeing good in others and doing good to others', which he really tried. Soon, he and his young subordinates started having more casual conversations about their private lives and fun stuff during breaks, and they felt closer to each other. Then the foreman's perspective shifted. He said, 'I naturally started to have a heart-felt intention that I wanted to help these boys be better at their work and let them grow and be my successors at the workplace.' He used to be very harsh in criticising the young ones for making mistakes. The young ones' improvement was very slow. But as his perspective changed, he started saying, 'It's OK, even if you make mistakes. I will make it up for you. So no worries. Do challenge!' That shift was so encouraging for the young ones and they showed surprisingly rapid progress in their job skills in response to the foreman's sincere expectation. When I heard this, I felt deep respect for this foreman and his subordinates and what happened between them.

After the interview I understood that much of what happened in the process of their workplace transformation was not the direct result of SF training as I had expected. Instead, it was more a result of a chain of natural positive responses. Somebody gives an OK message (appreciating, acknowledging or validating) to another person because he thought SF was to 'see good in others and doing good to others'. The receiver feels very good and naturally wants to do the same to others 'without being conscious' about it. This can ignite a positive chain reaction. It really happened at ZACROS such that it could be recognized as an organisational change. So I started to call that phenomenon a 'chain of natural positive response' or CNPR.

The new meaning of 'SF inside' is useful in being flexible and inclusive

I now regard the SF methodology as one of the switches to activate the resources inside people. A very effective switch, of course, but what's switched on is more important. When the switch is on, we can expect lively communication, cooperation, positive emotion, creativity and spontaneity. When people in organisations use SF successfully, often they start describing the end-result experience as 'SF' and not so much the methodology of how they do it. What they mean by

'SF inside' is that they are enjoying their own resources being activated, but not necessarily using a clear SF format in communicating.

Here is an example. A ZACROS team came to J-SOL2 (Second Japanese National Conference for Sharing SF Utilisation in Organisations) to do a presentation on their success of creating 'SF inside' their workplace with unique tools, which they had created themselves: hi-five greetings, SF notebooks, SF emails and so on. When they returned to J-SOL3 the next year, they said, 'We are no longer using those tools because we realised we can interact positively in an SF way without those tools. Using SF tools became redundant, so we discarded them. However, we do more of SF communication now.' It sounded like the guide wheels had been removed from a child's small bicycle.

If SF tools are only a guide wheel to be removed after the people in organisations realise they can interact with each other in mutually invigorating ways, we can be very flexible in accepting how people interpret SF. People want to talk about SF in the language they already have, whether in coaching, organisational development, psychology, positive management and so on. We can only utilise them to keep the bicycle moving. It does not matter if they use SF tools in the 'right way' or not. What matters is whether the bicycle is moving smoothly. You can see if the bicycle is moving smoothly by checking whether any CNPR phenomena are observed. So my meaning of 'SF inside' shifted from installing a ready-made program to finding already existing resources in client organisations that resonate with SF ideas and amplifying them.

44

MANAGING CHANGE AND ORGANISATIONAL CULTURE

Arvind Wable

Contradictions cohabitating in every sphere of life are what make India a uniquely exciting and challenging environment in which to operate. The modern and traditional, science and superstition, the global and local, extreme diversity and the underlying Indianness have all found a precarious balance in India. Indian businesses are an intrinsic part of this milieu, which is why the country and organisational culture play a key role in determining the performance feedback system in companies. The soft versus hard, indirect versus direct, and positive versus negative feedback are issues within any coaching intervention.

In my view, the solution focused (SF) approach with its inherent positivity and absence of a rigid structure suits the Indian context very well. The focus on solutions rather than problems creates a non-threatening environment to discuss issues and work towards a solution. In this chapter I outline two SF processes and their impact on an individual and with a team within the same organisation. In both cases the aspects of organisational culture were important ingredients to managing change.

Co-creation of desired changes within an organisation

A unique opportunity came when I introduced SF Coaching in an organisation where I had been a member of the senior leadership team and a member of the board.

The senior leadership team had been in the company for over 20 years, and the second line of leadership had all been recruited by the senior team and also had long tenures with the company. The company had evolved into a benevolent top-down culture, providing a secure, nurturing environment with the top leadership being the mentors to all levels. The succession planning required the second line to take over the top jobs in the company over the next few years, during which the top leadership would gradually pass on the mantle of running the company to the second line.

The board of the company felt that a specific intervention was needed to provide an objective assessment of leadership qualities among the second line leadership. Given this opportunity, I made a presentation to the board of the company on the concept of a coaching culture and specifically of the SF approach as distinct from other forms of coaching. What weighed the board in favour of the SF approach was its positivity and its ability to adapt to the specific situation and culture of the company. We discussed in detail what the board wanted, in terms of the desired outcome and organisational changes they hoped for.

The next stage was to introduce the idea of coaching to the second line leadership. This was done through an interactive group session followed up with one-on-one communication. The emphasis was on the benefits of coaching and how it was not a corrective but a positive intervention for self-development. The coaching interaction was voluntary so four of the five second-line leaders opted for it. For the purpose of this chapter I have taken one of the cases to serve as an example.

Organisational culture and leadership development

Ajay led the market research and insight division of the company. He was liked by all those who had worked with him. He was bright, was intelligent and kept up with the latest trends in his field. The areas he wanted to work on in the coaching sessions were 'low assertiveness and self-confidence'. He described situations wherein he had worked hard on projects but found it difficult to sell his ideas to his boss and clients. He said he found himself 'ever willing to give up his point of view at the slightest push back'.

Ajay said he worked best on his own and 'getting work out of others was not a strength'. He felt he needed to profile himself better within the company as well in the industry circles.

Ajay really opened up during the miracle question when he described himself as at 'his best'. He described himself as a morning person who would get up and go for a walk, listen to music and have an easy start to his day. He loved to read a new article or book (not necessarily related to work) while travelling to work. At the weekend, he enjoyed taking a break from work and spending time with the family.

Ajay rated himself a '4' on a scale, where 10 represented his best self. Ajay felt he could do a lot better and set for himself some specific next steps to move up from his current level.

We met a month later, and I asked Ajay what was better or different since our last meeting. He mentioned that his portfolio had been divided and the part he enjoyed the most had been taken away. He also talked about how his boss had been putting a lot of pressure on him, and hence he was not getting any free time. I asked Ajay about a time when he had been under a lot of pressure but had felt good about the work he had done. Ajay related a period a few years ago when he was in a similar situation and had worked independently and 'really slogged it out'. But it had been a great year with a 'lot of learning and exposure to new things'.

At the end of this session Ajay decided that his next steps would be: (1) to do some meditation to handle his stress, (2) he would think about what he really wanted from his work life and (3) he would ask for a meeting with his boss to calibrate his expectations and seek clarity about his role and future in the organisation.

I met Ajay a third time about six weeks later and asked him 'What is better?" This time, his response was 'I am feeling a lot more focused'. He also said he was feeling less guilty about doing things that he enjoyed! And even though his boss had indicated that he was now operating at 70 per cent, Ajay felt he was at 100 per cent and happy about it.

Ajay left the company two months later and took an assignment that gave him the freedom, flexibility and independence to do the things he liked. When I connected with Ajay a year later he mentioned that our coaching sessions had really helped him 'put his professional relationship under a scanner and decide that to come out of the victim mode either I change the dynamics of the relationship or end it'.

Reflections as a consultant and coach

What I found interesting, was that all the other coaching sessions with the second-line leadership shared a common theme. Almost all of them had received feedback from their superiors about being too soft, not being assertive or proactive, and in most cases, the coachee believed it to be fair feedback. This is what got me thinking. Was it that the entire second line had similar personalities, or was it something to do with the organisational culture? I suspected it had to do with the directive, top-down culture of the company, which had resulted in a second line evolving this way. I shared my impressions with the senior leadership who were open to relooking at their role in evolving a new culture. This resulted in a decision to work towards creating a more participatory culture in the company. A major outcome of this was in setting up a more transparent and participative decision making structure and handing over operational responsibility of running the company to the second-line leadership with the hope that greater empowerment will facilitate the emergence of future leadership.

Team-building process

A second SF process I introduced in the company came in the form of a team-building exercise. One of the offices of the company had undergone a leadership change. The newly appointed office head was the most senior amongst the four second line managers. The new appointment had ruffled some feathers and within a couple of months, two of the second-line managers left the company. Soon after, the office also lost a major business deal, which resulted in pressures to reduce the head count and overheads for the office. This created further friction within the team, and some unilateral decisions by the office head led to a breakdown in the cohesiveness of the senior team. Each functional head was doing a good job within his own area of responsibility, but there was little sharing of information and ideas across the teams. This was in sharp contrast to the previous culture of the office, which had built great team spirit and camaraderie over the last two decades. Repeated attempts by the office head to meet as a group and evolve a common vision had limited success. While the office continued to make strides in business terms, the undercurrents of a divided leadership team percolated down in the system, resulting in demotivation and increased attrition rates at the junior and mid-levels in the office.

At this stage, I facilitated a team exercise to break this deadlock and help the team work towards a common vision. The first session was a warm-up session, essentially to discuss the need for the senior team to meet regularly and raise and discuss issues facing the office. Anticipating that the office head would meet with resistance in organising the meetings, the responsibility of coordinating these sessions was given to someone who thus far had refused to participate in any group activity. Surprisingly, all subsequent meetings happened on scheduled dates and with full attendance. Being kept away from the decision making process had alienated the senior team. Involving them resulted in a positive and purposeful response.

In the next session, I facilitated a platform-building exercise with each one identifying three or four issues that the person felt were most critical for the team to address. The issues were then shared for all to discuss. The group, comprising nine people, came up with a list of 39 issues, including: 'lack of direction', 'we do not communicate', 'lack of pride in our work', 'no common vision', 'lack of cohesive spirit in the senior team' and 'lack of transparency'. Obviously, there was a fair degree of common concerns. The group then spent some time clustering the issues and arrived at seven big issues that they felt needed to be addressed.

The next stage was asking the group to visualise the perfect day in the company when all the above issues were resolved. The session started off slowly, but with my persistence in asking 'what else', it soon became a flood of outpouring and reminiscing about the good old times. The group was then asked to individually do a scaling exercise, where they rated the current situation that prevailed in the office, with the perfect day being a '10'. Each one read out their individual score. The scores ranged from a low of 2 to a high of 5.

Team reflections

After a brief break, the group reassembled and the conversation shifted to sharing instances when the team had worked together even during difficult periods and had shared successes. There were anecdotes of the company values which had built up a strong culture. It became evident that the entire senior team were committed to the growth of the company and were putting in the effort to meet their individual targets. What they needed was to communicate, share and work together as a cohesive group (which they had done in the past), which would resolve a lot of the prevailing misgivings and misunderstandings.

The session ended with each person identifying two or three steps they would take to contribute towards movement to the perfect-day vision that the group had visualised.

The significance of using the SF approach was that, in just two sessions, it had reconnected a group of people who had disengaged from each other, to the extent that they were reluctant to even meet and discuss the issue that impacted their work life. Many middle managers down the line said that they noticed a more positive interaction amongst their seniors after the SF sessions. Over the next few days it created a ripple effect in the office, even among those who had not participated in the group exercise.

Conclusion

In my experience, the use of the SF approach is very effective in countries like India, as it is a non-evaluative, 'soft' approach that works well in a culture where hard feedback is neither given nor received very well. The informal conversational style in the SF approach helps overcome the otherwise top-down, directive culture in many Indian organisations as it does not impose a rigid structure on the coaching interaction and can adapt to the diverse multicultural mosaic which is so typical of Indian organisations. The other significant aspect of SF, which was appreciated by both individuals and groups in this example, was the small 'next steps', which seemed manageable and easy to execute in the journey to bring about the desired change. Maintaining individual ownership of each step and designing a shared vision all enhanced the process of managing change and forming a more suitable organisational culture.

45

CHANGE YOUR CONVERSATION, CHANGE YOUR ORGANISATION

SF consulting leveraging strategic methods of collaboration

Denise Wright

This chapter focuses on the facilitation of culture change and working systemically within an organisational context. It offers an Asia-based case study of how the author used a solution focused (SF) consulting approach over an 18-month period, from initial briefing to celebration of achievement, and how it created a cultural energy conducive to generating shared ownership and shared leadership. The SF framework and complementary group methods applied will enable the reader to have a clear sense of how an SF-based program design and delivery, within an Asian context, was instrumental in creating a collaborative culture and cohesive high performance teams.

A blended approach: Solution focused and strategic collaboration

Two fields of work have particularly shaped how I have co-facilitated desired culture shifts in organisations:

*   The solution focused approach
*   Group methods of strategic collaboration

I have witnessed how an SF consulting approach to whole system change can be visibly transformative for organisations and teams in Asia. I feel very grateful to be able to share my perspective and experience on this topic.

An SF approach to group work creates an environment conducive to useful conversations and interactions. The focus on what is wanted helps to transcend actual and potential barriers whilst generating a rich picture of the preferred future and tangible progress clues for next steps forward.

The art of hosting groups through leveraging powerful methods of strategic collaboration ensures that all group members have the opportunity to share their hopes, questions and views. These group methods foster integration and cross-pollination across roles, seniority, ethnicity, gender and leadership levels during the generation of the rich shared visions and plans. This is extremely useful in multi-cultural Asia where respecting hierarchy, seniority and consensus is deep cultural value and can make working with diverse groups particularly challenging.

Group members choose which conversation they want to continue and which roles and responsibilities they own, building accountability. The degree to which employees assume ownership and responsibility can be impacted by societal cultural norms. Investing in building ownership as a core organisational value can be particularly impactful in predominantly Asian environments where strong traditional, collective values (perseverance, harmony, self-sacrifice and respect for authority) contrast with individualistic, more Western values (expressing personal autonomy, freedom to decide and speak out for oneself).

This blended approach creates an environment conducive to open, honest cross-sharing, which builds greater trust and connection and enables the more introverted, common amongst many Asians, to speak up and get their views represented.

Case study: Transforming our working culture

Background. In mid-2013 my team and I took a brief trip to work with an Asia-based R&D centre of a global pharmaceutical company. The project sponsor, a member of the senior management team (SMT), described their desire to shift the culture from the current small within-group style, to a more collaborative, systemic working approach. This was the beginning of an 18-month organisational culture change journey for the whole centre. We utilised an overarching SF framework at each stage. Our approach was somewhat emergent, building on shared learning and tailored to each stage and the systems involved.

Stage 1: Partnering with the SMT – clear direction. Our SMT clients were ready customers for change. They were clear that they would need to (a) listen to their people and (b) refine organisational priorities and their own practices.

Listening. We kicked off with my team conducting some interviews with a representative sample of 20 per cent of the whole site. We explored their best hopes for the future, mainly in terms of 'how things get done around here' (our broad definition of organisational culture), plus what was already in place and under way towards this preferred future. As a result of these research conversations, the SMT, agreed to certain objectives:

- To build whole system cohesiveness and contribute to the development of the R&D talent pool, particularly in the area of systemic team-working.
- To create an environment where site employees can express and act on their hopes, concerns and opinions
- To foster trust and inspire responsibility towards realising a shared preferred future of 'working effectively across and beyond the organisation'.

Refining the big picture. The SMT decided that providing all employees with a clear direction of the big-picture goals for the next three years was a key first step in this culture change process. I facilitated a full day off-site where SMT members discussed five SF questions to help them refine this big-picture direction:

What do we do well now? An exploration of what they already did well helped the SMT to ease into the process, build confidence to move forward to subsequent steps and create the space for open and honest dialogue.

What do we need to get right? We explored current and likely future challenges, and short- and long-term opportunities for them as a management team and as a site. Exploring this up front, before moving on to their shared preferred future, was helpful as the SMT were itching to discuss current challenges and needed changes.

What is our shared preferred future? We explored what they wanted to upgrade given what they do well now and what they need to get right. A rich collective description was elicited through various process questions.

What is already in place towards this preferred future? The team used the preferred future output to help them consider all that was already in place.

What are our immediate next step actions? The SMT prioritised several key actions they could take to move closer to their preferred future work culture.

Impact. The SMT members shared that the use of the SF framework created a positive, open energy that helped build trust levels between them and the inspiration to make the identified changes. Two valuable benefits particularly stood out for them:

Firstly, the detailed description of their preferred future gave the SMT a clearer idea of key objectives and progress clues towards achieving these, particularly in the area of high-performance, collaborative team-working. It helped them to focus on what was possible. The shared exploration of *what else* and *what next* in the short term was particularly helpful.

In Asia, recent success has been the norm, and relished prosperity can hinder future-focused inquiry and reinvention. It can also lead to a struggle to adapt to changing conditions. Hierarchical centralised leadership has been the tradition in Asia together with expectations that seniors, experts and 'gurus' will provide all the answers. Currently, however, the global challenge for organisations, including this R&D site, is to flex to a high-agility approach where shared leadership, working across boundaries and managing and valuing diversity are becoming increasingly necessary. This requires conscious evolution.

Secondly, the SMT shared that acknowledging what was already in place boosted their feelings of resourcefulness and their readiness to act. They realised that acknowledgement and feedback were visibly absent practices within their current organisational culture and they made a commitment to make positive changes in this area. An acknowledgment mind-set fits nicely with the Asian cultural value of honouring and respecting all and offered a much needed balance to the current problem focused culture.

Review. I met with the SMT for a check-in conversation a few weeks later. The SMT had been meeting more regularly and working more cohesively. They were energised and focused and had put into action many of the immediate next steps they had previously identified.

Stage 2: Towards greater cohesiveness and inspired accountability – whole site. With the SMT refined preferred future in place, we focused on how the whole site could best achieve the key objectives (inspiring working environment and collaborative, high-performance team-working). In June 2013 the whole R&D site team met off-site. An over-arching SF framework was combined with the use of two group methods that foster strategic collaboration – the World Café method and Open Space Technology (OST). Through this blended approach, we were able to create and model the mood, energy and behaviours that the SMT were aiming to foster internally, in terms of collaboration, being solution focused and inspiring accountability.

The World Café process involved three whole-system group conversations based on the following SF questions:

•   What possibilities can we see for the next three years in terms of how we (whole site) create an inspiring working environment and high-performance team-working?

- What is in place already towards this?
- What do we need to get right over the next 18 months?

This method created a safe space for both rich small-group sharing around these core questions and cross-pollination of ideas and integration as participants moved around to join new discussion groups. This method allowed the whole system to meet and yet avoid potential barriers brought by mixing different functions, generations and levels, transcending strong Asian cultural expectations around hierarchy and seniority. The small group size and several rounds of conversation created the space for intimacy and trust to gradually build, which typically takes longer with largely Asian groups.

Through the OST, we created a marketplace where everyone had a chance to propose a topic that they deemed important to be developed. Participants formed topic stations around the room, self-selecting which discussion they would join and sharing responsibility for work on that topic. Conversations focused on next 18-month priority actions sourced from the World Café process. This OST-style process helped to create a mood of passion, responsibility and ownership in line with key organisational objectives and move away from reliance on the traditional hierarchical leadership of the past.

The results of each discussion were compiled and shared with the whole site, and further topic taskforce meetings were arranged with a commitment to present ideas and action plans to the SMT six weeks later.

Impact: This stage 2 process was extremely successful in building and sustaining momentum towards achieving the desired preferred future culture. The mood of the centre shifted significantly over the next nine months, driven by inspired adoption of the SF language and principles we had collectively practised. Nine staff-led taskforces were operational and active for a nine-month period. All SMT-approved taskforce initiatives were put into action and completed. New practices were introduced for meetings, and the physical workplace space was redesigned and radically improved to nurture and sustain further collaborative, cross-boundary working.

The most felt progress clues nine months later were: staff confidently speaking out and engaging more with one another in group meetings and large-group social outings and activities, supporting each other (beyond the self mind-set of offering each other ideas and cover) plus greater interaction and more cross-pollination across departments. Two particularly noticeable positive changes were increased acknowledgement of what was already in place and appreciation of their colleagues, who had now become an integral part of the new organisational culture.

Stage 3: Towards greater shared leadership – top teams. Through on-going development and coaching work with the SMT and their direct reports, we were able to build further alignment, cohesiveness and shared leadership. The SMT had been operating as one system, and their direct reports had been focused mainly on their down-lines. Through various team development sessions we worked on building systemic working across the SMT-1 level (2nd tier cross-functional management level) and also together with the SMT (SMT + SMT-1 as one system). Team-working at both of these levels had been missing thus far. We worked on building self-awareness (individual and team), sharing behaviours, and giving and receiving feedback and on-going progress checks to build and sustain the habit of celebrating what was going well. The growing acknowledgment, mind-set and practice helped pave the way for greater courage to reinvent the organisation and regenerate, including having necessary difficult conversations, an important muscle to build amongst a culturally very polite predominately Asian workforce.

Stage 4: Celebration and on-going evolution — whole site. In March 2014 we (my facilitation team, SMT and SMT-1) held another whole-site planning session, this time focused on questions that inquired beyond culture and performance. We leveraged the opportunity to celebrate recent achievements and most appreciated shifts plus to model and reinforce relationship building and collaborative working practices.

Overall delivery impact. At the end of 2014, the feedback from the SMT indicated that they felt change not only in the area of desired culture change but in terms of increased results, productivity and strategic agility, which was extremely positive and encouraging.

The changes achieved were a win-win. The organisation gained from more effective team working at all levels in the organisation and beyond, greater diversity of input and increased productivity. The SMT were able to get more from their direct reports and from each other, expand their big-picture view, be less insular and feel more supported. Individuals and teams were generally having more fun and growing both their relational skills, and at the same time, their capacity to deliver results together, working systemically with others across and beyond the organisation.

In closing

I believe there is real genius in leveraging this combination of an SF framework, language and principles together with methods of strategic collaboration. This specific blend of ingredients works, as over time it creates a 'How can we best interact and achieve with one another?' mindset that builds a new more conscious organisational culture.

Organisations are largely their conversations, the sum of their conversations and interactions. If leaders and colleagues can support one another through helpful solution focused interactions, building on existing strengths, we are better placed to adapt, innovate and successfully navigate our future. Within the rich multi-cultural environments we operate in Asia, consciously managing the diversity and unity within our workforces and building collaborative, cohesive and committed workforces, through conscious, strategic design, can significantly and positively impact organisational culture and effectiveness.

46

'WORK SMARTER, NOT HARDER'

Debbie Hogan

To create a better life for all

(Company core value)

As a consultant and coach, specialising in solution focused practice, I have lived in Singapore for the past 28 years and work with organisations to help them deal with challenging issues and change management. In this chapter, I will share an example of how a solution focused consulting project helped a successful business owner in Asia develop his core leaders to work from a shared mind-set, which led to significant expansion and growth of his organisation, and describe the personal benefits and organisational changes that happened as a result.

Personal impact of coaching

Mr H. is a successful business owner of a holding company, with thousands of employees under his care, in five distinct areas, from textiles, furniture, property, and retail, to hotel management across Asia. When I first met Mr H., it was evident that he was a leader with a mission and possessed great leadership qualities. It was no surprise that he was a successful businessman with strong corporate values. Mr H. was a man with deep religious values, and his faith in God profoundly influenced his personal and business practices. He explained that in his country, business practices are sometimes questionable and personal prestige is pursued. Very little focus is on the quality of life or the wellbeing of families, who often struggle due to long work hours. It was very important to him to take care of his family and his employees.

In the year before this project began, Mr H. attended our solution focused coach training course and participated in individual coaching sessions. He had made personal changes since adopting solution focused practice as a leader, and the benefits were evident to his family and his employees. His interest was in learning how to 'work smarter and not harder' and how to model his company's core value, 'To create a better life for all'. He worked long hours as a CEO and wanted to spend more time doing what he enjoyed, which meant that he needed to delegate responsibilities and empower his staff. He enjoyed having more time with his family, and he became a more effective and efficient leader. He modelled ethical work practices and encouraged his employees to do the same. He discovered that his staff enjoyed taking on more responsibilities and they too, were learning to 'work smarter, not harder'. As a result, his company thrived and continued to grow.

Co-creation of a desired outcome: What do you want for your organisation?

Mr H. contacted me to explore leadership development and change management for his organisation, specifically, with the 11 directors of his holding companies who were responsible for the five business pillars. He wanted to encourage his directors to develop a coaching culture within their companies and thrive as individuals and take care of their staff. He wanted to grow the company, but more importantly, he wanted to develop his people.

To clarify what Mr H. wanted, I explored:

- What is your best hope for your organisation?
- What differences are you hoping for?
- What will it look like when your best hopes are realised?
- What is going well already?
- What resources are currently in place?
- What concerns do you have?
- What do you need now?
- What will be the small steps to accomplish this?

His hope was to build and expand his company holdings over the next two years. It was clear that Mr H. wanted to improve productivity as well as strengthen cohesion among the directors. He hoped a solution focused mind-set would enable his team to work from a common philosophy of change management and the personal benefits would impact all the employees. He wanted a different approach than the predominant problem focused and top-down leadership style that most organisations in Asia adopt.

After exploring these ideas with Mr H., it led to co-creating a leadership development program for his directors, in which a colleague, Dave, and I would facilitate. The directors were invited to attend sessions to facilitate leadership development and identify 'best practices' within their various companies. Phase 1 focused on training his directors in solution focused leadership coaching so they could coach their managers and develop their staff. Phase 2 included a team coaching process with the directors and training them in team coaching with their management teams, to help them effectively lead their teams and plan out strategies for growth and development. Individual coaching was offered to each director to support the changes they wanted to implement. This process took place over a period of 16 months.

Phase 1 – Solution focused leadership coach training

Dave and I, both solution focused consultants, met with the 11 directors for 2 days to train them in solution focused leadership coaching. It was important to first establish a platform based on trust and ownership in the process.

Clarity on personal objectives. The directors came from across Asia, and it was the first time they were all together. All the directors, who were Asians and Westerners, wanted to participate in leadership development and organisational growth – although they were not sure about the approach. After introductions, we facilitated exercises to build trust and an atmosphere of fun and openness. There were opportunities to share what was going well in their lives and work. Sometimes Asians are hesitant to speak up in a group and share what they did well, for fear of showing off. It was important to ensure all voices were heard and respected. We took time to identify individual concerns and their desired outcomes from these sessions. Some had already taken leadership training and were sceptical as to why they should learn another approach. Some had no previous training, and others were eager and ready to learn. It reminded me of the analogy of the stoplights. When approaching something new, some people are like a 'green light', eager and ready to learn. Some are like the 'yellow light' and approach with caution. Others are like the 'red light' and are at a full stop. The directors were in various states of readiness and openness to our approach. However, the atmosphere in the room very quickly became jovial and light. These directors knew how to have fun! There was no hint of the competition that is sometimes present in organisations in Asia. There was a noticeable spirit of camaraderie.

Throughout the two days, the directors learned and practised solution focused coaching. They learned coaching tools that enabled them to work individually with their staff. Whether it involved day-to-day operations or critical issues, they had coaching tools they could utilise. This enabled the directors to lead 'from behind' and draw from the expertise of their staff and empower them. They were beginning to shift their mind-set from problem-focused thinking to solution exploration. Lightbulb moments and laughter came when they understood their CEO's use of certain questions, such as, 'What do you want to be different?' or 'What else?' or 'What's better?'

The directors learned how to co-construct a coaching goal, identify what was wanted or needed to change and what was working, and come up with ideas for taking the goal forward. This facilitated cooperation and collaboration between the directors and their employees.

Reflections from phase 1. During reflection time, those who were sceptical became less sceptical. They began to see the differences in what they had previously learned and what they were learning. It slowly dawned on them that solution focused coaching was not just a technique, but a way of thinking about and interacting meaningfully with their employees and even family members. Some jokingly commented that they were going to 'SF' their wives or children. The overall takeaways for the directors were expressed by these common sentiments:

- I realise I need to stop 'taking the monkey'.
- I learned how to listen and stop trying to problem solve.
- I learned to ask questions and not just tell people what to do.
- I learned how to coach myself when I get into situations I need to change.
- I'm more aware of how I talk to people and pay attention to how I say it.
- Affirming or giving compliments is something I realise I need to do more.
- I see the value of noticing what's going well and not focusing on the problem.
- Using this approach, I see that my staff are capable and I can delegate more.

Follow-up coaching. Each director also participated in four to five individual coaching sessions with either Dave or me. By being coached, they felt it reinforced what they had learned about being a coach. They felt the coach training clarified what was important for them and convinced them they needed to make changes. During follow-up coaching sessions, they reported that not only had their personal goals been met, there had also been positive changes within their companies. They were intentionally acknowledging the contributions of their staff, and morale and retention were improving.

Phase 2 – Team coaching and change management

About 12 months after Phase 1, Dave and I met with the 11 directors for team coaching. It was important to clarify the desired objectives and outcome from the session with each director. A clear platform for ownership by all participants enabled us to work within the 'best hopes' of the group as well as facilitate the main objectives of the session. This time, there was 100 per cent buy-in and ownership from all the directors in the process and in the use of solution focused practice in their coaching and leadership. Clearly, this team of directors had embodied the 'work smarter not harder' mantra of their CEO and it had now become a company mantra.

Review of Phase 1. The directors were eager to share 'What's gone well?' since the beginning of their leadership development training. They shared positive differences and benefits they had gained through the past year. Some had already begun to expand their number of employees and added on more companies or started new companies. The energy and atmosphere was loaded with laughter as well as a high level of trust and openness. The directors were now a cohesive team working from a common platform. They were eager to learn how to be a 'team coach' as they had now seen the benefits of coaching one on one. They were also aware that at the end of this session, the CEO would be joining the 11 directors for a team meeting to discuss and plan out next year's targets to grow their individual companies and expand the number of companies.

Team coaching session. During the team coaching rounds facilitated by Dave and me, the purpose was to facilitate 'best practices' in team coaching by giving them an experience of actually doing it. Each director led their group through one step of solution focused team coaching. Solution focused practice has an isomorphic quality, in that the team coaching process is similar to the individual coaching process, and the directors were able to facilitate the process with a high level of confidence.

Team coaching agreement: Platform for change and desired outcome. Three groups were formed. The designated team coach for each group began by asking their group what topic they wanted to work on for their coaching goal, something that was important to them. Questions that helped the coach facilitate the discussion were, 'What will make our team coaching worthwhile today? What do you want to achieve as a result?' Each coach helped to define and refine the team coaching agreement by asking questions, until there was a common agreement for the 'best hopes' for the group project. During this phase, the team coach addressed potential challenges for the group project to ensure that concerns were raised. The coach asked questions, such as 'What do we need to get right?' or 'What do we need to pay attention to?' Each group went through the same process.

Miracle picture: Suppose your best hope occurred; what would it look like? The next team coach invited each member to imagine what it would look like, supposing their best hopes had really happened, which included the important aspect that 'all the problems and roadblocks were removed'. Flipcharts were used to create a visual representation. It became a very creative and energising process. The individual visual representations of 'best hopes' were shared with all the members in their group.

Scaling from 1 to 10. The next coach used the scaling tool to facilitate a conversation around: 'Where are you now with regards to where you want to go? What is working already? What's the next step? Who is going to do what?' Once the process started, team members were able to recall many things that were already working and could be utilised. Additionally, more ideas surfaced in terms of moving them forward and closer to their desired goals. Individual members agreed to take certain steps toward their desired outcome.

Highlighting strengths and competencies of the team. During the last part of the process, the coach and team members complimented each other on what impressed them and how amazed they were at what they were able to accomplish through good team coaching facilitation. They began to realise the potential and application of this process in other areas, such as coaching high-performance teams and facilitating effective team meetings.

Final reflections

We facilitated a time of reflection and individual takeaways from this experience. It became evident that a meaningful shift had taken place. For example, the directors were due to meet with the CEO after this session to plan a one-year strategy for growing the organisation. The directors had taken the opportunity during the team coaching session to actually work on this topic using the solution focused process. The results that emerged from this exercise were amazing.

The CEO joined the directors during the debrief and listened to them share some personal benefits from having been through this process. One director mentioned that he had never spent Christmas with his family due to work commitments, and he was now planning to do this for the first time. When the CEO saw all the creative and outstanding ideas the directors had developed, he realised that the work he was going to do with them was already done, and in such an excellent way. It became a testament as to how thoroughly they had embraced the process and philosophy of the solution focused approach and that they were now speaking a common language. The directors reviewed next year's plan with the CEO, which they subsequently implemented.

A follow-up meeting with the CEO indicated that they not only were on target but exceeded the number of new companies they wanted to develop. Organisational morale and retention was high. New leaders and directors had been identified and nurtured and were now directors of the new companies. This is not easy to accomplish in Asia, where some companies are scaling back and implementing retrenchment, and the work force are driven to work harder and for less money. Mr H. and his directors continued to flourish through their stand on ethical practices and in developing their people to 'create a better life for all'.

47

SEE IT AND MAKE IT HAPPEN!

Indry Wardhani

This chapter will highlight how a consulting approach with an organisation in Jakarta helped a top management team within the organisation realise their journey and their goal as being attainable and utilise their strengths to help them achieve it. I will share my experience of working with an Indonesian company, whose top management wanted my help to 'motivate' their team to grow the company. The chapter describes how a solution focused consulting and team coaching process was used to help the management team see their desired future in the vision, mission and goals of the company. The Indonesians are very visually creative people, and using their talents during training, and especially in answering the miracle question with creative methods, had a positive impact on the team. Visualising the miracle question can be helpful to reach every layer of a company, since it doesn't differentiate between levels of education, amount of knowledge or position in the company. As a result of this process, the individual team members recognised their own existing strengths and the importance of their own role in the bigger picture of the success and growth of the company and reaching their goals

Visualising words

> When we treat man as he is, we make him worse than he is; when we treat him as if he already were what he potentially could be, we make him what he should be.
>
> (Goethe, http://www.quotes.net/quote/42844)

Goethe captures the essential differences in two different perspectives. Where a traditional approach would emphasise the symptoms and problems at that moment, the solution focused approach wonders about what this person wants to be, what passions he has and what he can be.

I was asked by the top management of a large company in Jakarta, Indonesia, to coach the middle management team to be more 'motivated'. After meeting with top management to better understand their best hopes from our work, I then met with the human resources manager prior to the training to understand what they wanted as a result of the process. She described the things they struggled with and eventually said they wanted the middle management team to be more 'motivated' and, consequently, to motivate the people that worked for them. Morale was very low; they were getting stagnant, and the directors wanted to grow the company. The most common request I have from leaders of companies in Indonesia is: Can you motivate my people so my company can grow? This became the working goal or desired outcome for this organisation.

What is motivation?

How do you motivate your people so your profit will grow? How do you become a more motivating boss? These were some of the key questions presented by the top management of this company. In my work, I find that people will move toward a desired company goal when the employee has ownership and is a stakeholder in the process. In order to move all individuals to a common goal, it is important for them to feel connected to the employer, to their co-workers and to the 'dreams' of the company. A sharing and understanding of the rationale behind the 'dreams' of the company can help to get a team engaged.

Making the desired future visual

I initially spent time with the top management discussing and identifying what the common goals were and what they meant by 'motivation'. How would they know their managers were 'motivated?' What differences would that make for them and the company? As a result of being more motivated, what did they want for the managers, team and company? The top management team said things like: 'Believe in the vision and mission of the company'; 'all work together toward these goals'; 'show enthusiasm'; 'take initiative'; 'be creative'; and 'grow the company'.

The next day, during our first training day with the whole management team (top and middle management team), I asked the miracle question and gave all participants an opportunity to create it visually in their own unique way. In Western society we are more used to reflecting and 'imagining' our wishes. In Indonesia, it is my experience that most people are creative, artistic and very good with experiential learning. When I talk too much, I lose their attention. I learned that pictures do more than words, especially when you mix humour with doing unusual things. By participating in this process, they started to have fun and became more relaxed. They started to give their honest feedback to the bosses about their ideas of the company vision, mission, goal and which opportunities they saw. There were some brilliant ideas generated from these first small steps. Everyone was engaged in the process. There was ownership in the process of defining goals and identifying clear makers of 'motivation' and 'company growth'.

Making the miracle question into a visual piece of art enabled the top management team to transfer their vision to the middle management team, and also to connect to all levels of employees within the company. It didn't require a certain level of academic knowledge or a certain range of language skills. Everyone in the organisation participated in this exercise during our day together, which was the second day of training. I asked them to explore their own personal future wishes and goals. Even the security guard, who knew a lot about the current situation in the company, participated in the process and made a valuable contribution by sharing his ideas about the goals of the company. I learned that every individual in the company had good knowledge about the company, from their own job perspective. The visualisation of the miracle question enabled the employees to work together, have fun together and make significant progress in the process of achieving their desired future. Each employee felt their contribution mattered and that the company valued them. The visualisation of the miracle question required the team to really work together, have fun and yet make huge progress in the process of achieving the desired future.

We deveoped this further with another question: 'What will the company look like at the end of 2015?' I facilitated a big group discussion, and then I broke them into small groups to discuss their wishes and goals. As it was a construction company filled with people who were good with their hands and building things, I chose a 'Tampah', an Indonesian bamboo platter originally used to clean rice or to serve traditional snacks. Every group received one Tampah with lots of arts and crafts material to use to build their desired future of the company. Then each group presented their ideas of the desired company to the larger group and explained what they meant and which goal was their priority. Figure 47.1 highlights one of their creations.

FIGURE 47.1 The vision of the company for 2015. (Photo credit: Indry Wardhani)

From this point we collected the elements of the desired company, the common goals, a measure of the current situation (by using a scaling question) and the small steps needed to be just one point higher. We translated the desired situation into SMART goals. Because this was done in a fun and unusual manner, it made it more likely that people would remember it, which made realisation of the goals easier. As a famous French writer, Antoine de Saint-Exupéry, said:

> If you want to build a ship, don't gather people together to collect wood and don't assign them tasks and work, but rather teach them to long for the endless immensity of the sea.

Follow up

At the time of follow up with the company (one month and three months later), they had made changes in formatting the teams that made the communication between different departments better; the percentage of absence of employees was lower; the board of directors felt that they didn't have to intervene as often and, most of all, the top and middle management team reported a much more happier work environment. They kept the Tampahs of art at the office and continued to adjust and make new SMART goals to achieve their desired future together. The organisation continued to make progress in their initial desire to 'motivate their team' and 'grow the company'. The directors continued to be satisfied with the organisational improvements after the three-month follow-up meeting.

Dare to be different

One of the basic principles of the solution focused approach is: If it doesn't work, do something different. Therefore, when offering coaching or training, don't be afraid to try new things. Look outside the 'training' box and ask yourself: What is fun to do, relaxing and yet helpful in reaching your goal? Nothing is crazy. My experience is that people will participate and are willing to explore new activities. Being genuine and creative in the moment can encourage participants to think outside the box.

I love to challenge people into doing something different because it actually activates the brain more. More fresh ideas will come when you challenge people. But it is very important that you use their specialties to discover the strengths. For example, when I had a training day with a confection company, we visualised leadership qualities by writing on a white t-shirt and presenting that to the others. The desired future of the company was painted by the whole company, divided into small groups, on a very large piece of fabric (10 m × 2 m). When this was finished, it was held up, and everyone was amazed at the work they had achieved together. They recognized a lot of strengths of the company and each other and the importance of their own role in this bigger whole. The company had achieved all goals made that day and more.

Conclusion

The solution focused approach was a very powerful and effective process that helped both teams achieve what they wanted. It helped them see a way forward by engaging their imagination and collaborative spirit. Guiding them by using their own desires, wishes and strengths made them shine, not only in their jobs but also in the other aspects of their life.

The Indonesians are visually strong, very creative and naturally group-oriented and appreciate originality. Using these cultural strengths and combining them with products that are familiar to them (like the Tampah) really helped to make them think out of the box and yet feel comfortable doing it. Culture is an important variable in a person's life and in a company. Know the culture and use it so you can communicate in the same 'language'.

Making use of cultural strengths, asking solution focused questions and complimenting helped to give people hope and trust in themselves. By making the desired future and the company goals into a visual representation, it made the effect even bigger.

48

CONFLICT RESOLUTION GOES MOTHER GOOSE

Karen McDonald Louis

Humpty and Dumpty were working on a wall;
They had a 'falling out', and great was their fall!

This is a story about two NGOs in Asia who ran orphanages together until things started to deteriorate, and how a team of solution focused consultants facilitated a conflict resolution process leading to reconciliation. I used the characters of Mother Goose to tell the story of how these two bickering NGOs were able to work together successfully again, highlighting the strategies, questions and group work that took place during the process. The solution focused process facilitated conflict resolution with two organisations in culturally appropriate ways that fit the Asian values of harmony, being non-confrontational, being respectful and using an intermediary. The end result, culminating in a celebration with all stakeholders of both organisations, produced harmony for the 'boots on the ground' employees of the NGOs, brought peace of mind to the CEOs, and benefitted the recipients of the NGOs' work in Asia.

Once upon a time in the mythical country of Asiastan, there were two NGOs ('Humpty' and 'Dumpty') whose partnership in running orphanages had helped thousands of people and been mutually beneficial for decades. Their collaboration first began when 'Jack Horner' fell in love with Asiastan and decided to start an orphanage there. Searching for a trustworthy provider, Jack serendipitously came across Humpty and saw it had expertise in management, human resources, fund-raising and starting orphanages. He found seed money and hired Humpty to put the initial orphanage together, but still needed a reliable continuous source of funds. Dumpty was looking for worthy projects in Asiastan to support. From the time Humpty opened the doors at its first Asiastan orphanage, Dumpty gave over 50 per cent of the daily expenses of running the programs, and continued for years – what an effective partnership!

Round-one consulting: Damage control

The problem started when Jack Horner insisted on being publically acknowledged as the sole founder of the orphanages. He had just turned 70 and, according to Asian tradition, he felt it was his right that a man of his age be given seniority and honour. Humpty didn't mind, but Dumpty felt since it had donated the lion share of operating funds amounting to millions, if any person or organisation were going to be named as sole founder, it should be Dumpty! Humpty felt caught in the middle; true to his Asian values of being non-confrontational, not wanting to offend either side and hoping to maintain harmony, Humpty was slow to act. Dumpty then felt taken for granted and began demanding more of a say in how its money was being spent. Eventually, Dumpty pulled most of its funding, started new orphanages in other cities and hinted it might get Humpty shut down.

Humpty's head office feared the orphanages it had built through the years were about to be destroyed overnight. They had only a year of contingency money to run the orphanages with reduced funding. Humpty's head office agreed that they should call in a mediator, which is a common Asian conflict management style. They hired us as consultants, and notified the Asiastan-based head of their own organisation and that of Dumpty's.

Customer for change: Who wants what? The CEO of Dumpty in Asiastan flew to Singapore to meet with us. At this stage, not yet a 'customer for change', he just wanted to share his pain. As it turns out, a few years earlier, he had been part of Humpty's upper management in Asiastan but had been let go; he felt his views on corporate governance had not been appreciated. Initially we met with each CEO separately. In the Asian context, we wanted to be cautious about them not 'losing face' and making sure each felt respected. When we met with each CEO we asked, 'How would you know the mediation process was successful?' We knew it was important to find a common goal, one in which both parties would be invested in. We explored exceptions. 'Think of a time when things were better, even just a little bit.' One remembered the victories that had occurred when Humpty and Dumpty had worked well together in the early years. Both agreed that the optimal outcome for everyone would be if both organisations could work 'together in harmony'. They had now both become 'customers for change'.

When we first tried discussing a preferred future, one CEO said he would know a miracle had happened if he woke up and the other CEO had apologised and disappeared! The other CEO said his miracle would be 'if that group would get out of the country and let us run the orphanages our way'. We had our work cut out for us!

A few weeks later it was our turn to fly to Asiastan. We met with the CEOs separately, reminding them of their desired 'future perfect' – working together in harmony. We wanted to build on that vision, to get them to describe more about what that would look like.

Finding progress clues. We asked scaling questions, such as, 'Where would you put yourself, on a scale of one to ten, with one being not at all confident that you can work together in harmony and ten being completely confident that you will be able to work together harmoniously?' On the first day, both CEOs scaled themselves on the low side. We then revisited the miracle question so they could enlarge their vision. 'Tell me more about what working in harmony would look like.' 'What else?' 'And who would notice if that happened?' 'Who else?' 'And what would that do for your organisation?' 'What else?' And so forth. In some cases, their answers had to do with the other person changing, or the other NGO *not* doing something, so we asked questions like, 'How would so-and-so changing make a difference?'

With a firmer idea of their preferred future, the CEOs began to be excited about the vision of working together in harmony, and by the third day, when they were asked the same scaling question, they had moved significantly higher up the scale in terms of confidence.

In our last session we fleshed out even more details. 'What do you now expect?' 'What exactly do you want to see happen?' Each CEO wanted resolution; both wanted to feel heard and understood by the other.

Suggestions for next steps. We finished up with compliments and homework. We complimented the CEOs on their progress and how hard they both worked to help others, on their willingness to endure hardship and sacrifice and to get out of their comfort zone for these sessions. Their first homework was to consider what would help them feel heard and understood. The second homework was to think about what they could have done differently, and if they had done it differently, how that might have encouraged the other party. Since they said they wanted to be heard, we suggested that would probably mean the other side wanted that as well. Both sides agreed they would have to do their part to help both sides have the miracle. Processing this homework took two months, mostly consisting of weekly Skype sessions with the two different CEOs separately.

What's better? During the weekly Skype sessions, we asked questions such as, 'What's been better?' 'Suppose the other CEO were to do XYZ, how would that make a difference for you?' and 'Suppose the miracle had already happened, what might you be doing differently?' Not surprisingly, both sides discovered that in order to reach their miracle, they would need to value empathy and sensitivity in their communication with the other.

The day came when we did a Skype call with the two CEOs together. They set groundrules for themselves: a time limit for speakers, listening without interrupting, avoiding displays of unfriendly body language, and each party summarising what the other party had said. The CEOs began by sincerely apologising on an emotional level. Both shared what they knew they had done wrong. And both sides really tried to make healing statements that would satisfy the other party. I was impressed by the level of trust that had built up between them. To admit one's fault in Asia is very rare, especially to your adversary.

Reflections from round one. With the future of hundreds of vulnerable children at stake, we had felt we could not get the CEOs together until we were sure it would go well. Looking back, it seems that taking time, being patient and not rushing the clients ended up helping the 'coaching' to be brief. It may sound counterintuitive, but when we let them talk while gently guiding the questions, they seemed to feel more able to respond, and were more open minded about really listening to the other side. Of course, none of this could have happened if the two CEOs hadn't found a common goal in the beginning. Round one of the conflict resolution journey took about four months.

Round-two consulting: Other stakeholders

The Asiastan-based CEOs of Humpty and of Dumpty were all *gung ho* about repairing their relationship and figuring out how to go forward, but that was not going to matter in practice if they didn't get their respective head offices on board with some new terms. Individually, they asked us for guidance regarding approaching their bosses. We processed some options, spoke to several of their board members by phone and even had a session in person with one of the decision makers visiting Singapore. In keeping with their vision of a preferred future, the CEOs did a great job of winning over their head offices: Dumpty would immediately reinstate half of their funding, wouldn't insist on being the founder and obviously wouldn't jeopardise Humpty's orphanages. Humpty would honour Dumpty as a founder (rather than sole founder), and treat Dumpty not like a renegade NGO but as a partner. They both agreed to trust each other when there was an overlap of money, care giving or personnel. (And Jack Horner, who had started the mess, became ill and no longer participated in the discussions, ceding all decisions to Humpty.)

Round-three consulting: All stakeholders

We brought in four more consultants to help. Our team of six SF practitioners (one Malaysian, two Indonesians and three Americans) from three different Asian countries flew into Asiastan on a Friday afternoon. The team scheduled meetings for Saturday so we could use Sunday for last-minute talks, and fly out late Sunday night.

Saturday morning we met with the top 30 employees and stakeholders from all the orphanages, all but 2 being from Asiastan. We reviewed the process to date, and shared many stories about what was better. The powerful part came when the CEOs openly shared how they had realised their own issues had got in the way. They revealed how they had learned to become open to hearing from others, how they had made personal healing statements to each other and how they had both really felt heard. The two CEOs made fun of themselves ('That's when I went "nuclear"' and 'I'm sorry I became judgmental'), got teary-eyed and even hugged!

This moving experience empowered the various local leaders to share openly, as well as to get behind the harmony miracle. As the day progressed, the 30 stakeholders really enjoyed brainstorming, learning how to tap into their own resources and choosing how they wanted to go forward. Several things surfaced during this time. One was how the employees had seen some things in their bosses but had not felt 'safe' enough, or even worthy enough, to speak up. As Asians, it is not customary to speak to your superiors on this level. But because their bosses had invited feedback, a new level of trust was emerging. Another was that because of personal hardships, they had not felt the work troubles were such a big deal and had only recently realised how the stress caused by the disunity of the two organisations was affecting productivity and job satisfaction. The stakeholders promised to speak up more in the future for the good of the respective organisations and to not be so fearful of their bosses, no matter their nationality or title. During the afternoon break, we divided into smaller groups to help the few who were struggling and when we came back together, we shared progress and what was better, and gave compliments as a group.

On Sunday, our team had individual sessions with various groups of stakeholders, and we capped off the weekend with a unity dinner before heading to the airport. Once again, we closed out with compliments, and encouraged them to remember how wonderful it felt to work together the way they had over the weekend. They told us they had one more thing to do – jointly craft a unity letter to be read out to all the staff in every orphanage. We followed up on Skype, and the letter was soon read to all parties. From beginning to end, the whole process had taken six months.

As a practitioner, it was helpful for me to be conscious about the ways our team catered for certain cultural distinctions. In addition, I enjoyed witnessing the CEOs' postures shifting and the stakeholders becoming comfortable with speaking up, and once again seeing that, underneath the skin, human beings are more similar than different.

Humpty and Dumpty were working on a wall;
They had a falling out, and great was their fall!
They forgot about the children – their work hit the brakes;
They wasted bucks and time when they focused on mistakes.
Wise men and kings' men tried appealing to their soul,
But they only got together once they had a common goal!
Armed with 'future vision' and respect for others' pain,
Now Humpty and Dumpty are together again!

49

THE SOLUTION FOCUSED APPROACH IN A CHILDREN'S HOME

Edwin Choy

I am a solution focused (SF) coach and trainer from Singapore. I was approached by the super-intendent of a residential care home in Singapore that serves children and teenagers either who are abandoned or whose families were not able to take care of them. The superintendent shared his concerns regarding the care of these children as well as the staff who manage the home. In Asia, there is a lot of negative stigma and shame associated with abandoned and neglected children. Often, these children develop extremely negative self-beliefs and many become delin-quents. And the staff, if not properly trained, can often perpetuate these negative attitudes. His concern centred on 12 teens in his care, who were struggling with confidence issues and at times were disruptive and problematic. In our initial session, I explored his best hopes from our meeting and how he hoped it would make a difference. Being solution focused trained himself, he expressed that he wanted some kind of training or program to help build confidence in the 12 teens he mentioned and he wanted the staff to learn how to relate to the teens in a way that brought out the best in them. He was interested in developing a shared philosophy of care with all staff that would be solution focused and wanted it to permeate his institution and positively impact the children. He had also heard about adventure training, and wondered if this could make a positive difference for these 12 youths.

This chapter will highlight the process the superintendent and I created to develop a solution focused orientation in his organisation and the positive impact it made on individual staff mem-bers and the youths.

Together, we co-created a process that involved the whole organisation, based on his best hopes for the staff and children. Involvement of staff was also very high and they were keen on participating in this project. This process included the following aspects:

- The entire staff, including house parents and social workers, participated in four half-day sessions of training on the solution focused approach in managing and coaching these teenagers.
- The teenagers each received two individual coaching sessions and a day of confidence-building adventure training.

- I facilitated a follow-up session with the staff to explore what was going well and ongoing practical ways they could continue to utilise solution focused practice in their organisation.

There were many positive impacts and significant changes in the organisation as a result of these interventions, and these are described during the rest of the chapter.

Solution focused training for house parents and social workers

I conducted four half-day sessions of SF training for the caregivers and social workers at this home. I solicited their ideas on co-creating an environment for sustained change in the youths. Not only did we want the youths to view themselves differently, we also wanted the staff to learn how to notice their changes and support them in their strengths, not their weaknesses. The four sessions were designed to help care givers and social workers learn:

- The paradigm shift to the strength-based approach in connecting with the teenagers
- The power of direct and indirect compliments
- Basic solution focused coaching skills
- Applying SF practice in their organisation

The training helped them realise new possibilities in caring for these teens. They learnt to see the teenagers differently through the 'solution lens' – that by noticing what is right with the teenagers and giving them direct or indirect compliments, it motivated the teenagers to repeat positive behaviours. They also learnt to look for exceptions in the teenagers' behaviour – times when they did right instead of wrong.

This is counter-cultural in Asia. It is more likely, in the Asian context, that such teens are labelled as troubled teens and discipline often means catching them doing wrong and correcting them. Asians tend to adopt the 'spare the rod and spoil the child' principle and use more criticism than compliments. However, focusing on their mistakes often increases conflict and even aggression in the teens. It was certainly heartening to witness how these caregivers were consciously focusing on what the teenagers had done well and used compliments that encouraged positive behaviours, thus creating a nurturing environment for them. Some of the staff reported that it helped them in their own parenting at home.

At the end of each session, the staff were encouraged to look for opportunities to practise the skills they learnt with the teenagers during the week and provide feedback at the next training. They were excited to share how the simple concept of complimenting, looking for exceptions and highlighting them to the teenagers increased the teenagers' trust and collaboration with the staff.

Individual coaching: Solution focused strength interview

I met with each of the 12 teenagers for individual coaching twice – once at the beginning and once at the end of the entire programme.

Teenagers are usually reluctant to share with social workers and counsellors, but by re-labelling the interview session as 'coaching' instead of 'counselling', it created a positive atmosphere and put the teenagers at ease. The interview focused on their strengths and best hopes for the future. Some of the questions I asked in this first interview included:

- What are you good at? How do you use your gifts?
- What is one thing you have accomplished that you are proud of? How did you do it?
- On a scale of 1–10, with '10' representing your miracle future, what will be different at 10? How is this difference helpful?

This first coaching session revealed interesting strengths and best hopes from the youths. They responded to these questions with lots of smiles, and I complimented them on their strengths. The miracle question revealed interesting aspirations from these 'troubled' teens. They shared their desire to make progress in life. The increased energy level was palpable as they talked about their aspirations.

Focusing on strengths is quite counter-cultural in the Asian context. Asian parents, caregivers or educators are more likely to highlight the weaknesses of the teen, and discipline is often about punishing wrongdoing. We focus on the mistakes of the child and attempt to correct them in a punitive way in order for the child not to repeat the same mistakes. Focusing on strengths during this interview released positive energy and brought hope to the youths.

One youth, after a long pause, shared that the thing he was most proud of was when he defended his grandfather, from abuse by his own mum. I commended him for his courage in defending his grandfather, who cared a lot for him. In the Asian context it is unfilial for a child to go against his mum. However, in this instance, commending him for standing up for the weak led him to be more trusting and co-operative instead of being guarded. When asked for his miracle future, he shared his dreams of having a good job and earning enough to provide his children with a good education. It showed he had good dreams, which gave him hope for his future.

Powerful stories like these from the 'troubled' teens confirmed the value of the SF approach in an Asian context. When we focus on their strengths and what works in their lives, we build up energy for positive changes.

Adventure training and coaching

I designed a one-day adventure training for the 12 youths and incorporated SF coaching questions to process their learning points. I created three main activities in this programme

Rock wall climbing. After each teenager completed the rock wall, we had a coaching session to process their experience. I used the following solution focused questions:

- How high did you climb?
- How did you manage to climb that high? What skills did you use to do that?
- If you were to climb again, how much higher would you want to climb?
- How would you achieve it?
- If the wall represents your journey in life, when have you have felt like you have accomplished that much in your life?
- How did you do that?

These questions, after a challenging experience, enabled the teenagers to see their accomplishments and progress, thus strengthening their self-esteem.

High ropes challenge course. The high ropes challenge course consisted of three different challenge elements. When each completed the high ropes challenge course, I processed the learning points with them using the following SF questions:

- What was the toughest part of this challenge and how did you overcome it?
- What skills did you use?
- When was life toughest for you?
- How did you manage that?
- What did you learn that will help you to cope?

Dark adventure tunnel maze. The third adventure involved pairing the teenagers to go through a dark tunnel maze with different challenges. Each pair had to find their way out of the dark tunnel with only a tiny light stick.

There were situations in the tunnel in which the only way to clear the obstacles in the dark was to help one another. When each pair completed the challenge, I used these questions to process their experience:

- What did you experience in this adventure?
- How did you overcome the challenges?
- What strength did you notice about your partner?
- What did you learn that can help strengthen your friendship?

The teenagers loved the adventure training. It provided a great outlet to release their boundless youthful energy and at the same time enabled them to reflect on the strengths and abilities that they have and can apply in their lives to make progress.

I ended the adventure training with the 12 teenagers affirming each other on what they saw others doing well at this training. It lifted their spirits as they focused on what went well, and it bonded them as a team.

Follow up with staff

At the final session with staff, we brainstormed ways they could implement the SF approach in their work with the teenagers. Some simple yet great ideas emerged and were implemented. One idea was to adopt the SF approach for their weekly review meetings. In the past, they began their discussions with the problems they encountered with the teenagers. With this new approach, they started the review by asking what had been going well with the teenagers in their care. The more they recounted what the teenagers did well, the more hopeful the staff became.

They also agreed to compliment teenagers not in their direct care with the good things they heard about them from their caregivers at these meetings. This resulted in a positive environment where 'positive gossip' took place regularly. Another positive change for their meetings was in sharing what went well with their work and what they could do better. The social workers appreciated learning how to ask useful questions in their coaching.

Pre- and post-training review with youths

The teenagers did a pre- and post-training assessment to gauge the success of the entire adventure training and coaching programme, by rating the following statements on a scale of 1 to 10, with 10 being the best:

- I am happy with my life now.
- I know my strengths and my abilities.
- I know what I want for myself and my future.
- I can let go of the past and move on to the future.
- I am happy with this home now.
- I am willing to work with the care givers to make this home an even more ideal place to live in.
- I am willing to be a positive influence to the younger residents of this home.
- In future when I have the opportunity, I am willing to give back to this home by volunteering my services.

Almost everyone showed an improvement at the end of the entire coaching and training programme. The post-test gave me an opportunity to ask them how they were able to make progress in their lives.

Conclusion

After the training was completed, the superintendent of the home sent this feedback.

> The SF training for the residential staff helped them see how they can use the SF approach on themselves, in their own family setting as well as in their engagement and care of the residents. Teenagers who were generally loud and negative towards staff were surprised to see a change in the approach of the staff and they either toned down their voice or became cooperative with the staff. The training also helped the home to look for positive behaviour of the children and praise them, and develop a reward system based on good behaviour.

What began as an exploration for adventure training to increase self-confidence in these 12 teenagers developed into a more comprehensive, solution focused orientation for the whole organisation. The interventions were experimental in nature, and the superintendent and I were pleased that it had such a positive impact on the organisation. It is not common that staff training be included in an intervention meant initially for the teens. This makes sustained transformation more possible – that beyond seeing themselves differently, they also experienced similar strength based treatment from those who care for them on a daily basis.

I was very impressed with the leadership at this children's home. They have done a great job with the teens. I was told some of these teens made good progress. They followed up on their aspirations. One who showed great skill in art is progressively doing well and getting 'A's in his courses, and he was selected for a school leadership programme and earned an overseas reward trip to

China and Melbourne. Two of the youths pursued their aspirations in photography and had their photos in an exhibition in October 2015. Another took up his interest in fitness and is doing well in dragon boat races.

In the words of the Superintendent, 'the realities are that there are still those who need more work and guidance'. However, 'the transformation of those who came to them traumatised, abused, rejected, and told that they are useless . . . is really very encouraging'.

50

WORKING LESS, DOING MORE

Dave Hogan

At the very beginning of my first coaching workshop in Singapore with Peter Szabo, he gave each of us a neatly wrapped Swiss chocolate and, with a big smile, explained to us, 'In Switzerland we have an expression: "schoggi job" – a "chocolate job", meaning a "fun job". Solution focused (SF) coaching is a "schoggi job" and I love doing it and helping others learn how to do it.' He and co-authors Daniel Meier and Kirsten Dierolf make it clear that while SF coaching may be a 'schoggi job', it certainly does not mean the SF coach does nothing:

> As coaches we create a frame (of thought) for the client in which his or her goals, solutions, and first steps can shine. The frame constructed by the coach consists of goal-oriented questions, reinforcing feedback, present listening, and useful summary. The client can take space and time to sort out his or her thoughts, set concrete goals, become aware of resources, and plan next steps. It is the task of the coach to ensure that each client receives the appropriate frame.
>
> *(Szabo, Meier & Dierolf, 2009, pp. 1–2)*

This chapter chronicles one leader's journey in making progress in his life and work with his growing organisation over the course of four years. It was my privilege to have the 'schoggi job' of being a small part of the process as an SF consultant, trainer and coach. SF consultation in organisations is best understood as a process – using the SF tools and principles to enable clients to recognise 'what they want and do more of what works to deliver it' (Jackson & McKergow, 2007, p. 204). The SF frame enables them to do the hard creative work of 'painting' their desired future.

Jose Luis Calle, founder and Managing Director of Lifestyle Retreats, first encountered the SF approach to organisational development when he participated in a two-day coach training for leaders that my training partner, Debbie Hogan, and I were asked to conduct in Jakarta, Indonesia. As the participants began to learn and practise SF 'OSKAR' coaching (Jackson & McKergow, 2007), Jose's best hope, his platform for change, was clear: He wanted to find a way to manage his work better so he would have more time for his wife and two young children.

Reflecting on that experience four years later, he told me:

> At that time I was still based in Bali, operating three resorts and travelling extensively for sales and marketing as well as chasing new opportunities for development. I hardly spent time with my family and slept in the office an average of two nights a week. I was indeed a workaholic, yet accomplishing little despite all my efforts. My business partner could see I was out of balance and he thought that joining the coaching program would help me. I returned to Bali and started implementing all I had learned, coaching my leaders and letting go of some of the 'monkeys' I was carrying on their behalf. I also started spending more time at home.

Near the end of that same year Jose was back with the same group of leaders for another coaching workshop I ran in Bandung, Indonesia. This time the focus was on team coaching, and applying the OSKAR coaching model to team work in organisations.

A few months after this workshop, and well into the New Year, I saw Jose again when he was in Singapore for a business meeting and he wanted to meet with me for an individual coaching session. I remember waiting for him in a coffee shop in the centre of a food court in the basement of a large shopping mall near his hotel. It was early in the day, so the usual crowds had not yet a massed. When he arrived, he ran across the large, unusually empty food court to me, and when I stood up and extended my hand to offer a businesslike handshake, he smiled and exclaimed, 'Hey, Dave, let me give you a hug'. Before I could respond he suddenly bear-hugged me, lifting me off the ground. I looked at him and asked, 'Hey Jose, what's better?' He replied, now beaming, 'I knew you'd ask me that! Well, since I last saw you in Bandung I had a heart attack.'

'What?! How is that better?'

Over the next hour he explained in his animated, enthusiastic way how that was a critical moment in that it helped make this past year one of the best ever for him. The heart attack led to an important reflective time for Jose. His trusted partner in business invited him to move to Jakarta, where they could collaborate in new ways and he could take on a new leadership role in his partner's holding company in addition to continuing to operate the resorts.

He explained that when I had first met him at the coach training workshop in Jakarta, he was in the process of setting up several new resorts, and those projects were now under way. Best of all, he had experienced something new with his family:

> It was a quick move since we were living in Bali. By the 19th of December we were in Jakarta and I managed to celebrate Christmas AND New Year with my family for the first time. It was a great move since now I began travelling to Bali every second week and implementing active coaching with the leaders so we could spend less actual time but more quality time reviewing operations and also talking about personal stuff which helped us connect closer. On 31st December I wrote emails to my teams and also to the owners reflecting on the New Year and also thanking them for all their support. It felt great, and great for my family having me there.

At the end of our hour together, Jose invited me and Debbie to do leadership coach training at the Maya resort in Ubud, Bali, similar to the one he had first experienced, for the key leaders of his resorts in Bali to mark the beginning of their new year of work together. Later he told me:

> The training went very, very well and we all had a great time setting up the goal to continue together 'to not take the monkeys' – to empower staff to do more on their own and also to continue with our larger goal to set up more resorts.

By 'monkeys' Jose was referring to his tendency to take on all the responsibilities of his subordinates and to try to solve the problems for them.

The move to Jakarta helped Jose to focus on the expansion of the company over the next year. It also allowed him to detach himself from the day-to-day operations of the resorts. He became more determined to use his time with his leaders even better than he had when he was based in Bali. Meetings became shorter and more focused on their most important concerns. As the leaders took on more of their own responsibilities, it freed Jose to focus on his own priorities. He could now spend more quality time with his family, arriving home to spend more time with his children and even put them to bed, something he had not done since they were born. In Jose's own words, 'It felt amazing, and from that time onward I tried to be at home as much as possible, also making the decision to skip dinner work appointments as I had a very important one indeed – with them.' Jose's best hopes from the very first SF coaching experience were coming true: more time with his family while his company continued to grow.

After that year of expansion, Jose and I met again in Singapore for an hour of exploring 'what's better?' and 'what's next?' What was better: he said his leaders were empowered to do their own jobs better by coaching their own subordinates. He was now working in Jakarta so his times in Bali were focused on meetings with his teams. Though there could be as many as eight meetings a day, they were far more productive. What's next? I was amazed to hear that not only had he started two new resorts but he was about to start a new company with the owner of one of the resorts he was operating. This company would focus on energy saving and environmental conservation. A year and half later that company is now up and running in Bali and in Taiwan, with one more to be set up in Jakarta.

The last time I met Jose, I asked him what was different since that first meeting four years earlier. I was curious how SF coaching had helped him in his personal and professional journey. His response was:

> I can definitely say I am working less and doing more. I am less of a workaholic although I must confess that I still love working hard and I am passionate about everything I am doing at the moment, but spending time with family (three kids with the newest only 15 months old) is remarkable.

He explained he now operated six resorts and that another would be opening in Cambodia within the next eight months, with plans for two more to come.

I asked what differences he had noticed in how he worked with his leaders.

> When I was operating three resorts and prior to learning SF, I supervised leaders and also directed another 15 or 20 others under their charge. I was 'carrying everybody's monkey' in an organisation with 250 employees. But now, with 6 resorts and nearly 600 employees I am able to work less but do more.

I asked how he was able to do this. He told me he made structural changes. He started coaching 15 leaders in the entire organisation, who in turn coached their subordinates. Together they created a coaching culture within their organisation. He discovered that the SF approach had enabled their Indonesian employees to communicate more effectively, saving face, especially when dealing with shortcomings and challenges experienced in day-to-day operations. He stopped micro-managing.

> I schedule my time effectively and prioritise time for family and God as much as possible without compromising my responsibilities in my various company roles. By doing so I have managed to spend more quality time with a close group of team leaders and am actively looking to enhance the already amazing team and with great individuals that bring added value to my family.

Instead of three-hour meetings or as long as it took to cover every item on the agenda, Jose said he limits meetings to one hour or less, even setting an alarm! When time runs out for the top five priorities, he entrusts the team to carry on without him. 'I empower my leaders and let them make mistakes, take responsibility for them and learn. I gave up my Blackberry, which was a clear addiction.'

Final reflections

Traditional approaches to organisational consulting usually help leaders to identify problems and weaknesses and then prescribe ways solve them. In this example with Jose, we began with identifying what he wanted to accomplish in a coaching situation, and how the personal impact of a solution focused perspective helped Jose to make important changes within his organisation. Change happens between individuals, one conversation at a time. The changes Jose experienced impacted him personally, and also had far-reaching implications for his organisation. When one person is different, it changes the organisation at a micro-level. In that sense, organisational consulting was not a grand-scale plan designed to attack the problem of 'motivation' or 'balance' but, instead, it impacted one person at a time, therefore, changing the organisational structure. Addressing a person in their strengths and highlighting what they are doing well is a catalyst for significant change in the individual, between people and for organisational change. Jose wanted to find a way to manage his work better so he would have more time for his wife and two young children. Four years later he is 'working less and doing more' – effectively expanding his company by empowering his leaders and spending more of the quality time he values with his family.

References

Jackson, P.Z., & McKergow, M. (2007). *The solutions focus: Making coaching and change SIMPLE* (2nd ed.). London, UK: Nicholas Brealey International.

Szabo, P., Meier, D., & Dierolf, K. (2009). *Coaching plain & simple: Solution focused brief coaching essentials.* New York, NY: W.W. Norton & Company.

INDEX

Page numbers in italics refer to figures. Page numbers in bold refer to tables.